Not For Export

Not For Export:

The International Competitiveness of Canadian Manufacturing

Third Edition

~~~~~~

Glen Williams

M&S

Canadian Cataloguing in Publication Data
Williams, Glen, 1947-
Not for export: the international competitiveness of Canadian manufacturing
3rd ed.
Includes bibliographical references and index.
ISBN 0-7710-8846-9
1. Canada – Commercial policy.   2. Canada – Commercial policy –
History.   I. Title.

HF1479.W55 1994   382'.3'0971   C94-930830-7

Printed and bound in Canada

McClelland & Stewart Inc.
The Canadian Publishers
481 University Avenue
Toronto, Ontario
M5G 2E9

1 2 3 4 5   98 97 96 95 94

Contents

~~~~~~~~~~~~~~~~~~~~~~~~~~~~~~~~~~~~

To my wife Carol-Lynne, my daughter Anne,
and my mother Margaret.

Preface to the First Edition

~~~~~~

Not For Export was born in the traumatic bout of culture shock which afflicts many Canadians who return to their native land after working for some years in an underdeveloped country. In my case, I returned to graduate school in Toronto from a very rural area in Zambia in late 1973 to find my intellectual environment buzzing with the heady left nationalist rhetoric of Canada's colonial "underdevelopment" and the need to liberate it from the tentacles of U.S. imperialism. At the same time, a minority view took the more orthodox Leninist position that Canada was itself an imperialist country.

I had previously reflected on these questions many times when I was in Africa. So, while this debate crystallized an already awakened interest, I often found its expression by Canadians unsatisfactory. Both sides reflected important truths, yet they were so crudely formulated that they could not be reconciled by simply staking out a middle position. Rather, it was from the beginning necessary to transcend both arguments in order to come to terms with the central questions of Canadian politics, economic development, class, nation, and our position in the international hierarchy of wealth and power that each sought to address. This book, then, traces my intellectual search during the last decade for a more satisfactory approach to these pivotal Canadian issues.

Many have stimulated, informed, and encouraged me along the way. In pursuing my doctoral studies at York University and preparing the dissertation which forms the basis of over half of this book, I gratefully acknowledge the assistance of Tom Hockin, David Bell, Fred Fletcher, Mel Watkins, H.V. Nelles, Jim Laxer, Daniel Drache, John Saul, Rob Albritton, and Sten Kjellberg. In refining my ideas at Carleton University, I have greatly benefited from the advice and helpful criticism of my colleagues, including Jane Jenson, Wallace Clement, Lynne Mytelka, Maureen Molot, Dan Butler, and Leo Panitch.

In gathering material for my study, the libraries of the University of Toronto, York University, and Carleton University and the National Library in Ottawa have proved invaluable. The Public Archives provided every possible assistance and I especially thank Sandra Bell and Gilles Malette. The Department of Industry, Trade and Commerce gave me special permission to view certain of its files from the 1950s and 1960s without which the core of the later chapters would have remained speculative.

Finally, I acknowledge my debt to the patience and perseverance of my publisher and series editors, Ed Dosman and David Bell, through all the years and stages of its preparation. All shortcomings in the book are, of course, my own responsibility.

For those who will wonder if our title, *Not For Export*, was conjured up out of nothing by a clever copywriter of catchy phrases, I must report, unhappily for the national interest, that instead we have here a case of art imitating life. Some years ago, when Maureen Molot and I were collaborating on an article for another book, she directed my attention to her typewriter, the product of a well-known branch plant manufacturing in Canada. Just out of view and inside the frame, a label was affixed to her machine, which read as follows:

Patented 1936 1937 1939 1941
Made in Canada
Protected by American and
foreign patents
/NOT FOR EXPORT/

Glen Williams
October, 1982

Preface to the Third Edition

This edition preserves the basic historical outline of the original study while at the same time refining its interpretation and adding new material to bring the reader up to the present day. Chapters 2 to 5, based on original archival research, and covering the period from the 1870s to the 1940s, are reproduced without substantial change. Chapters 1 and 6 have been extensively rewritten to incorporate both new updated material and some material that appeared in other chapters of the previous two editions. Chapters 7 and 8 are, for the most part, new and have not been previously published.

I am grateful for the support of the readers of the previous two editions and to my publisher for this opportunity to retell the story of the political economy of Canadian manufacturing and trade policy. In the intervening years, much that was unclear about the contemporary economic transformations sketched in the previous two editions has come into fuller view. In shaping the arguments of this edition, I acknowledge the continuing influence of my graduate and undergraduate students, and to the list of collegues thanked I add Neil Bradford, Steve Dorey, and Barbara Jenkins. My heartfelt thanks as well to my family for their support.

Glen Williams
March, 1994

Chapter One

Introduction: Northernmost Region of American Industry

~~~~~~

The 1980s *and* the 1990s were both sung in by discordant choirs rehearsing funeral dirges for the Canadian economy. In the economic crisis of the early 1980s, Canadian bankers warned that the country faced defeat in world markets and economic ruin at home. Our politicians cautioned us to "live within our means" and accept "short-term pain" while promoting "mega" strategies to restructure Canadian industry and trade. Canadian industrialists and union executives openly wrung their hands in despair as manufacturing employment and output fell by over 11 per cent between 1981 and 1983.[1] Government researchers introduced new concepts like "deindustrialization" into the national economic discourse, accompanied by novel and unnerving suggestions that Canada was in danger of "regression toward economies like that of Chile or Brazil." This decline, some declared, would bring Canadians "inevitably to a condition of pastoral servitude by the middle years of the twenty-first century."[2]

Although temporarily muted by economic recovery in the mid-1980s, the intensity of the recession of the early 1990s amplified shrilly these alarums. Canada's industries were hit sooner, harder, and longer than those of its major trading partners. Canadian manufacturing output suffered a significant decline in 1990, falling back to 1987 levels, while output in Japan, the United States, and the European Community (EC) was still expanding. By the height of the recession in 1992, Canadian manufacturing had shrunk by a total of 12 per cent and output had fallen below 1985 levels. Although the economic downturn also hurt the output of manufacturers in Japan, the United States, and the EC nations, those countries finished 1992 *ahead* of their 1985 production levels by 15 to 20 per cent.[3] Employment in Canadian manufacturing was also devastated, with 340,000 jobs lost between 1989 and 1992. As an indication of the severity of Canada's industrial plight, our manufacturers were employing only about the same number of workers in the second quarter of 1993 as they had in the early 1970s.[4] Realtors estimated that 135 million square feet of industrial space lay vacant in 1993 in the greater Toronto area alone, the equivalent of more than 250 large factories.[5] As if to prove that the world business community was taking note of all this, Canada lost its fourth and fifth place standing of the 1980s in international competitiveness among industrialized nations. It dropped to eleventh place in the 1992 and 1993 annual surveys of the Swiss-based World Economic Forum.[6]

And so, as the 1990s were launched, chilling predictions that the standard of living of Canadians was at risk lost their fringe, radical novelty and moved into the corporate and establishment mainstream. A widely publicized 1991 analysis of the Canadian economy, prepared by U.S. economist Michael Porter for the Mulroney government and an influential business lobby, cautioned that "if the current trajectory continues, the standard of living of Canadians seems destined to fall behind."[7] Two high-profile government think-tanks, the Economic Council of Canada and the Science Council of Canada, issued similar warnings in their final reports before they were disbanded by the Tories in 1992. The Economic Council declared that "international trade is still vital to continued prosperity in this country" and stressed the need to make the transition from an economy based on "abundant raw materials" to one based in high-productivity manufacturing. This would "ensure that Canadian living standards will continue to rise."[8] The Science Council was more direct. After underlining Canada's $7 billion trade deficit in high-technology trade and the comparatively slow growth in our high-technology exports when compared to the United States, Japan, or even the newly industrializing countries of Asia, it concluded that it was

> clear that we are not adjusting to the new competition fast enough. . . . There is nothing magical sustaining the Canadian economy or the Canadian standard of living. Canadians can lose out. If we are to compete, we have to work and we have to invest – in our people and in our firms. We have to innovate.[9]

Fully 82 per cent of 300 Canadian business executives in a 1991 survey worried that Canada was not prepared to meet its new international competitive challenges.[10] A failure to improve Canada's diminishing international competitiveness, the Canadian Manufacturers' Association explained, "will mean a declining standard of living."[11] In Ottawa, a House of Commons committee on Canadian industry barked:

> Our economy, our quality of life, our jobs, our entire future depend upon our ability to compete in the global economy. Our failure to create and develop new technology will, within the next decade, lead to a significant decline in our standard of living. The time to act is now![12]

Canada's Place in the International Political Economy

For more than two decades, Canadians of contending ideological persuasions have been writing in increasingly apocalyptic terms about the shortcomings of Canada's manufacturing sector. It began in the late 1960s with the nationalist left. One of the most influential Canadian books of that era characterized Canada as a "rich industrialized underdeveloped country." [13] In the 1990s, as we have just witnessed, establishment Canada has taken up a very similar cry. By linking "competitiveness" and living standards, they are revisiting earlier nationalist warnings of Canada's potential de-classification from a rich to a very much poorer nation, warnings they had once ridiculed.

By its very subject, this book adds fuel to the catastrophism that so often permeates the discussion of the future prospects of Canadian manufacturing. Indeed, it would take a very determined optimist to find much to celebrate in the historical or contemporary record of Canada's industrial exports that will be presented here. Yet, this is an unintended consequence. I outline the case for frustrated potential, not potential catastrophe. It would be imprudent to deny the possibility of Canada's long-term relative economic decline. Still, speculation that we are on the margins of a poor, semi-industrialized future is of greater interest for what it reveals about partisan political conflict in Canada than for its analytical weight. As we will discover in later chapters, the international weakness of our manufacturing has proven to be an indispensable backdrop against which Canadian political partisans have tried to illustrate the logic of two mutually contradictory economic reform programs: state interventionist nationalism and neo-liberal continentalism. To explain the limits of these catastrophist choruses, it will be necessary to clarify our understanding of Canada's unique position within the world economy.

Since its European colonization and the dispossession of the Native peoples on its territories, Canada has been located firmly within the economically developed centre of the international political economy. Canada was a colony of settlement, an offshoot, of the European social formation and, from the beginning, shared many of its most important social, cultural, political, and economic characteristics. Canada's fusion with the two world hegemonic powers during the past two centuries, Great Britain and the United States, has yielded her a position near the top of the international hierarchy of wealth and power. Economically, Canada always enjoyed relatively high wages in comparison to the rest of the world. Politically, it possessed the elements necessary for the evolution of liberal-democratic political institutions. These factors have both been keys to the unfolding of Canada as a new country of the centre, and they will continue to set limits on any future decline in Canada's living standards. Let us take each in turn.

Canada was never driven into the underdeveloped periphery of the world economy as were the European colonies of military∘occupation and economic impoverishment, such as those in Africa and South Asia. On the contrary, most Europeans who immigrated to Canada, particularly skilled labourers, did so freely, induced by the opportunity to improve their material condition. Definite lower limits were placed on Canadian incomes by their ability either to move into independent farming or to immigrate to the more prosperous U.S. So it was that by Confederation, even before the formative years of our modern industrialism, Canada already possessed one of the highest standards of living in the world.[14]

Canada's high-wage economy, relative to the rest of the world, was to influence greatly the course of our industrialization. For instance, high wages made for relatively rich consumers and, accordingly, stimulated investment in our productive capacity. By contrast, manufacturing in the limited markets of the poverty-stricken periphery was starved of capital. Equally important, high wages forced the employment in Canada of the capital-intensive, labour-saving industrial technology that became typical of the central economies, rather than the craft, cottage, and labour-intensive techniques of the periphery.

Canada's integration within first the British and then the U.S. economy proved to be decisive beyond providing the basis for the development of a relatively wealthy modern centre economy. It also assigned specific patterns to that development. In manufacturing, this book will contend that Canada's initial bond with the British Empire accounted for its peculiar character (import substitution), while its later organization as a *regional* extension of American industrial production rendered its branch-plant and, more contemporary, continentally rationalized forms. In the more economically weighty natural resource trade, Melissa Clark-Jones has documented through her archival research the forging of a continental division of labour in which Canada's role became that of a "specialized (resource-producing) adjunct" to the U.S.[15]

During the last four decades, American owners have controlled more than two-fifths of Canadian manufacturing and mining industries, and the U.S. has been the focus for the overwhelming majority of Canada's international trade. Much of this trade is intra-firm, between American parent firms and their Canadian subsidiaries. As long ago as 1970, just over half of Canada's merchandise exports resulted from intra-firm trade and about two-thirds of Canada's manufactured exports to the U.S. were shipped to the American parents of Canadian branch plants.[16] Canada's provinces trade significantly more with foreign (mainly United States) customers than with each other. In 1988, 31 per cent of provincial goods were exported while 22 per cent were sent to other provinces.[17] Further, the trade of Canadian provinces with the U.S. is concentrated on geographically proximate American regions and states. For example, over one-half of the Atlantic provinces' U.S. exports in 1992 went to just four northeast Atlantic states and nearly three-quarters of Ontario's U.S. exports went to the eight states that border the Great Lakes.[18]

All in all, when investment, production, and trade are considered, the Canadian economy has appeared for some time to be more like a *zone* within the American economy than a distinct national economy. Indeed, Canada's economy is "national" chiefly in the sense that its formal boundaries are a political creation of the Canadian state system. In Canada, the economy is more visible politically than it is at the level of production. This is to say, the Canadian state system gives both shape and content to a "national" economy. It creates boundaries for the economy through publishing national economic statistics and regulating foreign trade. It also employs, with varying levels of effectiveness, its state sovereignty over economic matters in pursuit of policies that give a distinctive local character to our economic life.

Because of these strong links between state and economy, it is important to explore how the course of our industrialization was influenced by the development of Canadian liberal democracy. At variance with the direct administration of its colonies of military occupation by London, the U.S. War of Independence had ultimately opened the door to the propertied elites of the white Dominions for local autonomy in most matters. In the British North American colonies, the progression from representative to responsible government, and finally, to federal government, gave our political and economic elites considerable scope to make decisions about the course of their own economic future. Such opportunities were firmly denied to comparable elites in much of the periphery until the post-World War Two period.

This is not to suggest that, shorn of imperial control, the Canadian state simply became a mere instrument of a domestic ruling elite or class. In fact, just the opposite occurred. In the selection of our national economic strategy during the late nineteenth and early twentieth centuries the state required considerable autonomy to mediate and adjudicate the many substantive policy disagreements that arose among various groups within the capitalist class. Further, both the emerging industrial proletariat and the farmers were schooled, to some degree, in the British constitutional practices of free association and speech. Armed with an ever-widening franchise, these groups met with a measure of success in applying their weight to various sides in these debates.[19] To be certain, as in other centre political economies where it framed both social and economic reality, the logic of the capitalist accumulation process guided such major policy debates and decisions.[20] This limitation, however, should not obscure the significance of the liberal-democratic form in this matter. Canada's economic development strategy during its most formative early years was not externally imposed in any crude, direct fashion. Rather, as in other centre countries, it was shaped through the complicated interplay of social and economic forces mediated by the state. Liberal-democratic forms also mattered as the Canadian economy evolved into a zone within the American economy. In the main, Canada's political elites enthusiastically facilitated this transition not because they were constrained by U.S. economic, diplomatic, or military power but because they were convinced that this would secure a prosperous economic future for the nation as well as paying handsome electoral dividends.

All of this should not be taken to mean that, as an economically developed centre nation, Canada historically pursued the kind of industrial strategy typical of such centre successes as Germany and the United States. Indeed, the burden of the argument of this book is that Canadian development has been strikingly different insofar as it has emphasized resource extraction to the detriment of the manufacturing sector. Yet, if we are to draw the proper lessons from these differences, it is essential that we place them in their correct context from the beginning of our discussion. There are political and economic limits to any radical "de-classification" of Canada as a centre nation, at least in the short to medium term. The clashing catastrophist rallying cries of both the nationalist and corporate establishment elites are certainly dramatic and romantic. Nonetheless, they are extremely misleading in the Canadian case because they leave us with too few tools to understand what has happened in the past and what is likely to happen in the future. The disastrous effects of resource export dependency, so painfully obvious in the underdeveloped periphery of the world economy, are in Canada largely contained and modified by our special status as an economic zone within the world's largest and wealthiest economy. In turn, this zone is managed by a correspondingly developed state and class structure that has in the past demonstrated the ability to act in defence or promotion of what it perceives to be the national interest – capital accumulation with social harmony.

But there is no inevitability, no immutability implied here. Regions, even within very prosperous economies, can and do suffer economic declines. One might easily imagine a situation where Canadians became convinced that their elites were no longer politically able to leverage worthwhile economic benefits for their northern regional space through affirming a "special relationship" with the United States based on national sovereignty. If Canadians began to believe that a separate political future meant an increasingly dismal economic future, they might exercise the option of playing another of their historically unique trumps and sue for political annexation to the United States. As the public warmed its hands in the fire of Manifest Destiny to the rescue, the betrayed nationalist bellows of treason issuing from their about-to-be-disinherited political, economic, and cultural elites could go unheard.[21]

With this context now established, we can proceed with our inquiry into Canada's failure to develop a solid trade in finished manufactures. Our focus is admittedly far more specific than our discussion to this point. Nevertheless, it will soon become apparent that we have chosen a pivotal location from which to examine Canadian economic and industrial development.

Canadian Industry in World Markets: The Ledger

Scarcely any symptom of Canada's manufacturing weakness has received as much comment in the last two decades as its failure to export its products at a level appropriate to its developed modern status in the world economy. This failure has taken place in a century in which manufactured goods became established as the most dynamic sector of world trade.[22] Moreover, among manufactures, the most technologically advanced and highly finished categories have led the way. D.W. Slater calculated that transport equipment and machinery made up 12 per cent of world trade in manufactures in 1899 and 43 per cent in 1964.[23] With the continued rapid application of science to industry, motor vehicles and non-electrical machinery are now considered "medium"-technology manufactures. This medium category merely held its own in the total trade of the developed OECD countries during the last two decades with a 42 per cent share of 1970 trade and a 44 per cent share of 1990 trade. At the same time, the share of high-technology manufactures (including aerospace, computers, and electronics) trade increased from 16 to 23 per cent of the total trade of the OECD countries during this period, while the share of low-technology manufactures (including paper and printing, furniture, and textiles) decreased from 41 to 32 per cent.[24]

The twentieth-century success of manufactured exports has been so pronounced that it has led many observers to link it directly with economic development. Industrialization is said to be associated with economic development because it leads to increases in both labour productivity and real incomes. In turn, relative levels of industrialization and worldwide industrial competitive power can be measured through manufactured exports because industrial growth enhances trade potential. Not only is a high level of manufactured exports usually a feature of economic development, but underdevelopment is often associated with an export structure dominated by primary products and/or intermediate or semi-manufactures.

Table One
Newly Industrialized Countries among
the Leading Exporters of Manufactures

NIC	Rank in 1990	Average Annual Change 1980-1990 (per cent)
Hong Kong	9	14
Taiwan	11	13
Korea	12	14
China	15	16
Singapore	17	14
Mexico	20	18
Brazil	25	9
Malaysia	26	18
Thailand	27	20
India	28	11

SOURCE: GATT, *International Trade 90-91*, Volume II (Geneva, 1992), Table IV.2, p. 36.

In correspondence with these tendencies, by the 1960s international trade in manufactures was polarized, with a few developed and wealthy centre nations on one side and the many poor nations of the periphery on the other. Indeed, during the first half of the twentieth century, the ten largest industrial countries accounted for over four-fifths of the world's trade in manufactures.[25] In many important respects, this pattern persists into the present. When the focal machinery and transport equipment sector is considered, a sector that makes up one-third of world merchandise exports and one-half of world exports of manufactures, the developed countries still dominate international trade. In 1989, only one-eighth of world exports of these critical goods went from developing to developed nations or between developing countries themselves, while four-fifths of world exports were from developed to developing countries or between the developed nations themselves.[26]

Nevertheless, the rise of the newly industrialized countries (NICs) in the 1970s has gone some way toward blurring the stark divide in world industrial trade between the developed centre and the underdeveloped periphery. In the last two decades, a few developing countries have been able to take advantage of the decision of some U.S. and European multinationals to move part of their production process to low-cost locations. Seizing this opportunity, the NICs have attempted to transform their inward-oriented industries into export-oriented, technologically competitive manufacturing sectors producing mainly for the markets of the developed countries. Although varying degrees of success have been experienced by individual national economies, substantial development has been achieved within this group. Between 1964 and 1985, six NICs (Brazil, Mexico, Hong Kong, South Korea, Singapore, and Taiwan) increased from 1.6 per cent to 9.5 per cent their share of total OECD imports of manufactured products.[27] As can be seen in Table One, ten NICs now rank in the top thirty leading exporters of manufactures. Table One also demonstrates that during the 1980s the manufactured exports of all of these NICs grew significantly, often double or more than the 7 per cent world average. In some of these countries, this growth has been translated into rising incomes. In fact, per capita income in several of the Asian NICs is now comparable to that in lower-ranked OECD countries such as Greece and Portugal.[28]

This pattern of world trade shows the NICs wedged between the developed, manufactured-export nations on one side and underdeveloped, primary-export nations on the other. Three decades ago British economist Alfred Maizels first proposed a system of classification with interesting and important implications for Canada, given this current pattern of trade. He suggested that countries be divided into three groups – industrial, semi-industrial, and non-industrial – based on the value of their production of manufactures per capita and the proportion of their exports consisting of "finished" manufactures (products not normally subject to a further manufacturing process). In 1955, most industrial countries had at least one-third of their exports as finished goods. Up to 15 per cent of the exports of semi-industrialized countries were similarly finished. For non-industrial countries, the proportion was under 5 per cent.[29]

Table Two gives a picture of the export performance of individual countries assigned a classification by Maizels. Data on these countries have been brought up to date and have been supplemented by a record of their current imports of finished manufactures. In the decades since Maizels originally studied this question, international trade in manufactured products has intensified, as Table Two indicates. In the industrial countries, finished manufactures currently account for three-fifths or more of total exports. Semi-industrial countries are now performing at levels the industrials were achieving in the mid-1950s. Some non-industrial countries, such as Thailand and the Philippines, should now be re-classified among the semi-industrials.

As a corollary of his proposition that high exports of finished manufactures indicate high levels of industrialization, Maizels suggested that the larger industrial countries were less dependent on imports of

Table Two
Finished Manufactures as Proportion of Trade,
Selected Years (per cent of total trade)

			Exports			Imports
	1913	*1929*	*1955*	*1980*	*1990*	*1990*
Industrial						
Japan	31	43	64	71	83	32
Germany	46	54	65	60	68	53
Great Britain	58	49	62	50	63	59
United States	21	37	48	52	62	63
Sweden	23	26	33	53	59	63
France	44	47	38	50	57	55
Canada	5	14	11	32	43	68
Semi-Industrial						
India	13	19	31	35	48*	35*
Mexico	-	-	3	7	32	53
Brazil	-	-	1	24	28	37**
Australia	-	-	6	10	12	64
Non-Industrial						
Thailand	-	-	1	17	44*	48*
Philippines	-	-	1	14	24*	26*
Egypt	-	-	3	1	13**	33**

*1988; **1989.
SOURCES: A. Maizels, *Industrial Growth and World Trade* (Cambridge: Cambridge University Press, 1963), pp. 59, 64; 1980 and 1990 calculated from United Nations, *Yearbook of International Trade Statistics*, Vol. 1, various years.

manufactures than the smaller industrials, the semi-industrials, and the non-industrials. Today, these trends are moderated by a globalized production regime created by liberalized General Agreement on Tariffs and Trade (GATT) rules, regional free trade areas (such as the European Community), and the rise of the NICs. Nevertheless, it is still true that the two leading industrial countries, Japan and Germany, have significantly lower proportions of their imports as finished products than their exports. Other industrial countries tend to have roughly equal shares of finished imports and exports while the semi-industrials and non-industrials still tend to have somewhat higher proportions of finished goods among their imports than their exports.

On the face of it, Canada's claim to industrial status within Maizels's classification scheme seems quite weak. At only slightly more than two-fifths of total exports, Canada's proportion of finished exports falls far below the norm for the other industrials and has done so from the beginning of the twentieth century. As well, Canada is the only country among the industrials with a significantly higher proportion of finished imports than finished exports. Maizels also debated the appropriate category in which to place Canada. Important to his choice were the relatively high value of Canada's per capita production and also the relatively high proportion of our semi-processed but nonetheless manufactured exports, such as pulp and paper. In the end, and highly pertinent in respect to Canada's position in the international political economy, Maizels decided to place Canada among the industrials because of the extremely close relationship between the Canadian and American economies, a relationship so close that "in many respects," he said, "the two countries can effectively be regarded as a single economic system."[30]

An optimist might argue that Canada made dramatic progress in the thirty-five years after 1955 by increasing fourfold, from 11 to 43 per cent, the proportion of trade composed of finished manufactures. Unfortunately, this advance is less significant than it first appears for at least two reasons. First, and most obviously, most of Canada's competitors have been pressing ahead as well. As Table Two demonstrates, we remain at the bottom of the industrial heap in the 1990s, substantially below the three-fifths level marking the other developed countries.

In addition, direct comparisons in finished exports between the 1950s and later decades are suspect because of the peculiar effects of automotive trade between Canada and the United States. Since 1965, when free trade in automobiles and parts between the two countries was inaugurated, the Canadian proportion of exports of finished manufactures has risen dramatically. In the early 1960s, finished exports stood at approximately 13 per cent of total exports. This jumped to nearly 38 per cent by the early 1970s, settled back to 32 per cent at the beginning of the 1980s, and rose again to 43 per cent in 1990.

For the purposes of our inquiry, a good case can be made for excluding Canada-U.S. automotive exchanges from Canada's external trade picture. As we have been discussing it, the ratio of finished manufacture exports to total exports has meaning only because it is a rough indicator of a nation's ability to compete industrially within the world economy. Canada-U.S. automotive trade, however, tells us little positive about the capacity of Canadian industry to be internationally competitive as an industrial exporter because it is for the most part composed of intra-firm transfers of goods that incidentally pass over an international frontier. This may mean nothing more than the exchange of vehicles of different sizes, models, or colours from a Canadian subsidiary to its U.S. parent company. If, then, an adjustment is made to remove Canada-U.S. automotive trade from our total export trade, Canada's proportion of finished manufactures falls to 27 per cent in 1990. This represents only a meagre advance on the 22 per cent the same adjustment created in 1980. Further, in assessing the significance for Canada's manufacturing competitiveness of even this small advance, we must remember that an ever-increasing proportion of Canadian trade has no local footings but resembles the pattern of closely integrated, U.S. parent-directed, intra-firm trade in the automotive sector.

At this point our analysis could take two directions. One would return to a consideration of whether Canada's feeble export performance more appropriately ranks us among the NICs or semi-industrials than the industrials. The other direction would stress the limits in applying models that assume a national economy on what is, in fact, a regional zone or bloc within the world's largest and wealthiest economy. For reasons discussed previously, I have argued that the first approach leads only to a dead end.

From the *regional* perspective favoured in this study, Canada's weak trade performance in end manufactures suggests neither impending de-classification nor creeping underdevelopment. Historically, Canada has consistently played the role of industrial laggard while maintaining one of the highest living standards in the world. And so, the data we have just reviewed on finished exports simply reflect the relative strengths and weaknesses of the Canadian region (and its sub-regions) within the boundaries of the larger continental economy. Even today, resource exports remain the cornerstone of Canadian economic activity, our regional *raison d'être* within the continental economy. In spite of its potential to produce higher value-added exports with greater returns and higher employment levels, manufacturing continues to play second fiddle in Canada to resource extraction.

The resource export orientation of the Canadian economic region has added to the economic policy management woes of the Canadian federal state by aggravating two of the country's most persistent economic problems – balance-of-payments policy and employment policy. In only seven of the forty-three years between 1950 and 1992 has Canada managed a surplus on the current account of its international balance of payments. With only two surplus years in the most recent ten, from 1983 to 1992, Canada's cumulative current account deficit during those years was over $144 billion.[31] For several decades, then, we have been in a virtually constant state of deficit when all of our international transactions – such as merchandise trade, investments, and services – are considered. These deficits have been generated mainly in services, not in manufactures, and are thereby directly related to the high carrying costs of foreign investment in the Canadian economy. Nonetheless, trade in manufactures has also been a profoundly negative element in the health of the merchandise account of Canada's foreign trade. During the 1970s and 1980s, the cumulative trade deficit in fully manufactured end products was $310 billion. The first three years of the 1990s have jacked up this cumulative deficit to a staggering $400 billion. [32]

Our manufactured export shortfall has also had a negative impact on employment policy. In general, resource industries are capital-intensive while manufacturing industries tend to be more labour-intensive. Put simply, this means that historically Canada has sacrificed many potential jobs by emphasizing resource extraction rather than trade in end-product manufactures. As a result, the country has persistently maintained an unemployment rate near the top of the highly developed OECD countries. In not one of the twenty-five years from 1966 to 1990 did OECD average unemployment rates ever exceed Canadian rates. And in only four of these twenty-five years were Canadian unemployment rates equal to, or lower than, U.S. rates. To make matters worse, Canada also has a smaller than typical percentage of its national work force engaged in manufacturing employment. [33]

Toward a Political Economy of Canadian Industrial Competitiveness

There have been many attempts in the past to "explain" Canada's industrial weaknesses. Unfortunately, most have lacked the global and historical perspective necessary for the task, and, accordingly, have slipped into fairly crude determinisms of an economic/environmental or political/social type. These explanations include: our comparative trade advantage in resources that rendered an industrial specialization uneconomic; the unambitious character of our business elites and/or their willingness to betray the national interest to foreigners; our small domestic market that did not permit the production efficiencies necessary for industrial export; the protective tariff policies of successive federal governments that sheltered Canadian manufacturers uncompetitive in world markets; and, finally, external domination of the Canadian economy and state that chained the country in a resource hinterland role. Many of these interpretations have been mobilized and popularized in recent decades as part of an ongoing political and partisan struggle between state interventionist nationalists and neo-liberal continentalists. While these interpretations all have something to offer and will be more fully discussed in subsequent chapters, it will become clear that none by itself is sufficiently strong to be considered the prime cause of export impotence.

The reader is cautioned that a comprehensive theory of Canadian economic or industrial development is not being set out here. A great deal more investigative work in many areas still needs to be done before a summary work of that kind can be written. Rather, a political economy method of inquiry is being applied to a detailed examination of the failure of our manufacturers to take advantage of their twentieth-century opportunities in world markets. Through coming to terms with the puzzling evolution of our manufactured export capacity from its late nineteenth-century origins, this study seeks to make a contribution to that larger task of comprehensive summary and theory. The present inquiry will outline the complex interplay between the economic constraints and opportunities Canada has faced in the last century because of its unique position as a centre nation/economic region attached, in turn, to the British and American empires. It will also highlight the decisive factors influencing the choices, conscious and accretive, about industrial strategy made within the overall political process and also at the level of the individual firm.

Our study will proceed from a diagnosis of conditions in the womb of our modern industrial structure by examining the late nineteenth-century National Policy tariffs of Sir John A. Macdonald and the Conservative Party. Here, we will explore the selection of an industrial strategy that has shaped the development of Canadian manufacturing to the present day. Instead of adopting a policy of international specialization through the production for world markets of a number of technologically innovative lines, Canadian state and economic elites chose a much less ambitious alternative that is strikingly similar to that known in the underdeveloped periphery of the world economy as import substitution industrialization (ISI). This model relies on a protective tariff structure as an instrument for domestic manufacturers to capture primarily consumer-oriented sectors of the home market with a production process borrowed from foreign industrialists. Its two major components, import replacement and technological dependence, when fused, produce an industrial structure with little potential to grow beyond its domestic horizons.

With a conceptual model of ISI in hand and relying largely on previously unpublished archival material, we will explore five periods of Canadian industrial development as a regional extension of American manufacturing. Industrial export failure is shown to be characteristic of all these periods. The first period parallels the astonishing developments in Canada's booming "wheat economy" at the beginning of the twentieth century. In the second period, Canadian manufacturers failed to turn the extraordinary export opportunities provided by the Great War to their long-term advantage. In the third period, the "roaring twenties," a segment of our economic and political elite dreamed of making Canada the industrial workshop of the British Empire. The fourth period, that of export blocking through foreign branch-plant dominance of Canadian manufacturing, takes us from the late 1930s through the mid-1970s.

Spanning the 1980s and the early 1990s, the final period is one of great upheaval in Canadian manufacturing. This period features fierce policy debates between state interventionist nationalists and neo-liberal continentalists, a spatial re-orientation of Canadian industrial production, the ratification of the Canada-U.S. Free Trade Agreement (FTA), and the signing of the North American Free Trade Agreement (NAFTA). Setting the context for this upheaval has been trade liberalization under the Auto Pact and the GATT, as well as state-fashioned fluctuations in the value of the Canadian dollar. In the end, however, as this introductory chapter documents, Canada's participation in the keystone world trade in manufactures remains stalled and Canada persists in its regional role as a resource-producing industrial backwater of the North American economy.

Chapter Two

Import Substitution:
Strategy of Export Impotence

~~~~~~

An examination of Canada's industrial export frustrations could not proceed on any other basis than from a rigorous probe of the late nineteenth- and early twentieth-century foundations of modern Canadian manufacturing. The key to this formative period, it is generally agreed, is the National Policy tariffs that began to appear in 1879. Early commentators focused on the material achievements of an industrialization process they saw, either approvingly or disapprovingly, as being the artificial creation of the tariffs. [1] More recent analysis has highlighted the gaps and limitations in this strategy in order to account for the evolution of Canadian secondary manufacturing as an "inefficient, non-innovative, and backward . . . structure with a penchant for dependence on foreign technology, foreign capital, and state assistance as its sine qua non." [2] Our inquiry turns in this latter direction.

This critique of Canada's pre-World War One industrial strategy is not an attempt to find past scapegoats for present difficulties. Instead, our task is to piece together the logic of a decision-making process that in the end assigned a relatively low priority to the industrial side of our economic development. The leading actors of Canadian society found the industrial strategy that we will soon dissect both rational, from the perspective of profit and employment, and nationalist, within the nineteenth-century ideology of strengthening the British Empire. The pattern of expansion in our early secondary manufacturing fits an industrial strategy model – import substitution industrialization (ISI) – pursued much later in the underdeveloped countries. What sets Canada apart from the beginning is its favoured position as a young country of the centre. Accordingly, neither was the choice of ISI inevitable, in the sense that it was imposed by external economic or political structures, nor were the economic benefits of ISI to be confined within the disarticulated channels of underdevelopment. Rather, our relatively rich domestic market permitted ISI to proceed on a scale inconceivable on the periphery of the world economy and thereby to confirm the basically developed nature of the Canadian economy.

Import substitution industrialization was the industrial strategy most typical of the underdeveloped periphery during most of the twentieth century. It is essentially simple, rapid, and painless in execution. This accounted for its widespread popularity. At levels set high enough to make domestic production feasible, tariffs are placed on selected commodities that enjoy established markets formerly serviced by imports. This generally means consumer goods ranging anywhere from laundry soap to automobiles. Foreign technology (usually both machinery and processes) is freely employed by a domestic licensee or foreign-owned subsidiary to create an instant industry.

From the perspective of our study of manufactured exports, the limitations of the ISI model are clear. The new factories cannot compete on world markets as they have nothing distinctive to offer them. In addition, a condition of the use of the foreign technology is usually that production be restricted to the domestic market. Further, the ISI factory provides few backward linkages to the rest of the country's economy as it needs no domestic capital goods industry to keep it supplied with new processes and machines. In this regard, the continual demand for imported capital goods often creates new burdensome strains on the balance-of-payments accounts. Thus, the ISI manufacturing sector tends to stagnate as a mere supplement to other productive activities (usually resource extraction).

Not surprisingly, ISI appears to run contrary to the experience of such "late" European industrializers as Germany, Italy, and Russia, which initially stressed producers' goods over consumer goods.[3] While it is hazardous to oversimplify, the industrial strategy typical of such centre countries might be styled the specialized world competitive model. As we shall demonstrate later in this chapter, while Canada was following ISI in the early twentieth century, Sweden and Japan adopted a policy of developing world technological leadership in the production of a limited number of innovative lines. Although their domestic markets were used as a base, it was clear that efficient production runs required foreign customers. In turn, this demanded the local assimilation and adaptation of existing foreign technologies to the point where marketable technological breakthroughs made exports possible.

Occupying the Home Market

Having set out the essential characteristics of ISI, tariff-induced import replacement with extreme technological dependence, we are now prepared to examine the case of the National Policy. While the National Policy tariffs are familiarly, and correctly, discussed as a tool of national development policy, a device to increase government revenue, and as a measure to check the southward emigration flow by providing permanent employment opportunities, their relationship to import replacement and the balance of payments has been less well documented. In his 1878 pre-election speech to the House of Commons outlining the proposed new tariff of the Conservatives, Sir John A. Macdonald made it quite clear that Canadian industrialization would be based primarily on replacing imports in the domestic market.

> I believe that, by a fair readjustment of the tariff, we can increase the various industries which we can interchange one with another and make this union a union in interest, a union in trade, and a union in feeling. We shall then grow up rapidly a good, steady and mature trade between the Provinces, rendering us independent of foreign trade, and not, as New Brunswick and Nova Scotia formerly did, look to the United States or to England for trade, but look to Ontario and Quebec – sending their products west, and receiving the products of Quebec and Ontario in exchange. This is the great policy, The National Policy, which we on this side are advocating. . . .[4]

Later, we may assume, with the completion of the railway, the West was also to be brought into this domestic "union in trade."

S.L. Tilley, Conservative Minister of Finance, in introducing the National Policy legislation in 1879, explicitly tied the new tariffs to import reduction and balance-of-payments difficulties.

> Regarding the matter as I do, I think it is to be regretted that the volume of imports has not been materially reduced. I look upon the large imports, ever since the Dominion was organized, showing a large balance of trade against it, as one of the causes of the troubles with which we have to contend. . . . They have been decreasing to a certain extent, but are still very large, showing . . . that they ought still to be further diminished. . . . I think then, without entering into a discussion here of Free Trade and Protection, so far as it affects England and the United States, we may fairly conclude that the prosperity of the one country . . . is caused in great measure by the large surplus in its favour, and the depression in the other by the large deficiency. Under these circumstances it appears to me we should turn our attention to the best means of reducing the volume of our imports from all parts of the world.[5]

The "best means" of reducing imports was, of course, to increase home production.

From the manner in which he introduced the specific clauses of the tariff legislation, many of which came from the manufacturers themselves,[6] it can be shown that Tilley was not just making a theoretical point for the edification of the Honourable Members. For example, in imposing 25 and 35 per cent tariffs on various types of earthenware, Tilley observed "they [the government] did not anticipate any increase of revenue from the new duties, being satisfied that a large portion of the importations would be replaced by the home-made article."[7] In raising the tariff on candles and paraffin wax, Tilley said "it was very probable that a large portion of the candles formerly imported would [now] be manufactured from Canadian paraffin wax."[8]

It should be emphasized that the National Policy tariffs were not only designed to protect existing Canadian industries, but also to give manufacturers a chance to expand their operations or to establish a new plant to fill orders for goods that were formerly imported. Tilley stated:

> The policy of the Government had been that where an article was made in the country, where we had raw material in abundance here, it was considered desirable to give those industries not only such encouragement and protection to keep up those already in existence, but to encourage the establishment of others.[9]

Specifically, in imposing a tariff on clocks, Tilley observed "there were some manufactories in the country, the principal one being at Hamilton. The tariff would, no doubt, increase the production of this establishment, and probably might lead to the establishment of others."[10]

Eight years later another Minister of Finance used the same import substitution argument to justify his government's new tariffs on iron and steel imports. Pointing to the fact that there had been $288 million worth of iron and steel imports since Confederation, Sir Charles Tupper chided Canadians for allowing other countries to "reap this golden harvest that lies unconsidered at our feet." His answer? A tariff to "put this iron industry upon the same footing and foundation that you have put all the other industries of Canada, and you will sweep away to a large extent the balance of trade which stands against Canada up to the present time."[11]

One can readily find echoes of the logic of Tilley and Tupper in such business publications as the Montreal *Journal of Commerce*. In 1881, it mused:

> To us it seems somewhat extraordinary that, with raw materials near at hand, and every facility to manufacture, the bulk of the fabrics used in this country should continue to be imported. . . . The aim to promote home industry embracing the erection of factories to give employment to a large number of work people, must ere long greatly benefit this country. However persistently politicians preach agriculture as the proper vocation for Canadians, it is being more fully

recognized that while our money is sent elsewhere to employ others to manufacture our articles of consumption our progress cannot be satisfactory.[12]

Manufacturers also looked on the tariff as a means of substituting domestic production for imports. As early as 1883, *Canadian Manufacturer*, the organ of a leading group of Ontario industrialists,[13] pressed for higher tariffs on iron and steel imports on the grounds that

> The N.P. [National Policy] is good as far as it goes but it has not yet been carried far enough. So far it has gone that we need not today import a single yard of gray cotton or a pound of refined sugar; we can make enough of both at home. But we are still sending to England and to the United States for iron that we ought to be making at home instead.[14]

Indeed, during the 1880s and the early 1890s *Canadian Manufacturer*, in the context of this strategy of replacing imports, sang psalms of praise to the "home market" while downgrading the importance of export sales. For example, an 1883 editorial entitled "About an Export Trade" told readers that Canada's chances of exporting manufactures to the U.S. market were "about equal to those of getting to the moon by railway" and that the idea of selling surplus Canadian cottons or woollens "in any foreign market is about as visionary and impracticable as anything that could be conceived. . . . Both Old England and New England would meet us in every port and we would not have the ghost of a chance."[15] A similar sentiment was also expressed in 1885 by this periodical:

> In these days of over-production, when nation is fighting against nation for possession of markets, and when commercial war is hotter the civilized world over than ever it was before – what seems the most sensible course for us? Clearly this, we should say to hold our own – to keep a fast grip of the home market, the only one that we can hold, if we choose, against all comers.[16]

Like arguments were advanced in 1881 by the *Journal of Commerce* when it editorialized on the subject of Canadian trade in manufactured exports: "it is scarcely necessary to observe that it [export trade] has been and must long continue to be comparatively insignificant. . . . Canada can reasonably expect to do no more than supply her home market to a reasonable extent."[17] Two years later it derided an article in the Montreal *Gazette* lamenting that U.S. rather than Canadian manufacturers were establishing themselves in the Australian market: "So long as the United States manufacturers are able to supply our home market, notwithstanding heavy protective duties, it is vain to complain. . . . it is preposterous for them to expect to [compete] in the markets of the world."[18] In 1889, the *Journal of Commerce* again took note of the export successes of U.S. manufacturers, observing that they "certainly afford reflection for Canadians." However, the *Journal* cautioned that "nearby trade is all the more profitable and satisfactory owing to quicker returns, etc. . . . We do not advocate the abandonment of distant trade possibilities, but there is some danger of looking too far abroad and concentrating all our energies in one direction."[19]

By 1890, these practical arguments against developing foreign markets had been elevated to the level of economic theory. Readers of *Canadian Manufacturer* were told that "the nation that is self-contained, giving employment to its people and producing within itself all that the people require, may be enjoying the acme of prosperity, although it has never a ship upon the ocean and has no foreign trade whatever."[20] Later editorials more fully elaborated this autarkic theory.

> Before we worry ourselves about foreign trade in our manufacturing let us first fully occupy our home market. Let us make all such articles as we can manufacture to advantage at home, purchasing abroad only such things as we cannot produce here. . . . When we have done this it will then be time to consider the question of exporting our surplus manufactures, but not till then. . . . We should not desire to import any thing which we could manufacture to advantage at home, and we should not export anything which we ourselves could consume. This is the correct theory, and if it were elaborated and carried out to its fullest possible extent, our foreign trade might not be so large, but we would become richer and more independent.[21]

In accepting, indeed celebrating, the limited horizons of their domestic market, Canadian manufacturers were patterning a passive export model later adopted by industrialists in the periphery of the world economy. However, a minority of Canadian manufacturers, whose core was made up of agricultural implement producers, pursued the more aggressive export model typical of capitalists of the centre. One indication of this split can be found in the opposition of many leading agricultural implement manufacturers to the introduction of protective tariffs.[22] As late as 1876, Massey declared that "the existing tariff is satisfactory to us: perhaps even a little less would also be."[23] This unusual attitude was taken for at least two reasons. First, more than most Canadian manufacturers, agricultural implement producers were linked directly to prosperity in agricultural staples sales in world markets. Any drop in farmers' incomes due to tariff-related increases in the Canadian prices of other commodities could result in decreased sales of farm machinery.[24] Second, many of these industrialists were aggressive expatriate Americans who did not fear world competition and who, in fact, had not given up their dreams of access to the larger U.S. market. One such manufacturer had even gone so far as to work out a scenario for continentalizing the production of agricultural machinery in the event of free trade being negotiated with the U.S. He suggested that "there would not be so many manufacturers conflicting with each other here for we would strike out with particular branches of the trade, say in one or two articles, and after we had supplied Canada we would send the balance into the States."[25]

The difference in attitudes and emphasis toward export sales of the two groups of manufacturers is well illustrated by the reactions of *Canadian Manufacturer* to pressure placed by Massey-Harris on the Canadian government for a somewhat minor adjustment in the tariff. In order to protect his competitive position in world markets by maintaining low production costs, Massey threatened in 1894 to shift much of his enterprise to the U.S. if he was not given a refund on the tariff collected on imported raw materials that he re-exported as manufactured machinery.[26] *Canadian Manufacturer* originally supported Massey's eventually successful demands, but, significantly, when it became apparent that such tariff-free imports threatened the economics of import substitution production in the exempted articles, it reversed its stand. It noted that Massey-Harris had received $10,083 as compensation for 3,385 exported harvesters and angrily suggested that the interests of Canadian industry would have been better served if the government had simply handed the company a grant of $10,000. The effect of the tariff adjustment, it argued, was to force a drop in the Canadian price of the raw material to the lower U.S. level and, thereby, "to disorganize and demoralize the industry without one single compensating feature .to any Canadian industry, except that of the Massey-Harris people."[27]

Canadian Manufacturer and the group of import-substituting industrialists whose views it reflected did not really comprehend the desire of the agricultural implement manufacturers to maximize their sales by becoming internationally competitive in specialized lines. Their attitude toward export markets was, as we have earlier noted, basically passive – "while it is desirable to export our surplus products, that export should consist only of what we cannot possibly consume at home."[28] So it was that the agricultural machinery manufacturers were criticized for exporting before filling the "home market." For example, in 1901, *Canadian Manufacturer* was deeply troubled that $2 million of farm machinery was imported into Canada at the same time as this Canadian industry was exporting its products.

We are not of that optimistic temperament which allows us to see anything particularly desirable in the fact that the foreign trade of Canada increased to the extent of nearly $2,000,000 a year by the imports of agricultural implements alone. It is said of the Massey-Harris Company that they are the largest manufacturers of agricultural implements under the British flag; and there are a large number of other such concerns in Canada, but they do not supply the home market however much they may strive to increase the volume of our foreign trade.[29]

Technological Dependence

On the basis of our discussion to this point, it seems reasonable to conclude that the National Policy tariffs were rather more than simply the protection of "infant industries" that were eventually to become internationally competitive. Rather, they reflected a preoccupation on the part of state and business elites with the capture of the "home market" by substituting domestic production for imports. Another component of the ISI strategy, as it was earlier outlined with reference to the periphery of the world economy, is extreme technological dependence. To determine whether this feature was shared by pre-World War One Canada, we will now examine the circumstances of both the branch-plant sector, worth only approximately 9 to 11 per cent of the total capital invested in Canadian industry at this time, and the dominant Canadian-owned sector that controlled almost all of the remainder.[30]

A study of the relationship between technology and the development of modern industry in Canada must begin with the Patent Act of 1872. Before this date only Canadian residents could hold Canadian patents and the diffusion of foreign technology was accomplished by the theft of techniques, processes, and patterns and by the immigration into Canada of U.S. industrial entrepreneurs. Technology transferred in this manner was thereby assimilated by Canadian industry and adapted to local market conditions. The 1872 Act, however, made this learning process superfluous. It contained a "compulsory working" clause that allowed non-residents to hold Canadian patents on the condition that they or their representatives manufactured the article in question within two years of their submission of an application for patent protection. This liberalization came in concert with attempts on the part of many countries in the second half of the nineteenth century to rationalize their patent laws in order to cope with the flood of new technological innovations.[31] More directly, it was the result of many years of pressure on the part of U.S. industrialists and their government.[32]

The new Act opened the way to a deluge of imported techniques, which rapidly swamped Canadian industrial innovation. The proportion of patents issued to Canadian residents dropped from 100 per cent in 1870 to 35 per cent in 1880, to only 15 per cent by 1900. Not surprisingly, there was a corresponding increase in the proportion of patents issued to Americans – 70 per cent in 1900. In addition, in absolute terms, the total number of patents annually issued increased by a factor of fifteen between 1870 and 1900, while the number going to Canadians only doubled.[33]

The "working clause" of the 1872 Patent Act and the 1879 National Policy tariffs worked hand in hand to transfer U.S. technology and production to Canada. Much of this transfer was accomplished through licensing agreements with Canadian industrialists, as capital shortages often prevented direct U.S. investment in branch plants.[34] Notices, like the following, under the title of "A New Canadian Enterprise," frequently appeared in *Canadian Manufacturer* and demonstrate how the development of technological dependence was seen as a positive accomplishment of the National Policy.

> We always take pleasure in being able to draw the attention of our readers from time to time to new industries being started in our midst. . . . The party in power in Ottawa . . . showed their wisdom and foresightedness when they framed the National Policy and put it into force, and in proof of its success it has developed the country, increased its manufacturing interests to a large extent and covered the country with railways, so that we are in a more prosperous condition today than any other country in Europe or America. It is significant and to the point to notice that the well known firm of Henry R. Worthington, of New York, manufacturers of pumping and hydraulic machinery, have been obliged at last to make arrangement to make their goods in this country to enable them to hold their own. They have, therefore, entered into an agreement with the old established and well known firm of John McDougall, proprietor of the Caledonian Iron Works, Montreal, to manufacture and sell them, and to be known as their sole general and manufacturing agents for the Dominion of Canada.[35]

For Canadian industrialists, the short-run advantages of entering into such licensing agreements with U.S. firms were very clearly superior to the more difficult task of developing their own technology. First, these agreements provided relatively cheap access to an already proven industrial process. Second, only minimum delay would be encountered in exploiting innovations. This was of importance because if a Canadian manufacturer were to consider choosing the longer course of working up his own process in a similar line, he would be aware that a competitor might frustrate his efforts by simply picking up the licensed technology. Finally, those Canadian industrialists who entered into licensing agreements often gained a patent monopoly in the Canadian market that provided as much, or more, protection from foreign and domestic competition as the tariff. For all these reasons, then, the impact of U.S. patents and licensing arrangements on Canadian industrial capital was so great that, as early as 1892, W.K. McNaught, president of the Canadian Manufacturers' Association, was able to observe:

> Anyone who has studied manufacturing in Canada must be aware that our factories are largely duplicates of American industries, a large proportion of which are carried on by the help of patents which secure to their owners an absolute monopoly of their own market. Our manufacturers of articles patented in the United States, and "their name is legion, for they are many". . . .[36]

Preoccupied as they had become with "occupying" the domestic market, Canadian manufacturers demonstrated little concern for the disadvantages of technological dependence through licensing agreements. Perhaps the most serious of such faults is the risk that an industrial structure will lose the capacity to manipulate technology through the creation of its own marketable innovations if a serious effort is not made to adapt and transform at least a portion of the licensed technique. From the point of view of our study, however, the export barriers that typically accompany licensing agreements are of the greatest interest. M. Wilkins points out that manufacturing firms entering into licensing arrangements with U.S. firms during the pre-World War One era usually relinquished their export potential as they were allocated only a specified market territory by the licenser. U.S. General Electric is cited by Wilkins as a good example of an organization that carved up its international market by using licensing agreements. She notes that by 1914 U.S. General Electric had "associated" manufacturing operations in Canada, Great Britain, France, Germany, and Japan with ownership shares ranging from virtually complete to small minor holdings. Nevertheless, licensing agreements rather than ownership shares were the key factor in determining the marketing restrictions of the satellite firms. Wilkins observes that U.S. General Electric centred a network of exclusive rights, patents, and agencies that allowed it, effectively, to say to each affiliate, "You can't sell in a particular territory because we hold the patents – your patents, too – and have granted them to others."[37]

The source of new machinery going into industrial establishments can also be an important indicator of technological dependence or independence. In a typical ISI situation, it will be recalled, backward linkages to the domestic capital goods industry remain undeveloped while imports supply the necessary machine tools. Estimates by K. Buckley indicate that between 1900 and 1913, the key years in National Policy industrial expansion, nearly three-fifths of the total capital investment in plant were imported. The comparable proportion for the period 1914 to 1925 was over one-half.[38] By far the largest share of these imports was furnished by U.S. machine tool factories. In most years between 1885 and 1900 they supplied 80 to 85 per cent of this market. These figures increase to 85 and 95 per cent between 1901 and 1914.[39]

In this context, it is little wonder that Charles M. Pepper, a special agent of the U.S. consular service sent on a cross-Canada tour in 1905, was prompted to gloat:

> One striking fact is apparent, and this helps to explain why the imports from the United States have increased in spite of the steady development of Canadian industries and their partial success in supplying the home demand. Not a factory of any kind is built in the Dominion that the installation is not made very largely from the United States. This was the case with the steel works at Sydney and Sault Ste. Marie. The electrical works at Hamilton are a speaking catalogue of manufacturers of hoists, cranes and machine tools on this side of the border. It is the case with the flour mills. . . . It is also true of the lumber mills. In mining machinery the United States may almost be said to have a monopoly, and the great smelters are its contribution to Canadian progress. So long as Canada continues to build new mills and establish new industries, the installation of the plants will be done largely by the splendidly-equipped engineering works of the United States.[40]

According to Sir William Van Horne, chairman of the Canadian Pacific Railway, a considerable portion of this imported machinery may have been secondhand. *Industrial Canada,* the official organ of the Canadian Manufacturers' Association, quoted him as charging in 1908 ("with an authority that cannot be overlooked") that the use of machinery that U.S. manufacturers had "discarded" had resulted in a weakening of the competitive position of Canadian industrialists, even within their own tariff-protected market.[41]

Further, the approximate two-fifths of new machinery for industrial plants, which were Canadian in origin, cannot be assumed to represent an important sector of potentially competitive and technologically innovative production. In fact, a significant portion of Canadian machine tool manufacture during this period was undertaken by U.S. branch plants and licensed ventures.[42] In 1905, *Industrial Canada* surveyed the largely imitative foundations of the Canadian producers' equipment industry and the resistance to technical design innovation that kept it relatively backward:

Up-to-date United States patterns are followed almost exclusively, but our machinery is built upon somewhat heavier lines, though not so heavy as the British. The combination is very suitable to the needs of a country where manufacturing is not conducted upon so large a scale as in the United States and where manufacturers are consequently not so ready to abandon old machines to adopt new ones slightly better. [43]

Admitting that most specialized machinery in Canada continued to be imported from the United States twenty-five years after the 1879 introduction of the National Policy tariffs, *Industrial Canada* excused this deviation from import replacement by arguing that "naturally the making of machinery is one of the last industries to be developed in a new country." [44] As late as the 1920s, the *Monetary Times* could report little growth in Canada's machine tool industry:

It should be noted that much specialized equipment comes from the United Kingdom and the United States. Canada provides a sufficiently large field to permit the domestic manufacture of machines of such common use as small printing presses, concrete mixers, lawn mowers and gasoline engines. But for some of the more elaborate devices there are so few orders in a year that economical production in this country is impossible. [45]

By this point, it should be clear that the establishment of Canada's modern industrial structure was almost completely dependent on U.S. manufacturing for reproduction (through patents, licences, and machinery) of its means of production. Lacking any real commitment to the development of a more independent technological base by assimilating, adapting, and innovating on the basis of what it had borrowed, Canadian manufacturing from its point of origin was not in a position to become a competitive force in the world economy. Indeed, as we have seen, the possibility of international specialization had been rather scornfully rejected in favour of a more autarkic industrial model.

It is now appropriate to investigate the special role of U.S. direct investment in enhancing Canadian technological dependence during the formative years of our industrialization. An interpretation that would minimize the significance of the approximate 10 per cent of Canadian industrial capital controlled by U.S. branch plants is quite misleading because it fails to identify the sectors in which this investment was concentrated. In the pre-World War One period, a "second" industrial revolution was laying the base for modern industry in the United States, Germany, and Great Britain. Historian E.J. Hobsbawm identifies three major "growth industries" of this era: electrical industries, chemical industries, and industries based on the application of the internal combustion engine.[46] In the previous chapter we noted that the technologically advanced and highly finished products of these "growth industries" led the way in making manufactured goods this century's most dynamic department in world trade. We have just concluded a discussion of the barriers to Canadian industrial trade that typically accompanied licensing arrangements. Since U.S. branch plants were concentrated in these three "growth" sectors, then the negative possibilities of export blocking for Canada as a result of this more direct form of technological dependence can be readily deduced. Let us examine each sector.

Two electrical companies dominated production in Canada at the start of the First World War. One, Canadian Westinghouse, was a branch plant of a U.S. firm. The other was Canadian General Electric, nominally owned by Canadians but in fact bound securely in the orbit of U.S. General Electric through licensing arrangements. Some of the other U.S. branch plants manufacturing electrical goods in Canada by 1914 were Crouse-Hinds, Northern Electric, and Wagner Electric.[47]

U.S. branch plants were also well represented in the broad field of chemical production. In industrial chemicals we find American Cyanamid, Bird-Archer, and Canadian Explosives (a Dupont and Nobel joint venture that later became CIL Chemicals); in medicinal drugs, W.K. Wampole and Parke-Davis; in paints, Sherwin-Williams, Pratt and Lambert, and Glidden. Imperial Oil was already a leader in petroleum production. Goodyear Tire and Rubber was one of Canada's most important manufacturers of rubber goods.

From its outset, automobile production in Canada centred on the U.S. industry. Ford and Studebaker both had branch plants in Canada by 1914. One of the founding members of U.S. General Motors, Reo Motor Car Company, also had a branch plant here. Another important link with General Motors was instituted in 1908 by R.S. McLaughlin, who entered a licensing arrangement with Buick to import engines for bodies he was producing in Oshawa. Later, of course, his firm was absorbed by General Motors. In the same year, Canadian Cycle and Motor Car Company, which had prospered originally as the result of a licensing agreement with a U.S. bicycle manufacturer, began production of the Durant under licence. Finally in this sector, although Canadian manufacturers of agricultural machinery dominated production in Canada, U.S. branch plants such as International Harvester, Case, and John Deere had captured a significant share of the market.

While much can be inferred from the pre-1914 presence of U.S. branch plants in these critical sectors, unfortunately there are no statistics that would allow us to assess accurately the extent to which they had captured control of the "growth industries." We do, however, have a breakdown of

Table Three
Origin of Capital Investment in Selected Industrial
Enterprises in Canada, 1920 and 1921

Industry	Per cent of U.S. ownership		Per cent of Canadian ownership	
	1920	1921	1920	1921
Electrical apparatus	45	42	43	42
Paints, drugs, chemicals	60	55	33	35
Petroleum refining	63	36	36	63
Rubber goods, boots, shoes	36	40	52	53
Automobiles, auto accessories	69	78	31	22
Agricultural implements	39	24	50	52
Total	31	28	58	61

SOURCE: Dominion Bureau of Statistics surveys published in the *Financial Post*, December 1, 1922, pp. 17, 20, and October 19, 1923, p. 16.

the nationality of capital investment in Canadian manufacturing just after the Great War.

It would seem that the special requirements of wartime production stimulated a significant expansion in the value of U.S. investment in Canada as it reached approximately 30 per cent of the national total by the conclusion of World War One. An analysis of Table Three indicates that this U.S. investment was indeed concentrated in the "growth industries." In all these sectors, the level of U.S. investment is higher than its share of total capital investment in manufacturing (with the exception of agricultural implements in 1921). In automobile production, as well as in paints, drugs, and chemicals, U.S. capital is clearly dominant. If we accept that Canadian General Electric was a quasi-branch plant, then U.S. capital would also be dominant in the electrical sector. Only in agricultural implements, petroleum refining, and rubber manufactures is U.S. capital not dominant, although a strong base for later expansion had been established.

Industrializing within the Empire

To this point, our inquiry has argued that a particular set of individual and collective choices was made in late nineteenth- and early twentieth-century Canada by both politicians and businessmen, choices that, when put together, fit the ISI model of import replacement with unchallenged technological dependence. The growing power of the branch plants toward the end of this period merely further institutionalized ISI as the dominant mode of domestic industrial production, rather than signifying the liquidation of an independent, aggressive, export-oriented Canadian manufacturing sector. In order to better understand why these choices seemed appropriate to those who made them, we now shift our focus to an examination of the environment that conditioned them. This will require us to scrutinize the field of post-Confederation economic development with a much wider lens than we have previously employed.

The opening of the West, the building of a transcontinental railway, large-scale immigration, and the establishment of an integrated domestic economy through industrialization – all these were the objectives of Canada's ambitious, even visionary, national development scheme of this era. In this respect, our political and economic elites achieved no mean measure of success, thereby confirming both their entrepreneurial spirit and skills. How did these objectives emerge and what was the place given to industrial strategy among them? As we address this crucial question, it will become apparent that, more than any other single factor, Canada's attachment to the British Empire at this historic juncture seems to have structured the view of Canadian decision-makers as to the economic and political opportunities and constraints of their circumstances.

Let us survey first the economic context of Canadian industrialization. From the late nineteenth century until World War One, Canadian wealth was rooted in agricultural production for export to Britain. That country absorbed fully half of Canada's exports between 1875 and 1914, most of them agricultural. To illustrate, between 1900 and 1913 about four-fifths of Canada's exports to Britain were agricultural products. The importance of this trade to both countries can be seen in Table Four.

From the perspective of British capital, Canada's main function in the Empire was as a supplier of food products. Canada, India, and Australasia were dependable sources of cheap food and it was both for immediate profit and for future strategic security that British capitalists were eager to develop them agriculturally. Although the United States, not Canada, was Britain's main supplier of foodstuffs during this period, Canada was a principal imperial producer of some important staples, including meat and grains. Her contribution in this regard was greatly enhanced by the opening of the West. For example, in the first decade of this century, Canada accounted for two-fifths of Empire imports of wheat and wheat flour into Britain and nearly 16 per cent of Britain's total requirements by 1909.

While the Canadian bourgeoisie was becoming ever more dependent on British markets to digest its exports, it was also increasingly dependent on British investors to finance the massive transport infrastructure needed

Table Four
The British Market for Canadian Agricultural
Products, 1870-1913

Years	Canadian agricultural exports to Britain as a percentage of total Canadian exports	Percentage of total British imports of wheat and wheat flour supplied by Canada
1870-79	23	7
1880-89	29	4
1890-94	37	5
1895-99	43	7
1900-02	41	9
1903-06	43	10
1907-09	47	16
1910-13	39	n.a.

SOURCES: Canada, House of Commons, *Sessional Papers*, 1916, no. 6, pp. 12-15; Great Britain, House of Commons, *Papers*, "Food Supplies (Imported)," 1903, no. 179, and 1910, no. 278.

to move agricultural products from the Canadian West to London. A comparison will serve to illustrate the remarkable extent of this capital assistance. By 1911, there was somewhat more British capital invested in Canada than in India. Measured in per capita terms, it is apparent that as a young country of the centre, Canada was figuratively swimming in development capital. Reflecting the different regimen prescribed by British financiers for different parts of their Empire, the gap was dramatically wide – almost fifty-two pounds invested for every Canadian and less than 1.5 pounds per Indian.[48]

For those involved in directing Canada's economic development in this formative era, the availability of these massive infusions of British investment was at once an economic opportunity and a constraint. It was an opportunity in the sense that a dynamic capitalist accumulation process of economic expansion and transformation could run on extraordinarily rich fuel in pre-World War One Canada. Fortunes were being made and the country was booming. At the same time, it must be realized that this boom was being directed toward a very particular destination. By its nature, the swollen investment demand of resource staple extraction set a limit on the energy available to fuel other economic activities.

When we look at the record here we find that Canadian investment in

Table Five
British Investment in Canada, selected years, 1870-1914

Year	Value (million pounds)	Percentage of total British foreign investment
1870	20	2
1885	113	9
1902	205	n.a.
1911	373	11
1914	515	n.a.

SOURCE: A.K. Cairncross, *Home* and *Foreign Investment, 1870-1913* (Cambridge: Cambridge University Press, 1953), pp. 182-86.

the resource extraction sector dwarfed capital formation in the industrial structure even during the period of manufacturing's most rapid expansion before World War Two, 1901-1915. Based on Buckley's estimates, total rail investment during these years sucked up approximately 27 per cent of gross capital formation in Canada. Prairie farm investment represented an additional 15 per cent of domestic capital formation. After everything else was considered, this left only 7 per cent to be directed into industrial, electrical, and mining machinery and equipment – the means of manufacturing production. To place this small share in its proper perspective, it was only very marginally greater than that being invested at the same time in farm machinery. [49]

We are led inescapably to the conclusion that in comparison to the staples focus of both trade and investment, industrialization was placed basically in the position of being an afterthought of capitalist expansion in Canada. In the light of the near-monopoly of effort in the direction of resource export, the choice of a less thoroughgoing industrialization strategy, with a greater similarity to the ISI of the periphery than to the world competitive model of the centre nations, is hardly surprising. The economic objective of the majority of industrial adherents appears to have been merely supplementary to the main field of battle, resource extraction; namely, the creation of an "instant," technologically dependent, manufacturing sector to tap Canada's relatively rich domestic market. In proceeding in this manner, Canadian political and economic elites demonstrated little awareness of the long-term implications of their choice of investment priorities. In opting for limited, but above all rapid and cheap, industrialization they believed they were contributing to the creation of a more integrated and balanced national economy. They saw this as vital to Canada's economic development because the nation had to hold out the promise of industrial employment if it was to attract and keep immigrants in competition with its more developed southern neighbour.

This brings us directly to the issue of how the political opportunities and constraints of the Empire connection structured the views of Canadian decision-makers on industrial development. From our vantage point in the late twentieth century, it is possible to forget that the British Empire, for most of its inhabitants, was not simply stuffy pictures of Queen Victoria and pink blotches on a flat map of the world. Rather, it was a very nasty piece of repressive business that systematically subjugated hundreds of millions of people in the quest for world power and economic advantage. Typically, within the colonies, challenges to the economic domination of British commerce were thoroughly smothered by an unyielding application of legislative and administrative measures on the part of British authorities.[50]

Canada's National Policy industrialization presented just such a challenge. To Britain, Canada was not only a market for British manufactures but, as we have noted, was also a producer of raw materials for British factories and homes, as well as an outlet for investment capital. If the tariff assisted Canada to reach industrial maturity, she would no longer need to import British manufactures, would increasingly monopolize her own raw materials to serve her expanding industries, and would be searching for investment outlets and markets for her manufactures in competition with Britain. Indeed, National Policy industrialization was to hurt British exporters. Between 1880 and 1914, the British share of Canadian imports dropped from one-half to one-fifth.[51]

Yet, if the National Policy tariffs of 1879 were a "Declaration of Economic Independence," as suggested by F.H. Underhill,[52] it is curious that they provoked only mild disapproval from official Britain. The cabinet of the day sent a telegram to the Canadian Governor General informing him that "Her Majesty's Government regretted to observe that the general effect of the Tariff was to increase duties already high, but deemed that the fiscal policy of Canada rested, subject to treaty obligations, with the Dominion Legislature." Even *The Times* conceded that there was nothing Britain could do when it observed that "the election was the constitutional manifestation of the popular will, and that popular will must be obeyed. It must rule in Canada, and we have long since abandoned all power, even if we cherished the wish, to interfere with its supremacy there."[53]

To understand the reasons for the mildness of this response from the same imperial lion that was preparing to swallow large parts of the continent of Africa, we must briefly contrast Canada's position in the Empire with that of other British possessions during the last half of the nineteenth century. After 1776, Britain became cautious of re-creating the circumstances that had led to popular rebellion within colonies peopled by her "kith and kin." Thus, political and economic arrangements in the remaining white colonies tended to be more flexible than in the rest of the Empire as these colonies progressed through stages of representative and, then, responsible government, which featured home rule over domestic matters.

The 1837-38 Rebellions demonstrated that this policy of appeasement must be vigorously pursued in the Canadas if independentism was not to become a threat. Accordingly, the British reacted with caution to the growth of a movement among the Canadian bourgeoisie supporting annexation of the provinces to the United States after the destruction of their markets for agricultural produce in Britain with that country's introduction of free trade in 1846. The Governor feared that unless access for Canadian resource exports could be obtained in the United States, "there is nothing before us but violent agitation, ending in convulsion or annexation."[54] By conceding the ensuing Reciprocity Treaty of 1854, in which the Canadas were allowed to impose duties more favourable to a foreign country than to Britain, a precedent was established for the development of an independent Canadian tariff policy.

This precedent was extended by new tariffs in 1859, 1879, and 1887 in the face of angry storms of protest on each occasion from British industrialists who demanded that their government intervene to disallow this legislation on the grounds of "high economic and State reasons."[55] However, the British government did nothing more than frown. Sir Robert Herbert, Permanent Under-Secretary for the Colonies during much of this period, wrote that he was "satisfied that we (Colonial Office) shall have to give up all pretension to dictate, to such a country as Canada now is, the fiscal policy which is most acceptable to British manufacturers."[56] The British had little choice here. In the last half of the nineteenth century, Canada could not be held by military occupation. A serious rupture with Britain over trade policy could have led to rebellion and/or union with the United States. This had been made perfectly clear as early as 1859 by A.T. Galt, then Minister of Finance in the Macdonald-Cartier government, when he set the stage for a Canadian revolt by writing to the Colonial Office:

. . . in the imposition of taxation, it is so plainly necessary that the Administration and the people should be in accord, that the former cannot admit responsibility or require approval beyond that of the local legislature. Self-government would be utterly annihilated if the views of the Imperial Government were to be preferred to those of the people of Canada. It is, therefore, the duty of the present Government distinctly to affirm the right of the Canadian Legislature to adjust the taxation of the people in the way they deem best, even if it should unfortunately happen to meet the disapproval of the Imperial Ministry. Her Majesty cannot be advised to disallow such acts, unless Her advisers are prepared to assume the administration of the affairs of the colony irrespective of the views of its inhabitants.[57]

So it was that, in administering a colony of settlement, Canadian political and economic elites enjoyed far greater opportunities to shape their own economic development strategy than that which was permissible in most of the Empire. Nevertheless, it is apparent that the politics of Empire also framed constraints around our economic planners, even if these were largely self-imposed and more in the realm of ideas than material forces. It can be reasonably argued that the ideology of imperial nationalism (or, in the language of the time, imperialism), common to the discourse of the era, validated a Canadian ISI strategy and thereby stifled visions of a more thoroughgoing world competitive industrialization.

Let us consider the manner in which the Canadian government did all it could to soften the blow of its industrial strategy to the British. While not for a moment considering abandoning the protective tariffs it at least dressed them in imperial clothes. Two lines were pursued in explanatory communications to Britain. The first was that the tariffs were necessary because they were the only available method of raising needed government revenue. The second, and more important, put forward the position that the tariffs were principally aimed at foreign, that is U.S., suppliers of Canadian imports. For example, Galt stated in 1859 that "We have in Canada tradesmen who make goods similar to the Americans, but not to the Sheffield: and if our duty operates as encouragement to manufacturers, it is rather against the American than the English manufacturers, as any one acquainted with this country well knows."[58]

Tilley was even more encouraging in 1879, stating that the National Policy's "general effect must certainly be to decrease importations from the United States . . . while if it materially alters the measure of trade with Great Britain, it must be on the side of increase."[59] Tupper, in 1887, observed that U.S. iron and steel imports were gradually displacing British imports to Canada, and, therefore, his new tariffs on iron and steel products were trying to decrease Canada's "dependence on foreign sources" and were "on the whole in favour of British as against foreign industry." "In ceasing to be dependent on foreign sources . . . and by the development of her great natural resources," he told the Colonial Office, "Canada may hope to attain a more prosperous position and become a source of strength to the British Empire."[60]

One is tempted to dismiss these imperialist concerns as so much cynical rhetoric designed simply to defuse the criticisms of British capitalists. We have already noted, for example, that a primary purpose of the National Policy tariffs was to encourage the "foreigner" either to replace his export trade by licensing his product to a Canadian capitalist or to establish a branch plant in Canada. But in the curious world of turn-of-the-century Canadian nationalism, what can appear to us now as inconsistent or illogical may actually have conformed to the somewhat paradoxical world view of Canada's state and business leaders. We know that during this period Canadian nationalism meant both a strong adherence to the Empire and an equally firm rejection of things American.[61] Therefore, was it not possible to assist the Empire by transferring to Canada the production of U.S. commodities, particularly those in the "growth industries" in which Britain herself was not adept?[62] And, following this logic one more step, could not Canada serve imperial interests further by becoming the Empire purveyor of these "foreign" manufactures? In fact, as we will document in subsequent chapters, this rather befuddled strategy of import substitution for the Empire was to achieve an ever greater prominence until the Great Depression of the 1930s.

Industrialization outside Empire

It could be objected at this point that one need look no further than to the factors of time and size to explain why Canada's political and economic elites chose to emphasize the development of resource extraction and staples trade over manufacturing. Put simply, this argument would hold that our late start in the industrial race meant that we entered too far behind the leaders to be able to close the gap and effectively compete. In addition, any attempt to catch up was doomed by the inefficiencies of short production runs inherent in Canada's relatively small domestic market. With a total population of only 5.3 million in 1900, Canadians were outnumbered approximately seven to one by Britains, ten to one by Germans, and fourteen to one by Americans.

This line of reasoning has intuitive appeal but crumbles under the weight of an examination of the experience of two other late industrializers, Sweden and Japan. As we will see, the economic and political elites of these two nations, somewhat more removed from the considerations and temptations of Empire than their Canadian counterparts, selected industrial strategies founded upon the achievement of a significant level of technological independence and export competitiveness.

Sweden, with only 5 million inhabitants in 1900, was an economic backwater in Europe throughout the nineteenth century. Almost 70 per cent of her population remained agricultural as late as 1880 and living standards were depressed when compared to those of her larger, more successful northern European neighbours. In this period, Sweden's industries were concentrated in the traditional iron and timber resource export trades, which dated from the Middle Ages.

Sweden's "take-off" into modern industrialism, like Canada's, peaked between 1895 and 1920. Here, too, this period of rapid expansion of production appears to have been linked to the completion of a state-financed program of railway construction undertaken to improve internal communications in the latter half of the nineteenth century. Total rail kilometrage increased more than elevenfold between 1860 and 1880.[63] The enactment of tariff legislation in the 1890s also seems to have had some beneficial effect on the expansion of the domestic market.

For our purposes, of particular interest in Sweden's "second" industrial revolution is the rapid and early development of her high-technology engineering industries. To a certain extent, Swedish producers may have enjoyed a slight head start on Canadians in this key manufacturing sector as they had been able to satisfy a portion of the machinery demands of their iron and timber producers during the earlier part of the 1800s. Nevertheless, they were incapable of supplying the modern processes, techniques, and machines necessary for the "take-off" into modern industrialism. As in Canada, the greater part of this new technology initially had to be imported from more advanced centres.

Nor was it seen to be an easy matter to catch up to Germany, Great Britain, and the United States. Swedish machinery manufacturers understood that, despite tariff protection, their home market was "inadequate as a base for advanced, large-scale industrial operations."[64] However, the satisfaction of the demands of foreign markets, especially Russia, for specialized high-technology manufactures was seen from the first as a means of expanding their production runs to world competitiveness. The support of leading financiers associated with the timber and iron trades appears to have been a crucial factor in mobilizing the investment capital necessary for the intensification of manufacturing.[65] As one observer has noted, "these wholesalers, being both importers and exporters, had an international outlook. They saw the needs of the foreign market and reacted rapidly by founding or cooperating at the founding of new export enterprises."[66]

On the basis of this aggressive, outward-looking industrial strategy, Swedish engineering plants borrowed foreign manufacturing technologies and techniques; copied, assimilated, and adapted them; and rapidly came up with a number of innovations and inventions that were competitive on world markets – dairy separators, ball bearings, diesel engines, primus stoves, electric motors and generators, and others. The outcome was a growing volume of production in engineering goods after the turn of the century, which both largely supplied the home market, thereby reducing Swedish dependence on foreign imports of advanced technology and machines, and developed considerable foreign markets.

In less than twenty years, Sweden moved from import dependence in advanced high-technology manufactures to a position as net exporter, selling abroad nearly four times as much as she purchased in foreign markets in 1917. Overseas sales of engineering products reached 16 per cent of Sweden's export income in 1916.[67] The reader will recall that in this same era the official organ of the Canadian Manufacturers' Association was suggesting to its readers that "naturally the making of machinery is one of the last industries to be developed in a new country."[68]

Japan is perhaps the most dramatic example of a successful late industrializer. In 1887, nearly 80 per cent of the population still worked in the agricultural sector and only 10 per cent in industry. Here, as in Sweden, the key to success on the part of its economic and political elites was to link technological independence with the development of modern manufacturing. Here, too, the cultivation of foreign markets for industrial products held strategic importance from the beginning.

Held rigidly in check by a traditional feudal aristocracy, Japanese manufacturing was either extremely backward or non-existent in virtually all sectors until the collapse of the old regime in 1868. As a consequence, the Japanese bourgeoisie in formation was forced to rely completely on foreign technology in order to begin the construction of its modern industrial base. This was to mean the import of foreign specialists, the purchase of foreign machine tools, production under licensing agreements, and even a limited degree of direct foreign investment in pivotal sectors such as automobiles and machinery.

However, it was conscious government policy, in close co-operation with the growing manufacturing oligopolies, to use this borrowed technology to build up an independent Japanese technological capability. This translated into the adjustment and adaptation of foreign technology to meet local conditions requiring the labour-intensive production of cheap and often shoddy goods. The state established model factories and experimental stations using foreign machines and processes in order that Japanese manufacturers might imitate and adapt the technology they found useful. As one study has pointed out, this "process of imitation not only helped improve the understanding of the working of the technology involved but considerably strengthened, on account of the trial and error involved, the design and engineering capability of domestic machinery manufacturers."[69] The slogan used to highlight this policy was "the first machine by import, the second by domestic production."[70]

This approach rather quickly transformed the structure of Japanese industry. At the end of the nineteenth century traditional industries like foods, textiles, and forest products were dominant, with over 70 per cent of total manufacturing production, but by 1935 the modern machinery, chemicals, and metals industries made up more than 50 per cent of the total.[71] Imports of machinery equalled only 10 per cent of gross domestic output of these goods in 1936.[72] A "decidedly protectionist" tariff policy aided in the construction and consolidation of these modern industries.[73]

Foreign markets for Japanese manufactures held a strategic importance in this remarkable success story. In order to pay for the import of the raw materials and capital goods necessary to fuel industrial expansion, Japan had to sell the products of her industries abroad. In fact, both merchandise exports and imports were to expand more than forty-five times between 1887 and 1935. Here, too, state policy was of some assistance. The government encouraged the formation of export combinations, as well as providing technical assistance and commodity inspection.

The achievements of state and business export policies soon manifested themselves. By 1930, approximately 25 to 35 per cent of the entire product of Japanese industry was being exported. This represented nearly 20 per cent of Japan's gross national product. According to one source, while only 2 per cent of Japanese exports could be considered "wholly manufactured" in 1870, by 1930, over 50 per cent could be so classified.[74]

Conclusion

This chapter has employed a number of different directions to cut into the critically important formative years of modern Canadian industrialization following the proclamation of the National Policy tariffs of 1879. In so doing, we have confronted many of the more familiar interpretations of the failure of Canadian manufacturing to become competitive in the world economy. Our examination of the Swedish and Japanese cases helps to illuminate a number of the traditional explanatory myths that have surrounded the discussion of the issue. Clearly, by themselves, factors such as a late start, a small domestic market, a tariff-coddled production process, a high initial degree of technological dependence, and lack of comparative advantage in manufacturing cannot account for the failure of Canadian industry to climb out of its domestic market. Nor, in this early period, has foreign ownership yet become the crucial variable.

Neither do explanations that search for scapegoats among the business and government leaders of the era hit their targets. To illustrate, the post-Confederation Canadian bourgeoisie has been blasted for its alleged anti-nationalism, lack of entrepreneurship, and divisive intra-class rivalries between manufacturers and merchants. However, we have seen that the pre-1914 expansion and intensification of the resource export economy to include the West was, at once, nationalist, within the nineteenth-century perspective of Empire development; highly ambitious and successful as an entrepreneurial project; and, finally, a scheme that united, rather than divided, Canadian capitalists.

The concept of import substitution was injected into our discussion not to explain the course of Canadian industrialization but to help describe it. ISI serves as a framework to direct our attention to those internal and external factors that formed the investment decisions of individual members of the Canadian bourgeoisie into a collective strategy. The intent of the policy-makers, both inside and outside the state apparatus, was to build an industrial structure that would provide a supplement to the resource export economy – a quick and profitable return on minimal capital investment and a base for urban employment. A secure domestic market would be captured for local producers by means of a tariff-induced replacement of imports. Significantly, capturing the home market was not to be accomplished while becoming internationally competitive in specialized lines (with a few exceptions). Instead, an extreme and unchallenged dependency on foreign technology was to preclude from the beginning any serious attempt to move into foreign markets.

It has been suggested that Canada's position within the British Empire had a significant effect on the decision to pursue a more passive industrial strategy than typical in a centre country. We observed that political and economic considerations related to the Empire were important in influencing the decision to place maximum energy and investment in building a staples economy based on the production of western wheat. ISI, as a supplementary activity, was a strategic choice rooted in the logic of Canada's position in the Empire which, when made and carried out, became a constraint on future industrial development. It was to become progressively more difficult, even irrational, for individual Canadian manufacturers to swim upstream by risking investment capital in taking a more independent, export-oriented direction. This became especially the case as the branch-plant sector, for which import substitution was the *raison d'être,* gradually expanded into a dominant position in Canadian industry.

Chapter Three

"We Don't Need the Marts of Europe"

~~~~~~

The perplexing story of the failure of Canadian manufacturers to take advantage of their opportunities in world markets during the twentieth century could probably best be told directly from their own mouths. Unfortunately, this is unlikely to happen for a number of reasons. First, there are so many who could speak that the voices would deafen, forcing us to listen only to a sample. Since the fortunes and circumstances of firms vary so greatly over the more than 100 years of our investigation, it would be nearly impossible to select those few who could pronounce with authority for all. In addition, the perspective of individual firms, caught up in their own affairs, is typically too narrow for them to appreciate how they fit into the more general pattern we seek to describe. Then, too, we could not count on their record-keeping over such a long period of time to be anything more than fragmentary on the kinds of export policy questions we are addressing. Finally, firms are not different from individuals when it comes to revealing their own weaknesses. We could expect to find this to be particularly the case in an area as sensitive to national economic development as export trade. The temptation to stress minor successes in the face of more meaningful failures would very likely be irresistible.

Our method of inquiry, then, must of necessity be somewhat indirect. Rather than surveying the performance of individual manufacturers, we will excavate the historical record of their collective activities layer by layer. As we will discover, the core of these deposits can be extracted from the business publications of the time, and, more importantly, from the well-recorded interface between manufacturers and the branch of the federal state apparatus specifically charged with the responsibility of stimulating the foreign sales of Canadian industry, the Trade Commissioner Service of the Department of Trade and Commerce. This focus on government will also prove valuable at a later stage. It will lay the foundation for a theme to be explored more fully in the final chapters – the evolution of state export policy as a central aspect of an overall Canadian industrial strategy.

Export Promotion in the Post-National Policy State

In the last chapter we concentrated on the formative years of our modern industrialization. During that time, we argued, our political and economic leaders chose to direct their principal efforts and investments toward the expansion and intensification of the staples trade to the detriment of industrial development. Manufacturing was organized primarily as a supplementary activity with little sustained effort to cultivate an internationally competitive export capability built on a significant degree of technological independence. The reader might reasonably wonder how the Canadian government came at all to form a policy of stimulating manufactured exports during this early period. Indeed, as we will soon discover, it was far more on the basis of "muddling through" than rational planning.

Shortly after the re-election of his Conservative government in the midst of a worldwide depression in 1887, Sir John A. Macdonald introduced legislation to create a Department of Trade and Commerce. Influenced by the demands of business for more direct input into policy-making, Macdonald intended to split the functions of the existing Department of Finance, leaving it with the technical accounting duties and giving the broader national and international economic policy concerns to Trade and Commerce. However, by the time the Act was finally proclaimed in 1892, plans to grant such weighty responsibilities to the new department had been scrapped. Instead, Trade and Commerce was provided with an external trade orientation as it inherited a patchwork quilt of overseas part-time trade agents and subsidized shipping lines from Finance.[1]

At first, neither the new department's purpose nor its clientele seemed clear. Manufacturing interests had petitioned the government, from at least the mid-1880s, to furnish them with a foreign network of state export agencies such as those that had been available for at least a hundred years to capitalists in Great Britain and the United States.[2] Equally important in the introduction of overseas export agencies were the representations of land-based transportation companies, such as the Canadian Pacific Railway, as well as a number of influential Canadian merchants. These interests supported parallel programs of state subsidies to steamship lines that would connect Canada and a few selected foreign markets. The railways hoped to stimulate the use of their facilities for through traffic and the merchants were anxious to intercept the flow of Canadian resource exports that found their way to foreign markets through U.S. ports. Terminals of these subsidized lines were often selected as the sites of Canada's first external trade offices in order to drum up business for the shippers.

At the turn of the century, some manufacturers began to complain about the meagre quality of export services they were being offered by the few, mostly part-time agents placed in the haphazard manner just described. The reorganization and expansion of the Canadian Manufacturers' Association (CMA) in 1900 provided these industrialists with a platform from which they could air their grievances. Forming themselves into the Commercial Intelligence Committee of the CMA, they pressed the government to provide them with an expanded overseas service organized along the lines of "what is recognized as the most complete consular system in the world, that of the United States." They denounced then current Trade and Commerce efforts as "notorious . . . inadequate and disappointing."[3]

Criticism was focused on three principal areas: the poor quality of agents and their conditions of service, the meagre transmission of trade information between agents and manufacturers, and the small number of overseas trade offices. To begin, the committee argued that the system of part-time agents was inadequate as such men had "most of their time and interest taken up with private business." Consequently, Canadian "consuls" should be hired on a full-time basis. It was also recommended that these positions be given to candidates qualified in the field of export promotion and be removed from the patronage system that dominated public service appointments in this era.

On the question of information that agents were to gather on behalf of Canadian industrialists, it was proposed that they should be given more adequate funds for travel within their countries of posting and be periodically returned to Canada in order to bring them up to date on current business conditions. The committee contended that Trade and Commerce issued the reports of their agents too slowly to be of immediate use to manufacturers and suggested that in future the preparation of intelligence summaries should be more frequent and systematic.

Finally, it was recommended that Trade and Commerce establish "consular" offices in London, Sydney, Cape Town, Yokohama, Kingston (Jamaica), Paris, Hamburg, Rio de Janeiro, Calcutta, and Shanghai. They estimated that this new system would cost the government $75,000, fully four times greater than the established level. This substantially increased expenditure was justified along precisely the same lines used when the matter of state export agencies had first been raised by the industrialists of 1885.

We do not believe in relying too much on Government support or Government interference in trade matters. At the same time we feel that in a work of this particular kind success can only be secured through active Government co-operation. The practise of the whole world recognizes the correctness of this attitude. [4]

The Commercial Intelligence Committee was quite accurate in its assessment that government co-operation was essential to the advancement of Canadian manufactured exports. Had the committee's enthusiasm for trade matters been more widely shared by the general membership of the CMA, government intervention in this case might have been less crucial. However, it was far in advance of the majority of its colleagues. For example, the committee, wishing to mark the inauguration of a new government-subsidized shipping line from Canada in 1902, was forced to scrap a plan to send along a representative of its own to promote Canadian products in South Africa. After canvassing the membership of the CMA for financial support for this project, it could only find twenty-five interested firms, which collectively anted only one-fifth of the cost. In this indifferent environment, state assistance would seem the only logical alternative.

Largely as a result of this committee's efforts, the trade promotion facilities of Trade and Commerce were very significantly upgraded in the period before World War One. Although changes did not immediately follow on the heels of the committee's demands of 1900, the number of overseas postings of full-time agents was gradually built up. By 1905, the reports of these trade commissioners began to be published on a weekly basis. Continuing complaints about the quality of appointments brought a system of merit selections of university graduates in 1914.

The "Side Show"

Although evidence can be found in these representations to Ottawa of a desire to export among some manufacturers, for the great majority the home market remained almost their total focus of activity. This was the clear conclusion of a 1907 report of the Commercial Intelligence Committee on the subject of membership use of the CMA's own export services. Three programs were surveyed: requests for the reports of foreign commercial houses, applications for translation services, and the appointment of correspondent agents for the use of CMA members in "the principal cities of the world." As Table Six indicates, only a handful of manufacturers used either of the first two services. Because of general disinterest, the third program lapsed.

Throughout this report, the neglect of these export services by Canadian manufacturers was unfavourably compared to the performance of

Table Six
Membership Use of Canadian Manufacturers' Association
Export Services, 1904-1907

	1904-05	*1905-06*	*1906-07*
Reports of foreign commercial houses			
no. supplied	47	36	42
members served	30	26	16
Translations			
no. supplied	n.a.	57	43
members served	n.a.	18	14

SOURCE: National Archives of Canada, MG 28, I 230, vol. 36, nos. 154-163, Canadian Manufacturers' Association, Minutes of the Commercial Intelligence Committee, July 16, 1907.

their more accomplished U.S. rivals. To illustrate, it was pointed out that members of the National Association of Manufacturers had requested over 26,000 translations during 1906-07. With obvious frustration, the committee's secretary determined that little could be done to improve the export scene "under present conditions, with our domestic trade expanding at a rate which is taxing the capacity of many of our factories to the utmost, and with the consequent indifference displayed by many of our manufacturers to export trade."[5]

In 1912, the Commercial Intelligence Committee publicly conceded that the progress of Canadian manufactured exports in the previous decade had been slight because the rapidly expanding domestic market had made the "average" industrialist "indifferent" to foreign trade. Stress was placed by the committee on the many exporting opportunities neglected during these years. "Enquiries from abroad for Canadian merchandise have been distributed by the score," they lamented, "only to be met in most cases with the response that the parties addressed were too busy with domestic orders to quote on foreign business."[6]

Industrial Canada, the official organ of the CMA, had been forced earlier to conclude that "few manufacturers are willing to go in for an export business" after learning the results of an "experiment" undertaken in 1909 by the Commercial Intelligence Committee.[7] Each of the nearly 2,200 members of the CMA was asked for its co-operation in collecting information for the use of the government trade commissioners stationed abroad. No expense was involved for the individual firms as all that was requested was that catalogues and price lists be sent to the CMA for transmission. "Yet less than a hundred were interested enough to comply with the request," the journal reported.

Industrial Canada speculated on the reasons for the failure of more than 97 per cent of its organization's members to respond to this appeal. Big manufacturers had their own export facilities, it suggested, while the smallest companies were simply uninterested. Medium-sized firms were wary of foreign markets because "many feel that the same money and pains put into the local field would bring them just as ample and much quicker returns."[8] This was hardly an original conclusion. The home market bias of capital investment in Canadian industry and its negative effect on export trade had been earlier described in the pages of *Industrial Canada* by H. Watson, secretary of the Canadian Section of the Imperial Institute in London:

> Nearly all Canadian industrial enterprises were originally established for supplying the wants of the domestic market without, in most instances, any particular attention to the possibilities of export. . . . As a result, whereas capital has naturally been forthcoming for ventures from which local markets promised an immediate and profitable return, investment in other industries the product of which is more particularly suitable for outside markets has been, until recently, restricted.[9]

For its part, *Industrial Canada* frequently attempted to stir manufacturers to action, arguing that it was a short-sighted strategy to neglect export business

> merely because the unexampled prosperity Canada is enjoying gives them all they can do to fill home orders. . . . some day the manufacturers of Canada will be sorry that they regarded export business as a "side show", to be taken in when the other show was not running well.[10]

A sense of lost opportunities for Canadian manufacturers in foreign markets and a foreboding of a future in which Canada had missed the exporting boat permeated all the other important business journals of the era. The *Monetary Times* warned that "there is a danger of losing a chance to get into foreign markets . . . so long as prosperity remains, the purchasing power of Canada is high and the absorption strength of the home market is increasing."[11] Twenty years earlier, the *Journal of Commerce* had similarly observed that:

At present, possibly, the requirements of the home market are sufficient to absorb the whole of our Canadian industrial production.
But this will not always be the case. . . . Would it not, then, be wise to
exploit this new outlet for our wares [Australia] in time: so that we
may have a secure foothold there against the day when it may be of
vital importance for us to secure it . . . ?[12]

Such indirect appeals to action appear to have had little effect in altering the extreme domestic orientation of Canadian industrialists. Typical
were these sentiments of J.P. Murray of the Toronto Carpet Manufacturing Company, an important CMA militant. Murray argued that the "most
profitable market for a manufacturer is his home market" and that spending money on immigration was as important as spending money to break
into foreign markets. Exports were to be considered only after domestic
requirements had been filled.

We cannot hope to have much of a standing in foreign markets until
we are able to supply in a greater way our own requirements. To do
this properly we must manufacture much more largely, and we are
not warranted in doing so unless we have a larger home market.
Until we have reached that stage we cannot hope to export successfully.[13]

Readers should take heed of the sharp contrast between this statement and
the outward-oriented Swedish industrial practice of the same era outlined
in the previous chapter. There, it will be recalled, exports were, from the
beginning, used as a means of lengthening production lines and thereby
making them more efficient.

When we consider export developments in these years, we should not
lose sight of the fact that the general membership of the CMA was preoccupied with extending their reach only as far as the new markets of Canada's
western territories and the Yukon. For example, in 1903 over 100 manufacturers, including the president and other executive members of the
association, chartered a train to the west coast to survey business conditions for themselves. The train was decorated with such slogans as "Build
up our Home Markets" and "Canadian Goods for Canadian People," and
Industrial Canada boasted that it was "the heaviest passenger train ever
handled by the C.P.R."[14] Not surprisingly, this popular poem of Pauline
Johnson was heartily appreciated at many CMA banquets:

We don't need the marts of Europe,
nor the trade of the Eastern isles,
We don't need the Yankee's corn and wine,
nor the Asiatic's smiles.

For what so good as our home-made cloth,
and under the wide blue dome,
Will you tell me where you have tasted bread
like the bread that is baked at home?[15]

Abundant evidence that this poem was an accurate reflection of the viewpoint of the majority of Canadian industrial capitalists was readily available to both the business press and the general public in the published reports of the overseas representatives of the Department of Trade and Commerce. In fact, the trade commissioners frequently commented on the problem. "Nearly every letter from Canada in respect to propositions for new business here," one wrote, "has been a regret that the writer is unable to consider any foreign trade at the present time, as the improved demands in Canada require his full capacity."[16] Another government agent in Argentina was mystified by the industrial strategy of Canadian capitalists and their almost neurotic abhorrence of exporting.

From the inquiries received from Canada to date, it would not appear that much interest was being taken by manufacturers in this part of South America. One reads that factories are choked with orders for the domestic trade, which is highly satisfactory, but having assured a market at home, it would seem all the more reason that they should commence to show some interest in the foreign field. It is an inexplicable thing, but many manufacturers appear to fear the very thought of the export trade; they apparently harbour the delusion that it is full of pitfalls for the unwary, full of unknown risks, and that once embarked upon it there can be no return to domestic trade.[17]

All could not be put down to fear derived from ignorance, however. Even manufacturers who were well travelled told much the same story in regard to exports.

A manufacturer from the Maritime Provinces passing through [Japan] lately . . . was asked if he did not wish to look into the market here with the view to export to this country. . . . Being pressed, he said, well the fact was that unless things had gone wrong since he left home, his company had enough to do in their line to supply the home market. . . . Another Canadian manufacturer, largely interested in textiles, literally travelling for his health said . . . the demands of a rapidly developing home market were such that they could not pretend to offer business to Japan.[18]

Export Performance of the Manufacturers

In such a background of general apathy, it is hardly surprising that the *Weekly Report* of the trade commissioners provides a vivid catalogue of the many follies of Canadian industrial exporters. To begin, most manufacturers seemed to have attached so little importance to developing a foreign trade that they habitually neglected to answer letters from potential overseas customers in any meaningful fashion. Canada's first full-time agent, after two years in the Australian field, wrote:

> The greatest impediment to the success of the work here is in Canada. A few firms have a knowledge of what is necessary to be done to get entrance to this market, but the majority do not and writing seems to make small impression. On behalf of an [Australian] house, I recently wrote to a number of Canadian firms for information respecting their goods and of all the replies that I received, but one answered the questions in such a manner that would determine whether business could be done or not. [19]

Experiences in New Zealand and in other markets were even more graphically communicated to Canadians by the trade commissioners.

> In Auckland a large commission house wrote to eight Canadian paper mills soliciting their agency. One reply was favourable, the other seven stated they were selling all they could make at home at better prices than could be got in New Zealand. In Wellington, a firm had received but three replies to forty-two letters written to manufacturers of various lines, in only one of which was there a promise of trade. In Christchurch, a firm in a large way in boots and shoes, leather and leather goods had received five replies to over fifty letters. [20]

As we might expect, given the demonstrated reluctance of Canadian industrialists to reply to their correspondence, it was a rare occasion indeed when they would dispatch a salesman to directly canvass a foreign market. This sin of omission generated a good deal of critical heat from the trade commissioners, who made frequent and unfavourable comparisons with the performance of the firms of other industrialized countries in this matter. These comments were typical in this regard.

> Manufacturers' representatives from Great Britain make periodical trips and interview the business men and they invariably secure substantial orders. The resident agents of firms in Great Britain, Germany and the United States have regular customers upon whom

they call at stated intervals. Canada is at a great disadvantage in this respect. There have only been two instances within the past year when a direct representative of a Canadian firm has appeared in New Zealand, although the result justified the expense.[21]

Even in the much closer Bahamas, a Canadian salesman was said to be "a rara avis indeed, while from the United States he is a familiar object."[22] In Barbados, it was claimed that Canadian trade had not expanded as rapidly as that of Britain or the U.S. "due largely to the fact that Canadian commercial men do not visit the Island."[23] The trade commissioner in South Africa warned that unless direct representation was established in that country, Canadian manufacturers would continue to "receive the leavings of United States manufacturers, and tend to confirm the opinion of local business men that we do not take our export trade seriously."[24] The Manchester posting reported that U.S. commercial travellers were constantly pushing trade and canvassing orders for hot water heaters, furnaces, radiators, and plumbing supplies "in marked contradiction to our Canadian manufacturers, who are not represented and are totally unknown, hence the trade goes to their United States competitors, though the English dealer would prefer to trade with Canada."[25]

Unfortunately, even when the mountain journeyed to Mohammed, in the form of foreign sales agents eager to place orders in Canadian factories, our manufacturers frequently remained aloof. A Trade and Commerce agent in Australia recounted one such visit.

A number of Sydney houses sent representatives to visit Canada last year; those who have returned express disappointment at the results of their trip. They state that few firms seem to be interested in export trade, and fewer still were willing to make the sacrifice requisite to make a success. Some agreements were entered into which will lead, it is hoped, to business, but in the majority of cases little can be anticipated from their visits. They complain that even where contracts were entered into they have not been observed.[26]

Among those few enterprises that did make some attempt to break into foreign markets, participation was often token as it was limited to sending out copies of their Canadian order catalogues. This provoked a further set of complaints from the trade commissioners. As no revisions to the Canadian catalogues had been made, goods advertised in them were often completely unsuitable for sale in the markets to which they had been forwarded. For example, the Barbados agent recounted an early version of the "refrigerators to Eskimos" chestnut:

On more than one occasion, catalogues and price lists have been furnished by a Canadian manufacturer . . . without the least suspicion
apparently . . . that a different description of stove might be required
in the tropics from that used in the north. Not only have illustrations
shown stoves too large in size and therefore too hot to be successfully
used, but even furnaces and radiators for heating houses and
descriptions of hot water systems have sometimes accompanied
them.[27]

These catalogues were not usually accompanied by price lists of which the
potential customer could make any sense. Instead of quoting the cost of
goods landed in foreign ports, Canadian factory prices were provided.
More than one trade commissioner reported that "dealers will not even
pay ordinary attention to such scant unaccustomed information."[28]

When a Canadian manufacturer did decide to make a serious attempt
to enter a foreign market, the reason could very often be traced to causes
within the domestic market. A precedent for overseas dumping of surplus
stock in the face of a soft local demand or overproduction was established
within the first few years of the introduction of the National Policy tariffs.
The *Journal of Commerce* had noted at the time that "in spite of the glowing
accounts of mill managers, every consignment sent to Chinese ports had
to be sold at a loss."[29] From this point, the practice of dumping continued,
as reported by *Industrial Canada,* "not infrequently."[30] It was so univer-
sally denounced by the various trade commissioners that *Weekly Report*
took the unusual step of publishing a strong editorial blast. "To create the
impression that Canada is merely coquetting with foreign markets would
be most pernicious to our national reputation," it fumed.[31]

Trade and Commerce reports also related numerous incidents of the
export of substandard or obsolete products from Canadian plants. One
agent, stationed in Mexico, appealed to the higher sensibilities of the
offending manufacturers in pleading that they discontinue the practice.
"Any, who from personal motives, do not hesitate to send out an inferior
article should," he maintained, "at least from patriotic motives refuse to
do so."[32]

The lengthy delays that overseas customers encountered in getting
Canadian firms to fill their orders also received their share of attention
from Trade and Commerce agents. In 1910, the trade commissioner in
Australia estimated that only one-fifth of orders shipped outside of "established trade" were filled within a "reasonable" time.[33] Even if one
received a Canadian order without unnecessary delay, one could rarely be
certain of the condition in which it would arrive. Apparently, many manufacturers failed to pack their goods for export any more carefully than they

might for shipment between two Canadian cities. A trade commissioner in Argentina suffered personally from this habitual oversight. In a report detailing the "large" Argentinian market for imported furniture, he admitted that he was not "very sanguine" about the possibility of Canadian firms seizing this opportunity.

> The writer has recently had some experience of Canadian methods. The whole of the furniture for this office was purchased in the Dominion, from three separate factories, the idea being that . . . it might be an advertisement for the manufacturers. . . . the goods, although promised by a certain date, were late in shipment, or some of them, and were unaccompanied by the proper documents. . . . These things were not so serious, but on arrival the cases were found to be of old and inferior wood, and much damaged, and the packing to have been nothing short of disgraceful. The things appear to have been thrown in haphazardly. . . . As a consequence, the articles were in a shocking condition, requiring the service of two men for a week, to put them in repair, and even then it was impossible to restore all to their original condition.[34]

In Chapter 2 we suggested that the technologically dependent structure of Canadian industrialization placed important barriers in the way of developing a trade in manufactured exports. Licensees, we discovered, were often forbidden to export as a condition of using a foreign patented process in the Canadian market. U.S. branch plants, then as now, had to be content with a division of the world market determined by the priorities of their parent firms. It would now be appropriate to examine the extent to which the overseas agents of Trade and Commerce became aware, in their everyday work, of the structural barriers to export that, we have argued, were at once a cause and an effect of the almost exclusively domestic orientation of Canadian manufacturing.

It must be admitted from the outset that there is not as much discussion of the problem of export blocking in the trade commissioners' reports as one might initially expect, given the considerable extent of technological dependence. Certainly, all of the follies detailed above are far more pervasive themes. Yet, this is perhaps natural, given the perspective of these men. Physically removed from the Canadian scene, they were far more likely to comment on the concrete performance of industrialists with whom they had direct contact, rather than with any set of what were often highly invisible export restrictions imposed at the Canadian source.

Nevertheless, there is sufficient evidence to suggest that a number of the trade commissioners encountered the problem frequently enough to become aware of its negative effects. For instance, occasionally cases of direct export blocking, such as the following, were reported:

> During the past few years several Canadian enterprises have commenced the manufacture of skewers and have worked up a certain amount of British trade . . . in several instances, no sooner had a regular trade been established . . . than the Canadian manufacturer sold out to the United States Skewer Trust and no further supplies have been available from that particular source. Chiefly from that cause Canada has not obtained anything like the share of the British skewer trade which might otherwise have been secured. . . . Only recently a couple of Canadian concerns which had concluded arrangements with United Kingdom firms – and in one case made contracts ahead – have sold out their plants and gone out of business. [35]

That this may have been a fairly common pattern is indicated by a similar account originating in Australia.

> One of the difficulties in getting good agents to take up [Canadian] lines is the fear that after they have gone to the expense of building up a trade their Canadian principal enters into an agreement which prevents them from shipping goods to Australia. Two cases of such hardship occurred in our trade. United States firms finding their Australian trade cut into, went to Canada and purchased the rival factories and put an end to Canadian export in these lines. [36]

In this regard, there is some evidence that the constantly heard cry of "home demand" may have simply been a popular euphemism for export restrictions. One trade commissioner narrated the story of an Australian buyer who had made supply arrangements with several Canadian firms.

> In one case, after he had done this he received a reply that the home orders were increasing and the firm had concluded not to attempt an export business just yet. In a second case, he received information that they were unable to go any further, as they had been negotiating for some time with another firm in Australia and could do nothing until a conclusion could be reached in such negotiations. In both of these cases the firms were branches in Canada but owned abroad and the possibility is that the branches had been stopped in their proposition to do an export trade from Canada. [37]

Some notice was also taken by the trade commissioners of the undesirable consequences of licensing arrangements on Canadian industrial exports. Under the title of "cannot export," one observed that "a number of large factories in Canada are operated on arrangements with patentees or others which prevent their exporting to Australia, though the article may not be patented here."[38] Two years later the same agent pointed the finger at Canadian manufacturers of electrical goods "able to export" but forbidden to do so because of their "arrangements."[39] Another trade commissioner, working in Japan, also demonstrated his awareness of the territorial limitations of Canadian licensees.

> The practical nothingness of the Canadian bicycle trade here is consistent with the impression that I received in Canada before leaving; that the bicycle trade, like the wire trade and doubtless others, was not free but bound; that it had its allotment of territory or its measure of output, and must rest and be thankful, which is an industrial condition very well understood now-a-days.[40]

Industrial Capitalists and the Trade Commissioners

With all that has been recorded to this point, it stands to reason that the disinterest, incompetence, and even dishonesty of Canadian industrial exporters gradually eroded the enthusiasm of many trade commissioners with some years of service, often leaving them discouraged, frustrated, and cynical. In 1908, J.S. Larke, perhaps the most diligent of the early appointees, lamented that the dismal record of Canadian exporters in Australia had made it "more difficult to sell Canadian goods today than it was ten years ago." He cited these examples of how past performance had destroyed future prospects:

> I have endeavoured to get firms interested on behalf of two Canadian exporting houses. One firm wrote that he would not communicate with Canadian houses, as he, unfortunately, had had the experience of the uselessness of so doing. Another, a prominent manufacturers agent, who was very desirous a few years ago of taking on Canadian lines, stated that he did not care to touch the Canadian trade. He had been so disappointed in what he had tried to do through mistakes made in shipping and failure to meet conditions or even to reply to correspondence that he did not wish for any further experience.[41]

A Trade and Commerce representative in South Africa also deplored the "half-hearted business methods" of Canadian firms, which made much of his work futile:

> Any firms desiring to compete in a new market should study the trade statistics which appear in the Weekly Report. . . . customs duty,

preference if any, c.i.f. prices, the particular kinds of articles required, the methods of marking and packing, terms of payment, etc., all of this information can be received through the Government Trade Commission Service free of charge. But in spite of the valuable and disinterested information which is contained in the Weekly Report, instances occur time and again which indicate that this journal is never studied, much less read, by the manufacturing firms.[42]

The Japan posting was equally frustrated by the export apathy of Canadian manufacturers and their failure to use the information provided by Trade and Commerce to learn from past mistakes.

The manufacturing interest of Canada has had the benefit, for nearly thirty years, of a system of tariff aid that must have come far short of its pretensions, since, upon their own confession, they are not yet in a position to offer business to so accessible a market as that of Japan. . . . After four years experience here, I know of nothing Canadian offered to this market at a price that would compete with similar products supplied by other countries, with the further fatal disadvantages of uncertain supply in the event of a demand being worked up. Although I have from time to time placed this same statement of fact, variously worded, before the Canadian public in these reports, I still find public opinion as expressed in parliament, and upon the platform, and echoed by the press, uninformed as to the situation, and continuing to cry out its surprise that Canada's share of the trade with Japan is not greater.[43]

That such critical remarks piqued some Canadian manufacturers is evident from a 1911 article in *Industrial Canada*. In it, exception was taken to the charges of the trade commissioners "over our apparent lack of aggressiveness in foreign markets." This CMA organ counselled patience, submitting that Trade and Commerce agents "should not grow discouraged if the results come somewhat slowly" because industrialists were now preparing the base for a move into world markets.

. . . the great majority are utilizing their capital to the utmost to meet the demands of the Canadian market. Canada is growing rapidly. The West is developing more than any region in the world today. . . . So in most cases every effort is being made to cater to the home market and to meet the extraordinary demands which are being made upon producers in every line . . . there can be no cessation of the fight to maintain supremacy at home. . . . As, however, firms grow in strength and experience more and more will follow the lead of those companies which have built up a valuable export trade. . . .

Meanwhile, the ground is being prepared by the investigations of trade commissioners. . . .[44]

Thus, in the space of a single decade, we have seen the CMA move from the offensive, in regard to the overseas services of the Canadian state, to the defensive. There can be little doubt, however, that during this period the Department of Trade and Commerce moved firmly into the orbit of industrial capital. As we have already learned, after 1900 the Commercial Intelligence Committee of the CMA became both increasingly active in formulating demands on Trade and Commerce and successful in translating these demands into policy outputs. In addition, it would seem that Trade and Commerce progressively developed its services in the field of stimulating manufactured as opposed to primary exports. To illustrate, R. Grigg, who made a tour of inspection of the department's European offices prior to his appointment as director of the trade commissioner service, concluded that little could be done by Trade and Commerce to assist the sales of Canada's "natural products such as wheat, flour, cheese, timber etc." Greatly pre-dating the establishment of the department, the trade in such staples had long possessed its own channels. It was, Grigg stated, "the universal opinion among the highly competent body of men" who conducted it that there was no need of "help" from the trade commissioners. He suggested that a more useful role for the department could be developed in pushing industrial exports in "rising markets either in the Far East or in non-manufacturing countries such as South America, Australia, New Zealand, South Africa, and Russia."[45]

Import Substitution for the Empire

There was one quarter in which some Canadian industrialists expressed genuine export interest during this era and even lobbied for government action to further their cause. These enterprises sought Ottawa's assistance in gaining preferential tariff entry into the markets of the other white Dominions (and even Britain if it could ever have been persuaded to abandon free trade). These markets held a number of unique qualities that generated considerable excitement among Canadian manufacturers, especially U.S. branch plants and licensees. First, these countries had little domestic production of their own to compete with Canadian products. As early as 1894, *Canadian Manufacturer* noted that export possibilities in Australia and South Africa were favourable because "in their market our manufactures would not suffer from home competition."[46]

This, of course, was also true of much of the world at that time. What made the white Dominions particularly attractive to Canadian manufacturers was their position near the top of the international hierarchy of wealth. In the same article, *Canadian Manufacturer* contrasted the "limited" markets of the less prosperous parts of the Empire with the fact that the white Dominions were "large consumers." The *Monetary Times* posed the problem more bluntly:

> What can the millions of Hindoos whose labour brings only a few cents a day buy from Canada? . . . They would not take our manufactures, for they can buy British on better terms. When the elements of trade exist, distance can be overcome; but when you reach poor customers, at whatever distance, you will find a million of them go a very short way compared to an equal number of more prosperous people.[47]

Thus, while the colonies of occupation were less important in the preference plans of our industrial exporters, they did not completely ignore them. The rich harvest reaped by their resident colonial masters made a lucrative target. For example, a 1902 "Mission of Inquiry" to the West Indies led by the president of the CMA noted that

> It is always necessary to remember the class of people in the islands and their purchasing power. . . . The black is lazy and independent. . . . He is generally a contented man and his requirements are few. . . . At the larger islands the wants of the white population are, however, important, and in the large stores the range in all lines of goods is very wide.[48]

Clearly, as rich non-industrialized markets, the white Dominions held many natural enticements for Canadian industrialists. However, their strongest attraction may have been the taste these countries had begun to acquire for U.S.-manufactured products. Licensees and branch plants in Canada sensed an opportunity to undercut their U.S. and European rivals in these markets if a system of Empire tariff preferences could be instituted. *Canadian Manufacturer* expressed the strategy in this manner:

> With the . . . possibility of a preferential commercial policy amongst the colonies, there is every likelihood of an expansion which may yet be deemed marvelous. Lacking that great impetus to commerce, the United States has built up an [Australian] trade of $20,000,000 a year. With it, there is no reason why Canada should not establish herself as a successful rival of the Republic in many lines and a successful middleman in others.[49]

This imaginative form of ISI by proxy that Canadian industrialists dreamed of introducing to the white Dominions and Britain was, as we outlined in the last chapter, tightly wrapped in the Union Jack. Canadian manufacturers used self-interested sentimental appeals directed toward

Empire unity to justify their campaign.[50] In the face of fierce competition from the more technologically advanced U.S. and German manufacturers, concern was also raised over the failure of Britain to hold her position in the international trade of the sophisticated products of the "second" industrial revolution. R. Munro, 1902 president of the CMA, told the annual meeting of his organization that "Where Great Britain has held the bulk of the trade, her percentage is being attacked at every point and that by the most scientific methods. Canadian manufacturers càn do much to retain in British hands the trade of other British possessions."[51]

Canadian manufacturers felt that their government should use the fact that Canada had granted an unconditional preference on certain classes of Empire goods in 1897 as a lever to persuade the other white Dominions to offer corresponding concessions. For example, the Tariff Committee of the CMA in 1907 requested that Ottawa negotiate, "at the earliest possible moment," a preferential treaty with Australia:

> ... by virtue of the fact that Canada was the first to raise the standard of Imperial preference, we ought to be accorded equal privileges in the Australian market with our fellow-subjects from Great Britain. Given such a preference we could secure a large share of the business that is now going to the United States, as the lines which these two countries produce is almost identical and are of a kind that Australia requires.[52]

Australia, however, did not follow until the 1920s the example established in 1904 by New Zealand and South Africa in extending to Canada the privilege of their British preferential rates.

Unfortunately, a number of Canadian manufacturers rapidly fouled their own preferential nests in these white Dominions. A New Zealand correspondent of *Industrial Canada* reported in 1907 an increase of the tariff preference on a number of U.S. manufactures in which Canadians might now be able to substitute their products. However, "will manufacturers now avail themselves of their opportunity," he asked, "or are they going, as has been done before, to raise their prices so much that practically the whole of the preference goes into their pockets?"[53] Some months later his question was answered when Canadian clothing manufacturers, with a preference of 20 per cent, were caught *raising* their prices to the level of their competitors. As a consequence, the New Zealand government removed this particular preference and

> the business is going back to the United States. Even if Canadian manufacturers reduce their prices again to the level of the foreign manufacturer the business will go past them as merchants are disgusted with the manner in which the Canadian manufacturers have

appreciated a benefit which was given to them, not for the purpose of filling their own pockets, but to keep the foreign manufacturer out.[54]

International Competitiveness

This chapter could not properly be concluded without some mention being made of the small minority of Canadian industrialists who seriously pursued export trade. These firms, which did not accept the logic of the mass of their compatriots who argued that the home market must always come first, became the darlings of the trade commissioners. Contrast, for example, the tone displayed here in complimenting the aggressive tactics of one Canadian firm with that found in the comments we have previously reported.

> After a determined and tactful effort made by the direct representative of a leading Canadian corset manufacturing company to introduce their goods – hitherto unknown, this line has been successfully introduced to Australian wholesale importers. Large initial orders are going forward . . . in a line which competition is most marked . . . [and] are attributable to the exceptional ability of the travelling salesmen in overcoming the prejudices of conservative buyers.[55]

The agricultural implement manufacturers were the leading force in this minority, although it may be noted that they, too, on occasion provoked complaints from trade commissioners about sloppy performance in some less important markets such as Mexico.[56] In Australia, however, these firms were so aggressive that, by 1910, Canadian agricultural machinery held the largest share of the import market. According to the Trade and Commerce agent, the manufacturers had achieved this success as the reward for establishing Australian sales subsidiaries with ample stock, good salesmen, and effective local management. They had also provided consistently high quality commodities adapted to local conditions in Australia. "The result achieved is an object lesson to Canadian manufacturers of other lines of merchandise," he submitted, "as to what can be obtained in distant overseas markets by persistent effort while holding an equally prominent position in the home markets."[57] In South Africa, the export performance of one agricultural implement firm was actually held up to favourable comparison with its U.S. and British competitors. "If one Canadian firm can make a success, why not others?" the trade commissioner demanded.[58]

Conclusion

The creation of a federal government agency charged with a specific responsibility for stimulating exports can be traced to the lobbying efforts of various business groups desirous of a Canadian equivalent to the consular services long enjoyed by their counterparts in other countries. Before 1914, the growth of this agency was fundamentally incremental in nature. It was greatly influenced by a steamship subsidy program, the creation of an independent organizational base in the Department of Trade and Commerce, and the close relationship it developed with industrial capital because of its redundancy in the staples trade. From the reports of the trade commissioners, it is clear that Canadian manufacturers had many export opportunities in this era but failed to take advantage of them. Numerous instances of disinterest, incompetence, and dishonesty were catalogued. Interest in upgrading the foreign services of Trade and Commerce appears to have been limited to a select few at the core of the Canadian Manufacturers' Association. Ironically, as the trade commissioner service became better organized, industrialists found it necessary to defend themselves from its criticisms of their export apathy.

Our examination of this period largely confirms the analysis of the nature of Canadian industrialization undertaken in the last chapter. Although it could be alleged that a general lack of entrepreneurial spirit was operative here, it is more likely that the ISI milieu of Canadian manufacturing, with its limiting world view of import replacement and unchallenged technological dependence, was at fault. In this context, we should bear in mind that other relatively small nations, such as Sweden, were having considerable success during this same era in establishing a more export-oriented and technologically independent industrial strategy.

Among those few manufacturers who did export, three levels of intervention in overseas markets were identified: import substitution for the Empire; dumping of surplus production during depressed domestic conditions; and international competitiveness in specialized lines of production. Regrettably, this latter group was no more than a fragment of Canadian industrial capital.

Chapter Four

War and Peace:
Opportunities Averted

~~~~~~

Statistics, we are often reminded, never tell the entire story. So it was with the export performance of Canadian manufacturers during and directly after World War One. On the surface, it appeared that our industrialists took advantage of the unusual circumstances of these years to improve dramatically their standing in world markets. To illustrate, for almost all of the pre-war era covered by the preceding chapter, only 3 or 4 per cent of Canada's exports could be considered "finished" manufactures. By contrast, in the period we will now consider, this category jumped to approximately 25 per cent of total exports.[1] Nevertheless, as we will soon see, these achievements neither heralded a fresh outward orientation nor yielded many long-term benefits for Canadian industry.

Nearly all of the remarkable increase in exports just described can be attributed to the sale of war munitions. During 1916 and 1917, almost one-third of Canadian manufacturing output resulted from the production of shells and explosives. By the conclusion of hostilities, total exports of these weapons were valued at more than $1 billion, a figure equivalent to approximately two-thirds of the total Canadian war expenditure.[2] Prime Minister Sir Robert L. Borden reported that in early 1917, at the height of wartime manufacturing, 630 Canadian firms with a total labour force of over 304,000 workers were involved in making munitions. As a result, Canada was then producing more munitions than had any country before the Great War except for Germany and was supplying over a quarter of all the artillery shells used by the British armies.[3]

To a considerable extent, these impressive export successes must be credited to the federal government. Ottawa's heavy involvement here included the procurement of foreign contracts, the financing of war credits needed by overseas purchasers, and even the production of some vital components through the establishment of "national factories." The Department of Trade and Commerce, however, was only marginally drawn into all of this activity.[4] The reader may well wonder at this. After all, have we not documented how the department grew into its role of representative, spokesman, and agent for the export concerns of Canadian industrialists by 1914?

The answer to this little puzzle signals the reason why the massive wartime trade did not stimulate a reversal of the manufacturers' introverted outlook. As it unfolded, the munitions trade had little use for the specialized services painstakingly developed by Trade and Commerce after 1900. In fact, it was an export trade *in destination only.* Contracts were allocated within Canada to firms through official state agencies – the Shell Committee before November, 1915, and, subsequently, the Imperial Munitions Board – on the basis of orders submitted by the British Ministry of Munitions.[5] Canadian industrialists, therefore, did not face the difficult task of cultivating overseas contacts in order to make sales; competition was mainly with domestic rather than foreign producers, products did not have to be adapted and advertised to suit exotic tastes, and deliveries were generally to Canadian points.

"A State-induced and State-regulated Business"

Let us examine this munitions trade more closely. As we might have anticipated from our discussion of the pre-war period, the initial interest of Canadian manufacturers in overseas arms contracts owed a great deal to soft demand in the domestic market. A severe depression had erupted in 1913 and unemployment was still high in some regions in early 1915.[6] Not surprisingly, then, Ottawa was bombarded with requests for munitions contracts. Prime Minister Borden complained in mid-1915 of the "continuous pressure from companies and firms desirous of undertaking this work."[7] Typical was this appeal by the Imperial Steel and Wire Company of Collingwood: "We would not be so insistent if we had other business to look forward to but unfortunately, we have a large plant lying idle with heavy overhead expenses and little prospects of new business owing to the general depression in the country."[8]

Even though munitions work was greatly coveted by the manufacturers, a considerable number were unwilling to risk their capital in retooling for production. This is highly consistent with the reluctance to invest in export opportunities that we noted in the last chapter. For example, the Ordnance Adviser to the Shell Committee reported that

> when the Minister of Militia and Defence induced the manufacturers of Canada to consider shell manufacture several of them would not undertake the risks involved while others were prepared to do so although with some reluctance. It was a new class of work for the

manufacturers, the execution of which involved expenditure of money in new plants and risks of rejection of materials until their employees became skilled.[9]

Many manufacturers demanded that the government provide guarantees that they would not lose money before they were willing to invest in the necessary machinery. J.R. Shaw, president of Canada Furniture in Woodstock, promised Borden that he would increase his firm's shell-making capacity tenfold "if any definite assurances could be received in respect to the continuance of demand." He claimed that he had discussed the matter with "half a dozen gentlemen controlling large engineering plants" who were also ready to expand their wartime operations "only provided they can receive definite contracts for definite deliveries which will warrant them turning their plants into this work."[10] That this hesitant approach was pervasive is confirmed by these remarks of F. Nicholls, president of one of the foremost industrial enterprises in the country, Canadian General Electric. He recorded that he had offered at the beginning of the war

to invest two million dollars in a special plant to manufacture munitions provided we received a moderate guarantee of orders spread over a term of five years, but the Government did not entertain this proposal on account of the financial responsibility, although they were not asked to take any capital financial responsibility but only to accept delivery of the goods.[11]

Some smaller concerns unsuccessfully requested advances to purchase the equipment required for munitions manufacture, "as these special machines would be of practically no value, except for this particular work, and would simply be so much junk at the expiration of the contract."[12]

The weakness of Canadian industrial technology was also highlighted in wartime arms production. Work proceeded in two stages. In the first year, almost no finished shells were fabricated by Canadian firms because their capabilities did not extend beyond the provision of simple empty casings. Because of the intricacies of fuse and cartridge manufacture and the high cost of acquiring the necessary production equipment, manufacturers sought U.S. supply sources for these components. After mid-1915, however, the British refused to accept deliveries of any more unfinished shells and Canadian manufacturers were forced to secure the more complex skills and machinery.[13]

It would appear that many, if not most, of the machine tools required for both stages of production, as well as the specialized techniques necessary for their use, had to be acquired in the U.S. Writing some years after the war, the Shell Committee's Ordnance Adviser observed that Canada simply "had not the equipment and had not the facilities for its supply." Nevertheless, from the beginning of the war, U.S. machine tool factories "expressed" their products to Canadian manufacturers "with a commendable speed."[14]

In spite of this dependence on foreign technology, by the end of the war technical advances had been made in a number of fields. Still, many of the most complex processes (including the manufacture of airplanes, fuses, and explosives) were carried on in seven "national factories" established for war production in Canada by the Imperial Munitions Board. When the U.S. entered the war in 1917, some of the technical knowledge developed in Canada was shared with American manufacturers, although Canadian firms continued to purchase specialized machinery in the U.S. Thus, while munitions production may have increased the size of Canada's industrial establishment, it did not seem to have provided the stimulus necessary to induce Canadian manufacturers to sink independent technological roots. Time constraints were obviously an important consideration here, but it seems reasonable to suppose that fewer innovative spin-offs were achieved than might have been the case if Canadian industry had possessed the capability of producing its own capital goods at the start of the hostilities.[15]

In summary, the munitions trade provided Canadian manufacturers with uniquely painless export opportunities. It was a "state-induced and state-regulated business"[16] in which the buyers sought them out in a period of slack domestic demand. There was also little need to disturb the established patterns of minimum capital investment and extensive technological dependence in order to make a success of the trade.

Other Wartime Exports

Export orders for other military supplies (including clothing, bedding, soldiers' kits, etc.) did not fall quite so easily into the hands of Canadian manufacturers. The Allies tended to look first to the U.S. rather than Canada for their import requirements because, as one trade commissioner put it, "the greater out-put capacities of her industries makes her position more elastic for meeting exceptional demands, while her export experience and organization are superior."[17] Consequently, in striking contrast to the munitions experience, Canada was generally overlooked in the establishment of direct purchasing agencies for these other war materials. As a result, Canadian industries had to deal directly with Allied governments in Europe or with their purchasing commissions in the U.S.

In this quite different situation, the export expertise of Trade and Commerce was quite naturally called upon by the interested firms. Trade and

Commerce Minister Sir George Foster sent Borden a forceful letter in mid-1915 communicating the unhappiness of the manufacturers that no satisfactory purchasing agencies had been appointed in Canada by the Allies. Industrialists complained that representations to Allied procurement bodies in the U.S. had met with the obstacle of paying "hosts of middlemen," each seeking a "comfortable commission" before orders could be secured. They submitted that they "ought not to be reduced to the alternative of getting no business from these countries or of taking it through middlemen and jobbers." In London, Foster stated, manufacturers reported "long delays" and a "certain averseness to doing business with Canada." As a result, many had returned empty-handed. [18]

In the first months of the war, manufacturers were desperate for these orders because of the unhealthy condition of the home market. For example, the Canadian Clothing Manufacturers' Association asked Foster to intercede on their behalf to procure orders from the British War Office because "our factories are at present either entirely at a standstill, or at best working from 20 to 30 per cent capacity." This "general depression" had thrown "thousands" out of work. [19] For their parts, Borden, Foster, and Sir George Perley, Canada's High Commissioner in London, pressed the case of the manufacturers to the Allies at every opportunity. Canadian firms, they argued, should be given patriotic preference over those of the "neutral" Americans. Borden told one wartime meeting in London that "nearly everything that comes from the U.S. could also be produced in Canada at prices which would bear favourable comparison. . . . All that Canadian manufacturers desire is that they may be given a reasonable opportunity of producing goods so far supplied from the U.S." [20]

In spite of these representations, little progress appears to have been made during the remaining years of the war. To a considerable extent, Canadian manufacturers may have been the authors of their own misfortune. Not only did they fail to show initiative in expanding on the export opportunities resulting from government efforts, [21] they also burdened themselves with a reputation for producing shoddy goods. At the conclusion of the war, Borden's office compiled a report detailing many of the negative experiences suffered by Allied purchasers of Canadian industrial goods. The sloppy performances recorded there are consistent with what we already know about the poor export habits developed before 1914: numerous cases of failure to respond to orders or to fill promised orders; lengthy delays; and the shipment of defective and substandard goods. Comparisons with the export performance of U.S. firms were almost always unfavourable. In fact, they were quite likely at the root of the "certain averseness to doing business with Canada" of which the manufacturers were complaining to Foster. For example:

There have been many complaints as to the unbusinesslike methods of packing, shipping, etc., and although the most precise instructions have been sent out as to what is required, the [British] War Office states that they are not followed. The Contracts Department contrasts their experience with Studebakers [U.S.] and with the Canadian manufacturers. The former have always delivered to time, have so packed, shipped and advised the consignments, that a boy could undertake the distribution to the various depots, and the quality of goods has, with one exception, been all that could be desired.[22]

During this period, Canadian manufacturers continued to demonstrate their reluctance to accept the ordinary business risks of the export trade, often viewing it as an abnormal activity forced upon them in times of depression, something that could be safely abandoned when domestic market conditions strengthened. A good illustration of this attitude can be found in a letter from G.M. Murray, secretary of the CMA, to Foster in early 1916.

Mr. King, in common with other Canadian manufacturers of boots, complains that the manner of handling this [war export] business heretofore has been so unsatisfactory that he would not care to interest himself in the business further unless a firm offer were made to him. On previous occasions the time that was allowed to elapse between the invitation to tender and the closing of the contract was unduly long: tenders submitted on the basis of current market quotations for leather could not be lived up to with profit to the manufacturer if his tender were not accepted until three months later, by which time the price of the leather had materially advanced. Moreover if other business became available in the meantime manufacturers accepted it and were consequently unable to guarantee deliveries.[23]

We will now turn to an examination of the wartime export trade carried on by Canadian industrialists outside of the provision of munitions and other military supplies. For its part, Trade and Commerce was very optimistic in 1914 that the war would shake the manufacturers out of their exporting torpor. Foster, in an editorial in his department's *Weekly Report*, called on Canadian firms to launch what amounted to a holy crusade to capture those export markets now cut off from German industry.

Whilst a comparatively small number of our manhood fights the battle for Imperial existence and control of our ocean highways, those who remain should with spirit and energy throw themselves into the task of taking possession of the markets from which our enemies have been driven and supply them with the products of our own fields and factories. Here is a peaceful field of operation in which we can carry on a bloodless but most effective and profitable warfare. . . . Here are markets for hundreds of millions of dollars of products, the making of even a portion of which will keep our industries going and give employment to hundreds of thousands of our people.[24]

The CMA also expressed some interest in moving into markets Germany had been forced to quit, particularly South America. It printed a number of informative articles on the subject in *Industrial Canada* with material provided by Trade and Commerce. In addition, the CMA offered assistance to its members in forming "syndicates" of non-competitive manufacturers to share the expense in sending a sales representative to scout South America. However, since "comparatively few" industrialists responded, it abandoned the project.[25] The CMA leadership was also alert to the potential of former German markets in Russia. They persuaded Trade and Commerce to place a "Commissioner with two or three assistants . . . on the ground" to study that country's commercial possibilities.[26] However, the interest there, as in South America, was to prove to be mainly academic.

Undaunted, during the early years of the war the department spared little ink in pointing out the considerable value of markets lost to the Germans and the opportunities thus afforded for Canadian initiative. At the end of 1914, it published a 110-page report that reprinted articles on this subject. In addition, the trade commissioners frequently noted in the published market reviews of their posts the excellent prospects of replacing specific German goods.[27]

In general, Canadian manufacturers showed themselves to be incapable of seizing any extensive advantage from these favourable circumstances. They excused this failure by pleading transportation difficulties and the pressure of wartime production.[28] An examination of the trade commissioners' reports, however, indicates that this, like the plea of "home demand" that had preceded it, may have been in many cases simply a convenient apology for avoiding export business.

To begin, Canadian firms continued to shun the practice of sending out salesmen to establish direct representation in foreign markets. In contrast, U.S. enterprises had, in the words of one Trade and Commerce agent in South Africa, "flooded the country" with commercial travellers during the war.[29] Some time later, this same individual warned that it was vital for Canadian manufacturers to establish an active presence in foreign markets, even if only token for the duration of the war, so that a base for future expansion could be secured. "It is true that the conditions of extra business in many of the Canadian plants may prevent all possibility of immediate business," he reasoned, "but surely the management must give an occasional thought to future trade."[30]

This declaration captures a frustration experienced by many trade commissioners. To illustrate, the Bristol posting recited from a similar chapter and verse:

> Although Canadian manufacturers of the various kinds of steel products are busy with the filling of orders arising from the exigencies of war, yet this would appear to be the time to look into the opportunities for the sale of their products in the United Kingdom after the war. The United States firms are making energetic efforts to secure the trade in bolts, nuts, screws, nails, wire, etc., and . . . almost every boat entering the port of Bristol from the United States carries large quantities from that source.[31]

Even such exotic markets as India were showered with attention from U.S. industries during the war, while "Canadian commercial travellers were never seen." The readers of *Weekly Bulletin* were informed that as a result of an aggressive wartime sales campaign on the sub-continent "very strong American vested interests . . . are growing up among the importers, and unless Canadian producers take early steps to cultivate this market by personal visits and systematized propaganda work, they will find that it will be impossible to secure their fair share of the trade later on."[32]

Not only did Canadian manufacturers seem uninterested in matching the more venturesome sales tactics of their U.S. competitors, they continued to prove themselves unenthusiastic about even replying to mail from potential foreign customers. The trade commissioner in New Zealand transmitted the unhappiness of a number of importers in that country, previously agents for German firms, who, when the war came, were anxious to switch to Canadian enterprises "even at a slightly higher price." Initiatives from New Zealand were, nonetheless, met with silence from Canada. In this case, "the difficulty is not to secure orders but to get them filled . . . after exhaustive letters are written, no reply is received."[33] The problem became so acute in Great Britain that in 1917 one Trade and Commerce representative maintained:

> The neglect of correspondence on the part of Canadians has been mentioned by English firms more than any other feature in connection with their trade with Canada. . . . As an instance of neglect of correspondence the manager of a Bristol firm who . . . represents high class Canadian firms and yet could not get even an acknowledgement of letters enclosing remittances of money for goods sold.

During the months of May, June and July he sent 107 letters to Canada, about 90 of which required answers. He has received only 32 answers, 15 of which were received from one firm which always answers its letters. The other concerns practically ignored all correspondence. This is just one instance of many. It is realized that many Canadian houses have been extremely busy on war orders, but if they wish to build up a trade for the future there is no excuse for this neglect of correspondence.[34]

The columns of *Industrial Canada* also carried regular complaints on this subject. On one occasion, toward the end of the war, its editors became so exasperated that they indignantly lectured their readers: "Even if you don't wish to engage in export trade or are unable to carry out suggested arrangements, at least have the decency to say so, politely and cordially. Let Canadian manufacturers at least have the reputation for courtesy."[35]

During this period, Canadian manufacturers continued to lose export business because of the stubborn unwillingness of many of them to quote the prices of their goods landed in foreign ports. Deviating from the procedure customary among the exporters of other countries, these firms quoted only in Canadian or U.S. dollars at their factory gates. The trade commissioner in Paris suggested that Canadian firms were missing opportunities in France because "to ask a Frenchman to buy his goods in America or Canada in dollars is like squeezing blood from his very heart." The Birmingham post concurred that Canadian-dollar price quotations made it "almost impossible to transact business" in Great Britain. While British purchasers held a sentimental preference for Canadian over U.S. exporters, this was largely negated by the more "accommodating" U.S. attitude in matters such as these.[36]

Buy Canadian

In spite of the unusual opportunity that came in the wake of the wartime disruption of German trade, we must conclude at this juncture that there was little positive improvement in the apathetic export behaviour of most Canadian industrialists. Even *Industrial Canada* was moved to criticism. "But after all," it editorialized, "it is an old story. Ever since *Industrial Canada* started publication there have been complaints that the Canadian [manufacturers] have been slow to bestir themselves. The war might have been expected to wake up the tardy ones but it does not seem to have had that effect even yet."[37] Near the conclusion of the war, it probed the psychology of Canadian industrial capitalism in an attempt to discover an explanation for this export lethargy. "We must confess," it submitted, "that we have not developed the mental avidity which is the necessary accompaniment of vigorous and overmastering action."[38]

As might have been anticipated, however, *Industrial Canada*'s criticism of the continued home market obsession of Canadian manufacturers was far less forceful than its defence. This CMA organ, reflecting the views of its membership, saw more opportunities for the replacement of German goods in the Canadian market than in foreign markets. An illuminating contrast can be drawn from a comparison of Foster's earlier noted war editorial in *Weekly Report,* in which he called for a crusade to capture Germany's external trade, and *Industrial Canada*'s war editorial trumpeting a "Buy Canadian" crusade.

> This is no longer a commercial appeal. . . . It is the duty of Canadian citizens to spend every possible dollar at home during the war. Sending money abroad in payment for foreign goods indirectly helps the enemies of Britain, because such action weakens ourselves. . . . It is evident that a flood of goods, from neutral countries deflected from the ports of belligerent nations, will threaten to overwhelm our markets. . . . This is no time to indulge whims, prejudices, or fancies in favour of foreign manufacturers. . . . Fight the enemy by buying at home.[39]

In what could have been a response to Foster's early September, 1914, call to export action, *Industrial Canada*'s October, 1914, issue counselled Canadian firms to be very cautious in moving into the foreign markets Germany had been forced to vacate. Citing the numerous difficulties of export trade – intense competition, capital shortages, transportation delays, and language barriers – the journal argued that a threatened influx of imports from the "neutral" U.S. into Canada made it essential that industrialists give first priority to domestic trade and to replacing imports formerly made in Germany.

> The exclusion of goods formerly imported from nations at war goes hand-in-hand with determined efforts to flood our home market with the manufactures of neutral nations. We can begin to manufacture some goods formerly imported, but the processes are difficult to master and establish. We can try and capture foreign trade, but the obstacles in the way are serious, though by no means insurmountable. Canadian manufacturers are performing a great feat by merely holding their own under existing conditions.[40]

The industrialists were soon to lobby Ottawa for assistance in more effectively substituting domestic production for the excluded German imports. In early 1915, an "influential deputation" urged Borden and Foster to organize exhibits of foreign goods that could be inspected by manufacturers interested in import substitution. [41] As a result, Trade and Commerce mounted a show of German toys in Toronto in the spring and summer of 1916. This was followed, in the fall of that year, by a six-city tour of over 8,000 Austrian and German commodities borrowed from the British Board of Trade. Trade and Commerce was even able to arrange with the railways to grant reduced fares to manufacturers who wished to visit the display. By the war's end, a more permanent exhibit of replaceable foreign products had been situated in Ottawa. [42]

Fear of Flying (alone)

As the war progressed, Canadian manufacturers began to worry openly about a collapse of their export trade at the conclusion of the war. For example, in mid-1916 the Tariff Committee of the CMA correctly noted that the recent vast increases in overseas sales of industrial goods were largely due to shipments of munitions and other war supplies. "When the demand for these articles ceases at the conclusion of peace, how will the present volume of exports be maintained?" this committee wondered. [43]

By 1917, these concerns had crystallized into a resolution passed at the annual meeting of the CMA calling for a government inquiry into the "best methods for conserving and increasing our domestic and overseas trade, to the end that our present prosperity may not unduly suffer when the stimulus resulting from orders for munitions and other war supplies is removed." [44] After appointment to the Senate in 1917, F. Nicholls, one of the nation's leading industrialists and a lifelong CMA militant, took it on himself to ensure that this resolution was acted upon in Ottawa. In his maiden speech before the Upper House, he pleaded for a "systematic method of state aid" for Canada's industrial exporters. To him, this meant the establishment of a peacetime government agency to continue the job done during the war in bringing "export" orders to the doors of Canadian factories. Such an agency, according to Nicholls,

> would actually sell Canadian products in foreign markets and distribute the orders received amongst Canadian producers. . . . A Government department as a sales agent would carry more weight than an individual corporate body could. It would also be able to finance trade credits on a much lower basis of interest and thereby create a trade that it would be impossible for the individual to develop. [45]

Nicholls was able to secure the appointment of a special Senate committee to study the problem of post-war trade and was successful in getting it to recommend many of his proposals to the cabinet.

The Canadian Industrial Reconstruction Association, drawn from a most illustrious list of prominent capitalists, also placed pressure on

Ottawa to pick up once again the export ball on behalf of the manufacturers after the war was finished.[46] In mid-1917, its president, Sir John Willison, suggested that each individual Canadian industrialist "acting alone cannot hope to get such a foothold in foreign markets or such a share in the reconstruction of the devastated portions of Europe as may be had by co-operation and organization." He recommended that Canadian manufacturers act with "vigor, foresight and courage" to form trade cartels if they hoped to compete with their rivals from Germany, Great Britain, Japan, and the United States. Further, since the governments of these countries "freely afforded" many valuable services to their exporters, "the movement which Hon. Frederic Nicholls has inaugurated in the Senate for a Canadian Trade Corporation should have liberal aid from the Government and the active, organized support of the industrial and financial interests."[47]

The institutional machinery eventually settled on by the Borden cabinet to handle European reconstruction trade held many important similarities to the Nicholls plan. In late 1918, a Canadian Trade Mission was headquartered in London. It was charged with "the purpose of securing for the agricultural and other productions of Canada their appropriate share in the markets of the world during the period of reconstruction."[48] Any orders obtained in Europe were to be funnelled to the parallel Canadian Trade Commission in Ottawa. This Ottawa body, in turn, was to pass these foreign orders to the appropriate Canadian firms to submit bids.

Scarcely a week after the formation of the Canadian Trade Commission, Finance Minister Sir Thomas White, who was left in charge in Ottawa with Borden and Foster in London to prepare for the Peace Conference, chaired two meetings of a Reconstruction and Development Committee. This committee was made up of a number of important industrial and transport capitalists. White was warned of serious disruptions to occur as a result of the collapse of the munitions trade. These business leaders pleaded for various types of subsidy schemes to assist them in making the transition to peacetime trade. F.H. Whitton, president of the Steel Company of Canada, was more direct than most, but his comments fairly reflect the imperious tone of these meetings. He stated that:

> as Canada had contributed to the war in Europe, we had a right to demand a share in the reconstruction business that would follow. If Canada's prices were too high on this business, our manufacturers should have the right to call on the Government to make up the difference . . . and boats must be provided at once in order to get our goods delivered overseas.[49]

White was clearly shaken by what he heard. The day after these meetings were completed he fired off a cable to Borden in London passionately urging immediate action on behalf of the manufacturers.

> It is of utmost importance to Canada that you should immediately and strongly impress upon the British Government necessity of having new orders placed in Canada for manufactured products required for overseas reconstruction purposes replacing the volume of munitions business which is now being rapidly demobilized. Within six weeks over one hundred thousand operatives will be dismissed. We are taking every step to provide for their absorption but overseas orders for our manufacturers imperatively necessary to prevent unrest and discontent over the war.[50]

Reconstruction Trade

Meanwhile, those in London were discovering that post-war Europe was by no means the captive market it had been during the hostilities. Soon after arriving to take up his position as chairman of the Trade Mission, L. Harris, an industrialist himself, warned that "business over here is not going to come as easily as the munitions business came, and the manufacturers must not expect that we are going to get immediate results."[51] Foster and Harris both concluded from an early point that in order to capture any significant share of the continental reconstruction trade, the Canadian government would have to extend purchase credits. Harris was particularly cheered by possibilities in the less industrialized markets of Rumania, Serbia, and Greece and spoke of the "splendid results" that could be anticipated if credits were extended to these countries. "They require so many things," he opined, "that it would be possible to keep Canadian industries busy for some months to come."[52]

Finance Minister White, who had long supported the idea of Canada extending reconstruction loans, was concerned nevertheless that the weak financial position of the Balkan countries might result in defaults. From the beginning, White had also insisted that credits should only be extended for manufactured goods as Canada's raw materials and agricultural products would "probably find a market for themselves" in Europe.[53] Consequently, when credits of $25 million were eventually extended to France, Belgium, Rumania, and Greece, it was on the condition that more than half the money be spent on Canadian manufactures.

In spite of the extraordinary state efforts to assist Canadian manufacturers in developing their post-war export trade, it appears that the results obtained were less than satisfactory. By the end of 1919, for example, almost two-thirds of the export credits remained unclaimed by European purchasers.[54] The manufacturers themselves may have been at least partly to blame for this state of affairs. Harris complained to the CMA that the traditional sloppy business tactics of Canadian industrial exporters, including their unwillingness to send catalogues overseas or even to reply to their foreign correspondence, had cost them reconstruction sales. In addition, Harris accused a number of manufacturers of missing opportunities through delays caused by their attempts to adjust prices to take advantage of the strong European demand for certain commodities. To illustrate, Harris related the case of a British trade inquiry he had channelled to a Canadian firm through the Canadian Trade Commission in Ottawa. The manufacturer cabled London to say "anxious to get order, ascertain price we have to meet and cable quick so we can answer Ottawa on your inquiry." Harris concluded disapprovingly that "if a man has got stuff to sell surely to God he ought to have a price on it. Some of our people just want all the traffic will warrant."[55]

The state structures put in place to handle the reconstruction trade were also unsuitable. While centralizing the acquisition and distribution of wartime munitions contracts may have been highly effective in the munitions trade when it concerned only a small number of government purchasers, such centralization proved unnecessarily cumbersome for the more varied and flexible requirements of peacetime trade in which bureaucratic delays could prove fatal. After a year's experience in the field, Harris advised Borden that following each of the necessary steps between the Trade Mission in London and the Canadian firm consumed so much time that "before we could get prices and deliveries back to London other sellers were able to secure the business."[56]

Almost certainly aware that state assistance here was proving to be counterproductive, White cabled Borden in April of 1919 that it was wise to pass once again the initiative in the reconstruction business to the private sector. "The sooner we compel business houses to rely more upon themselves and less on government the better," he argued. "Our business firms and banks can do much more to help themselves than they are doing."[57] White felt secure in making such a recommendation because the predictions of economic disaster placed before him in his meetings with industrialists in late 1918 had failed to materialize. The domestic market was strong and sales of manufactured exports had not totally collapsed due to the exceptionally strong reconstruction demand. Although exports of manufactures were nowhere near their wartime volume, at least until early 1920 there was evidence of a significant gain over pre-war levels.

This mini-boom in industrial exports provoked considerable chest-thumping among manufacturers. T.P. Howard, president of the CMA in 1919-20, proudly informed his convention that in spite of the halt in munitions exports "we have held the greater part of our export trade, and instead of unemployment, we are now experiencing a shortage of labour."[58] Conditions appeared to be so favourable that one CMA official was prompted to compose an "Answer to the Critics" of the past export performance of Canadian industrialists. He stated that:

> in the two years since the signing of the Armistice there has been more money spent by Canadian manufacturers in endeavouring to develop export trade than in any ten years previous to the war. Not only has more money been spent, but more people have been engaged. Where there were probably between two hundred and three hundred manufacturers doing considerable amounts of export trade before the war, this figure will now easily exceed one thousand.[59]

Self-congratulatory remarks of this kind proved to be premature as exports of Canadian manufactures were to sink in the early 1920s to a level not strikingly in excess of pre-war averages. The reconstruction trade, like the munitions trade before it, was based in the exceptional circumstances brought on by a world war. Although some firms undoubtedly made progress, evidence that the majority of industrialists had not yet undertaken the needed fundamental adjustments can be found in the reports of the trade commissioners. Even in the midst of the reconstruction boom, export trade once again was sacrificed on the altar of the home market. Take, for example, this report from the important Australian post:

> In recently interviewing some of the departmental buyers for the largest wholesale dry goods importing warehouses in Sydney and Melbourne, stress was laid upon their inability to obtain anything like prompt execution of orders placed in Canada. The reasons given by the manufacturers in the Dominion were that the domestic demand was so active, and their inability to secure the necessary mill and other operatives. Under the conditions outlined, the buyers (who prefer to obtain "made in Canada" goods) are compelled to place orders of great magnitude with countries which make prompt shipment.[60]

After the war, as during it, Canadian manufacturers continued to allow their competitors to foreclose their future export opportunities in new markets. To illustrate, sixty U.S. firms, some of major size, established direct representation in China in 1919, according to Canada's long-time resident trade commissioner in that country. In marked contrast, he testified that Canadian manufacturers had *never* made any serious attempt to obtain orders in China.

Canada has had direct steamship communication with China from the port of Vancouver for more than thirty years, yet in all that time not a single Canadian business firm have established themselves or had agents in this country; and very few Canadian business men have evinced any but the most perfunctory interest in this market, or thought it worth the trouble to visit it and investigate conditions for themselves. The most that was done was to write letters in the hope of selling goods, and when this method failed in results – which it was bound to do – (for in the meantime some live agent from another country was here with his samples, and of course secured the business), they condemned the market as being of no value. [61]

The trade commissioners were not alone in their unhappiness. Another state enterprise, the Canadian Government Merchant Marine, had its own cause for complaint about the reconstruction performance of Canadian industrialists. As we will recall, the manufacturers had blamed a portion of their export sloth during the war on their inability to obtain ocean transport. Pressure from the CMA, the Canadian Industrial Reconstruction Association, the railways, and staple producers led the government to form a state merchant marine to carry Canadian exports during the reconstruction period. Fully sixty-three vessels were built to service all parts of the world.

However, overcapitalized and underutilized in an international context of excess shipping capacity, the line began to run aground after 1920. C.C. Ballantyne, Minister of Marine and Fisheries, singled out the manufacturers for particular blame. In 1920, he made a "public appeal to the Canadian manufacturers to bestir themselves and show more interest in the export trade of Canada than they have shown during the past years." [62] The following year saw him express his "disappointment" that industrialists had not heeded his "urgent appeal." "Canadians must not only look after the home trade but must reach out aggressively for foreign markets," he argued. [63]

For their part, the manufacturers saw little need for concern. Reasoning that the Merchant Marine should be written off as a "trade builder," they counselled patience. *Industrial Canada* asked rhetorically, "What does it matter, if, by running the lines at a slight operating loss for a few years, an expanding market is obtained for Canadian products which by the traffic it creates will ultimately make the actual carrying profitable?" [64] Nevertheless, faced with staggering losses, the Canadian Government Merchant Marine decided in 1923 that it had no alternative but to dispose of almost half of its fleet. [65]

Conclusion

World War One and its aftermath presented Canadian manufacturers with a unique opportunity to establish a strong and permanent base for future expansion of their export trade. Yet, on the whole, they failed to seize the occasion. Other industrial nations were not so shortsighted. It must be remembered that, in these early formative years, every decade Canada fell further behind made it all that much more difficult for the country ever to catch up.

While massive and vital to the war effort, the munitions trade in shells and cartridges produced few long-term benefits. Any significant structural improvement to the base of Canadian manufacturing was vitiated when its proprietors followed their traditional course of minimum capital investment and maximum technological dependence. In addition, since munitions purchasing was carried out within Canada by a state agency operating in a context of feverish demand, industrialists were not forced to sharpen their competitive skills by making direct representations in international markets. Indeed, rather than being stimulated to strike out on their own after the war, the manufacturers pleaded for the creation of a new government body to generate their peacetime "export" orders. This effort, predictably, was doomed.

If anything, outside of the munitions trade the picture appears even more dismal. In supplying other war materiels for the Allies, Canadian manufacturers injured their future prospects in foreign markets by dispatching considerable quantities of shoddy goods. Activity in ordinary export channels was equally lethargic. Specifically, it would seem that few serious attempts were made to match the active, comprehensive U.S. campaign to prepare for post-war trade in overseas markets. Even when foreign customers sought out Canadian industrialists during the war, many habitually declined to reply to their correspondence.

There are many indications that the vision of the majority of manufacturers in this era did not extend far beyond substituting domestic production for excluded German imports. Although they argued that transportation difficulties and the intense demands of munitions production prevented them from giving serious attention to export development during the war, their uneven performance in the subsequent reconstruction period largely confirms our thesis concerning their extreme home market orientation.

Chapter Five

Import Substitution for the Empire

~~~~~~

The rhythm of our narrative greatly changes as we enter the interwar period. The firing of the last Canadian shell in 1918 signalled a new growth plateau for industry in Canada. With production both deepened and intensified, its future development seemed secure. In addition, as explained in Chapter 2, foreign owners were poised to capture, if they had not already, the export dynamic "growth industries" of our century: electrical industries, chemical industries, and industries based on the application of the internal combustion engine.

Until now, our investigation has paid testimony to the unhappy inability of the mass of Canadian manufacturers to field internationally competitive products capable of gaining a foothold in the rapidly expanding world markets of their era. For most, an unchallenged technological dependence and an obsession with the home market were to preclude a serious attempt to export. So it was, then, that their forays into foreign markets were either dilettantish or non-existent. Only a minority of our industrialists could be said to be making an organized effort to reach broader horizons.

To be sure, incompetence and lack of interest continued to characterize the external relations of many manufacturers.[1] But this steadily became less significant in the more general pattern we are trying to trace. Canadian-owned amateurs, hampered by the innovative vacuum that typified their licensee production facilities, are no longer the main story. Between 1914 and 1960, foreign capital tripled its share of control over Canadian industry, moving from one-fifth to three-fifths of total investment. Accordingly, our attention will be focused on the new order. In this chapter, which roughly covers the 1920s and 1930s, we will scrutinize the branch-plant export strategy of imperial import substitution. In the next chapter, which takes us from World War Two into the modern era, the relationship between foreign firms and the blocking of Canadian-manufactured exports will be probed.

A "Permanent Basis" for Manufactured Exports

In Chapters 2 and 3, we outlined the export strategy we have styled import substitution for the Empire. With it, U.S. branch plants and licensees in Canada hoped to gain preferential tariff entry into British Empire markets so as to gain price advantages on their American and European competitors. Imperial sentiment, we noted, was the basis of their preference appeals. Manufacturers also argued that their Canadian-based firms could strengthen the Empire by compensating for Britain's weakness in exporting the sophisticated "growth industry" products. They persistently pressured the Canadian state to become involved on their behalf because only the government could provide the institutional framework and legitimacy necessary for the conduct of trade negotiations with other Empire governments.

Ottawa and the manufacturers achieved some early success in this area, gaining tariff access in 1904 on British preferential terms in New Zealand and South Africa. In addition, a reciprocal trade agreement that included some Canadian manufactures was concluded with a number of the smaller West Indian islands in 1912. The Great War, however, brought the question of a wider extension of Empire preference to the fore. In 1916, worried by the prospect of a post-war collapse of their munitions export business, the Tariff Committee of the CMA called on the federal government to pursue "wisely arranged preferential tariffs." They were particularly keen on Australia.[2]

Shortly after the conclusion of the war, the manufacturers applied more pressure in the form of a letter to Finance Minister White "unanimously endorsed" by the executive of the CMA. In this remarkable communication, the strategy of imperial import substitution was argued to hold three principal benefits for Canada: it would advance the goal of Empire unity, broaden Canada's industrial base, and provide a "permanent" foundation for industrial exports. All of this was set forth in the most enthusiastic and visionary terms.

> The noblest aspirations that animate the intellect, for the vitality and honour of one's country, can be satisfied by a system of reasonable tariff preferences within the Empire. . . . As regards Canada, under such a system, there would be immediate and extraordinary increases in industrial production. It would ensure the large expansion of Canadian exports on a permanent basis. Before deciding whether or not to establish branch factories in Canada a number of United States industries are waiting for British countries to determine their policy on this subject. Were British preferential tariffs the rule, great numbers of United States industries would have to

establish large works in this country in order to hold their export trade with British countries. [3]

The manufacturers were soon to see many of their prayers for a framework of Empire tariff preferences answered. In 1919, the British government extended preferential treatment to a number of Canadian-manufactured products. During the early 1920s, the 1912 agreements with the West Indian colonies were considerably augmented by expanding both the list of commodities covered and the number of islands included.

This left Australia, the richest white Dominion market excepting Canada, as the only major holdout. The industrialists continued to lobby Ottawa for action. A CMA deputation reminded the cabinet of Prime Minister W.L.M. King in early 1922 that "a large proportion of the goods supplied to Australia by the United States could have been supplied by Canada" if preferential tariff rates had been secured. [4] King responded by dispatching J.A. Robb, his Minister of Trade and Commerce, to Australia to see if some progress could not be made in obtaining tariff concessions. Nevertheless, it was not until mid-1925 that agreement was reached on a limited number of items.

On paper at least, 1932 was the high point of the imperial import substitution export strategy. By then, Canada had established some form of preferential agreements with Great Britain, the other Dominions, and Ireland, as well as with the scattered outposts of Empire including the West Indies, the Rhodesias, the Malay States, Cyprus, Ceylon, Malta, Hong Kong, and even Fiji. This had been the work of the Imperial Economic Conference of that year in Ottawa. Here, Prime Minister R.B. Bennett promised Canadians a way out of the Great Depression through what he called "family" arrangements for Empire preference in the exchange of both manufactured and primary products.

Canadian industrialists were particularly keen for such agreements; they sought a mechanism not only to revivify their collapsed enterprises, but also to renew their temporarily lapsed tariff privileges in the New Zealand and South African markets. Bennett left no doubt that he was in complete sympathy with their objectives. His announcement of the Ottawa accords echoed what the manufacturers had been saying for decades.

> Canada is the only part of the British Empire with the factories equipped to manufacture for export to the United Kingdom many of the manufactured articles heretofore supplied to that market by foreign countries. The possibilities of increased activities in Canadian factories and transportation routes with corresponding decrease in unemployment, as a result of these preferences, is unlimited. We should not fail to note the additional advantage of transferring to

Canada the industries formerly carried on in these other [foreign] countries. . . . [5]

As the interwar period got under way, the fruits of imperial import substitution appeared delicious to its proponents. In 1919 alone, nearly 200 U.S. firms established branch plants or acquired an interest in existing Canadian industries. [6] While most of the new branch plants were set up to exploit the domestic market, many also hoped to engage in export trade within the Empire. [7] Under the stimulus of imperial preference, foreign enterprises contributed the largest share in a new surge of "finished" manufacture exports from Canada. This category doubled its share in overall Canadian trade during the 1920s and reached over 10 per cent of Canada's total foreign sales. Approximately half of these finished exports consisted of transport equipment, mainly automobiles and their parts. [8]

With these boom conditions, it is hardly surprising that the political elite of the time became convinced that an industrial strategy combining U.S. branch plants and imperial preference had indeed rendered a "permanent basis" for Canadian manufactured exports. In 1923, Trade and Commerce Minister Robb argued that not only were manufactured exports making the structure of Canadian trade more diversified, but these improvements were fully in step with developments in the United States. Breaking down Canadian trade by a formula that was to become commonplace for decades to come, he concluded that

> the exports of raw materials of the United States were 39 per cent, and of Canada 44 per cent. Of partly manufactured products the exports of the United States were 11 per cent, and the exports of Canada 14 per cent. Of manufactured products, the exports of the United States were 49 per cent, while those of Canada were 41 per cent. . . . Canada is not only a large exporting nation of agricultural products, but she is becoming an exporting nation of manufactured goods. [9]

A later Minister of Trade and Commerce went so far as to predict in 1928 that Canada would eventually become the world's second largest producer of manufactured goods. [10] In reviewing this situation, Prime Minister King, as well, was prompted to deliver a glowing account of Canadian industrial success:

> the percentage of wholly manufactured commodities which we have been exporting is continually increasing. In other words, we are getting away from the stage of a country which is simply selling its raw materials to the stage where as a country we are developing a large manufacturing industry as well. . . . we have reached a higher stage in

our manufacturing development in Canada, having regard to the age of the country and its population, than has, I believe, any other country in the history of the world.[11]

As previously noted, the branch plants contributed the most to the increasing importance of manufactured exports. While partisan differences between the Liberals and Conservatives developed during the interwar period on the degree of processing the branch plants should be induced to undertake in Canada, there was little suggestion from either party that the branch-plant political economy brought with it limits to industrial expansion or trade. Prime Minister Bennett's hopeful confidence, as expressed in these 1931 remarks, was typical of the era:

> All young or underdeveloped nations have been dependent on large capital investments by outside countries for the development of their natural resources and for assistance in the establishment of the diversified industry necessary to all-round national development. Without such assistance, industrial progress would be slow and desperately difficult. . . . Fear has sometimes been expressed that these outside nations by starting industries in this country . . . are obtaining a menacing position in our economic life. The facts of the case reveal these fears to be entirely unfounded.[12]

Industrial export progress in the 1920s was so remarkable that even contemporary detractors of foreign investment, who might otherwise criticize Bennett's naiveté here, have been dazzled. For example, J. Laxer recorded the massive trade in automotive products that resulted from Empire preferences. By 1929, he observed, Canada was capable of building over 260,000 vehicles and exporting over 100,000 of these. "A nation of under ten million people out-produced all the great nations of Europe including the United Kingdom, France and Germany," he concluded with some apparent pride.[13]

In spite of the fact that many indicators point to the success of import substitution for the Empire as an export strategy, it will soon be demonstrated that appearances were very deceptive. A close examination of the evidence (most of which was readily available to the decision-makers of the era) indicates that not only were the achievements of this export strategy superficial, but its duration was certain to be temporary. With its collapse, first noticeable in the late 1920s, we can witness the destruction of this CMA vision of a "permanent basis" for industrial exporting.

Canadian Content

Far less actual manufacturing took place in Canada because of imperial import substitution than at first might be imagined. At the beginning of the 1920s, many U.S. firms found it convenient to establish rather primitive assembly operations in Canada to take advantage of Empire tariff preferences. Under these schemes, they were only required to demonstrate that 25 per cent of the factory price of their commodities was composed of Empire labour. When firms experienced difficulty in reaching this target with actual production costs, it was not unheard for them to inflate Empire content by adding various Canadian "administrative" charges.[14]

There is considerable evidence that many, if not most, of the branch plants engaged in preferential trade worked at the margins of Empire content regulations. Whenever these labour quotas were raised by Britain or the white Dominions (for reasons that will be discussed later), Canadian trade was considerably disrupted. One notable case involved the export of photographic equipment. After Britain increased its Empire labour requirements for these goods to 75 per cent in 1927, the value of Canadian camera exports plummeted from 130,000 pounds in that year to just over 2,000 pounds in the following year.[15]

When Britain raised her general Empire labour requirement to 50 per cent in 1933, Trade and Commerce was deluged with scores of inquiries from both the CMA and individual manufacturers seeking the most lenient possible interpretations of the new regulations. The CMA itself prepared "hundreds" of Canadian content cost analyses on behalf of its members.[16] Unquestionably, the export business of some firms was curtailed. For example, Goodyear Tire and Rubber complained that it had "an opportunity of doing a considerable business in shipping tire molds to England and could qualify quite easily under the twenty-five per cent rule but the fifty per cent requirement makes it extremely difficult."[17] Still, not all U.S. branch plants were unhappy with the new 50 per cent level. Those who could already meet these requirements hoped to gain an advantage over their competitors. Those who could not were angry. One threatened that "any increase in the quota would result in withdrawal of fully half of these plants from Canada" because it would be "unprofitable for them to operate in the Dominion."[18]

The standard-bearer of Canadian-manufactured exports in this epoch was the automobile. Its industry group dominated sales to the Dominions. The actual level of Canadian content in these products was uneven and greatly depended on the policies of individual firms. Ford, both the largest exporter and Canadian producer until 1926, also had the highest share of

Table Seven
Canadian Trade in Automobiles, Trucks, and Parts,
and its Relationship to Gross Value of Domestic
Production in these Commodities, 1920-1938

Year	Exports ($ million)	Imports ($ million)	Exports (percentage of domestic production)	Imports (percentage of domestic production)
1920*	19.2	36.1	(n.a.)	(n.a.)
1921	18.5	29.1	-	-
1922	9.4	24.3	-	-
1923	29.5	32.0	-	-
1924	37.0	33.3	-	-
1925	31.0	28.6	-	-
1926	43.1	48.2	-	-
1926**	38.5	61.4	26	42
1927	32.0	75.7	22	53
1928	36.2	101.2	20	56
1929	47.3	93.7	23	45
1930	20.6	49.3	17	41
1931	6.7	26.7	9	37
1932	7.1	17.4	13	31
1933	9.9	16.0	18	29
1934	19.7	26.8	20	27
1935	24.4	33.3	18	24
1936	23.2	36.9	17	27
1937	27.0	54.7	15	30
1938	25.1	39.9	16	26

*Fiscal years.
**Calendar years.
SOURCES: Canada, *Trade of Canada*, and *Canada Year Book*, various years. Parts include engines but exclude rubber tires.

Canadian content. It claimed its products were over 75 per cent domestically produced as early as 1920. Controlled directly by the Ford family, Ford Canada was technologically dependent on the U.S. operation for patents, designs, and engineering. This dependence appears to have acted to reduce the level of Canadian input toward the end of the 1920s as models grew in complexity.[19]

The branch plants of the other U.S. automakers in Canada were unable or unwilling to match Ford's attempt to manufacture locally the largest share of their products. Many of their operations were simply sophisticated assembly plants that added a Canadian body and minor parts to a U.S. chassis and engine. As a consequence, while Canadian automotive export sales were quite formidable during the period, imports of these commodities were also massive. Table Seven demonstrates that only in two years, fiscal 1924 and 1925, did Canada manage a slight surplus in automotive trade. In 1929, Canada's best foreign sales year, imports were running at almost twice the level of exports. In that year, imports of parts and engines alone exceeded total automotive exports by just under $7 million.

The assembly nature of the automotive trade became a source of both foreign[20] and domestic embarrassment to the Canadian government. This became an important factor in King's major automotive tariff adjustments of 1926. Finance Minister J.A. Robb explicitly stated that his new regulations were designed to "compel the manufacturers of automobiles to cease having simply assembling plants in Canada. If they are in Canada to enjoy the advantages . . . of the British preference . . . then we submit it is only fair they should manufacture at least 50 per cent of their products in Canada to be entitled to that concession."[21] King spoke contemptuously of the "so-called Canadian manufacturers of automobiles." The new tariff provisions, he claimed, told them "if you wish to enjoy the advantages which our tariff gives you of getting into the British Empire market, then produce in Canada fifty per cent of your car with Canadian labour from Canadian products."[22]

While the intent of the King cabinet may have been clear in its own mind, the policy instruments it used to accomplish its objectives were, at best, somewhat obscure. To begin, the general tariff on automobile imports was significantly reduced, especially for the popular lower-priced models. Further, duties on a number of imported parts were either reduced or eliminated entirely. These moves, according to Robb, would stimulate the export sales of Canadian automakers in the following indirect manner. Since the domestic retail prices of Canadian automobiles were considerably higher than U.S. prices for similar models, and since for customs purposes in Empire markets Canadian cars were assessed on their "fair market value" in Canada, the preference advantage had been "practically wiped out on some Canadian cars."[23] The lower Canadian retail price resulting from these tariff reductions, it was hoped, would restore Canada's advantage.

In a related attempt to lower the "fair market value" of Canadian

**Table Eight
Manufacturers' Claims to Canadian Content
in their Automobiles, 1931-1932**

Company	Model	Canadian percentage
Chrysler	Plymouth	50
	Chrysler	50
	Dodge	50
	DeSoto	50
Dominion	Frontenac	50
Ford		66
General Motors	Chevrolet	40-67
	McLaughlin Buick	32-47
	Pontiac	59
Studebaker		50
Willys-Overland		71

SOURCE: NAC, RG 20, vol. 94, no. 22693:E, August 15, 1932.

automobiles, while encouraging the branch plants to increase their Canadian content, a 25 per cent rebate on duty paid on imported parts (domestic drawback) was offered to Canadian manufacturers who could establish at least 40 per cent Canadian content before April 1, 1927, and 50 per cent after that date. This domestic drawback was available for all cars sold in the domestic market, provided the content requirements were met, and was not dependent on re-export. Interestingly, no attempt was made to impose a similar content restriction on the more directly relevant 99 per cent export drawback that Canadian automakers had enjoyed since 1920 on foreign parts they assembled and re-exported.[24]

The offending automobile manufacturers, spurred on by these Canadian drawback regulations and higher Empire content quotas in Australia and New Zealand, gradually increased the Canadian component of their products. This is reflected in the lower percentage of the value of domestic production taken up by imports after 1932 (Table Seven). According to claims made to Trade and Commerce, by that time nearly all firms had reached the 50 per cent mark (Table Eight). However, most cars were still one-third to one-half foreign manufacture and no firm was producing a product that was even three-quarters Canadian.

There are indications that Canadian content claims such as these may have been exaggerated. For example, investigations of British customs at the Oshawa plant of General Motors revealed that this company had misrepresented the Canadian content of some of its vehicles as being over 50 per cent in order to qualify for preference.[25] Even if this particular incident was exceptional, automobile manufacturers certainly had a strong incentive in the domestic drawback requirements to inflate their content claims. To some extent, this tendency was encouraged by liberal customs regulations. Parts purchased in Canada could have up to 25 per cent foreign content and still be considered all-Canadian. Administrative charges and 75 per cent of the duty paid on imported materials could also be included as Canadian costs. Entire plant production was the basis of content calculations, not individual models.[26] The scope for flexibility under these regulations was illustrated by testimony of an executive of Hudson and Essex Motors before the Advisory Board on Tariff and Taxation at the end of the 1920s. In considering whether to establish a Canadian branch plant, this company had determined that economic production was only possible with an actual Canadian content of 32 per cent. However, if "some of the [domestic drawback] laws were looked at broadly and perhaps stretched a bit without breaking them, we could come up to 38 per cent."[27]

In summary, a significant portion of Canada's exports under Empire preference were actually re-exports of U.S. goods that had been subjected to varying and often minor degrees of Canadian processing and assembly. Certainly, this was the conclusion reached by many in Britain and the white Dominions. For example, this understanding led one Labour member of the Australian House of Representatives to object to a preference for Canadian imports. He informed his colleagues that he had

> studied this business fairly closely, and I find that business people in the United States of America are investing capital in Canada and opening up factories there, where parts of machinery manufactured in the United States of America are assembled in order to get the benefit of the preferential tariff granted by Britain to Canada. As soon as the Americans know that preference is to be granted to Canadian goods by Australia, this country will be flooded with articles of Yankee origin.[28]

This widely held opinion led the Australian government to fix its Empire content requirement at 75 per cent for goods from Canada.[29]

Resentment over the issue of Yankee-Canadian re-exports was also at the root of New Zealand raising its Empire content standard from 25 to 75 (later lowered to 50) per cent in 1924. The New Zealand Minister of Customs stated that the 25 per cent quota was "too easily complied with, and that articles of an essentially foreign character are treated as British for tariff purposes when only a comparatively small part of the manufacture has taken place within the Empire." This point was illustrated with a specific reference to the case of Canadian automotive exports.

> The chassis, which may be considered as the really important part of the car, may be made in a foreign country. Suppose it costs 150 pounds: by the addition to it in England or Canada of a cheap body, costing as little as 50 pounds, making the total cost at 200 pounds, the complete car qualifies for tariff preference.[30]

Not only was the degree of Canadian content an issue in the Dominions, but the mere fact that many Canadian exporters were U.S. branch plants was enough to raise suspicions that the principle of Empire preference was being abused by the Canadians. J.A. Robb, while Minister of Trade and Commerce, discovered the strength of these feelings on his unsuccessful 1922 mission to Australia to obtain preferential concessions. He reported to King:

> There seems to be an organized campaign through the public press against Canadian trade, the principal argument being that Canadian industries are controlled by United States capital, and that any concession granted to Canada is indirectly a concession to the United States against whom there is a very strong feeling throughout Australia.[31]

As an example of Australian hostility to the import substitution for the Empire strategy of Canadian industrial capital, Robb appended an editorial, "English Sovereigns or American Dollars," from the Sydney *Sun*. This newspaper opposed an extension to Canadians of the Australian preference already granted British manufacturers:

> Today American money dominates Canadian industries. . . . Preference given to Canada at the expense of Great Britain, therefore, mostly means pouring good Australian money into American safes, already choked with gold; while England will be that much poorer and that much less able to help Australia if war should come in the Pacific.[32]

Similar logic was frequently employed by the Australian legislative opponents of tariff preferences for Canadian manufacturers. One, who was later to become Minister of Trade and Customs, suggested that much of the benefit of a Canadian preference would "largely go to the United States of America, and the money may be re-invested there in other businesses that may compete with British manufacturers."[33]

Canadian manufacturers were stung by these criticisms that they were acting as Trojan horses for their U.S. parents, but they were unable to counteract such accusations effectively. For their part, English industrialists encouraged the spread of this idea in order to influence favourably the purchases of their more public-spirited customers. T.A. Russell, president of Willys-Overland, complained to the Toronto Export Club in 1928 of "a very offensive type of propaganda" prevalent in Britain. This suggested that "a car was not British unless assembled in the British Isles from materials acquired there." "In other words," he continued, "it denies to the product of this country classification as British."[34]

Despite such protests, Canadian manufacturers appear to have made little headway in convincing consumers of their "British" standing. Over the years, Trade and Commerce documented the widespread public resistance to this notion. For example, the English distributors of Moffat ranges reported that in "ninety-nine cases out of a hundred the consuming public in Great Britain classify Canadian products as being of United States origin." Wahl Evershape Company of Toronto stated flatly that "the British public do not regard Canadian products as British. . . . Retail shops particularly are inclined to regard Canadian goods as American."[35] Unfortunately for Canada's interests here, and the interests of our bona fide exporters, this impression was grounded in a reality that transcended uninformed prejudice. As late as 1950, Trade and Commerce agents were to report "certain shipments of so-called Canadian merchandise" being presented for entry under imperial preference. It was observed that "these are nearly always American goods which find their way to Canada, perhaps to some subsidiary company there, who decide to re-export them to the United Kingdom."[36]

Imperial Preference and National Self-interest

We have witnessed how Canadian manufacturers had to struggle to convince everyone save themselves that imperial import substitution was an act of patriotism on their part. Emotional acceptance of this strategy in their intended Empire markets was limited both by the assembly nature of Canadian production and by the considerable dimension of its foreign ownership. In addition, certain miscalculations by the manufacturers in the early years of the 1920s, notably, quoting their prices in U.S. funds, may have exaggerated these problems.[37] The ultimate collapse of the strategy, however, cannot be blamed entirely on its inability to rally Empire sentiment. Other, more fundamental weaknesses located in the economic structures of Britain and the Dominions doomed the project from its inception.

British acceptance of the theory of imperial preference was both delayed and partial. In the last half of the nineteenth century, free trade had been the economic orthodoxy in Britain. The easy access to markets and raw materials promised by that theory has often been in favour in nations confident of their ability to dominate world trade. Imperial preference, with its return to a type of tariff-protected mercantilism, only gained currency when British industry began to run out of steam. In conceding a very limited degree of imperial preference after World War One, the British government hoped to arrest some of its economic reverses. According to the "Imperial Visionaries" in that government, British prosperity could be ensured by a determined effort to rejuvenate the Empire. The extension of a preference to the Dominions by Britain was a principal feature of the vision. As a response to the already existing network of Dominion preferences for British goods, it was a price that had to be paid to ensure that these governments would remain willing to accept the continued export of surplus British capital, labour, and manufactures. This vision assumed a natural division of labour within the Empire. Britain would produce manufactures and the Dominions and colonies would supply mainly primary materials.[38]

This British idea of imperial preference bore little relationship to the scheme of Canadian manufacturers to become the Empire purveyors of goods that might otherwise be imported from the U.S. Britain was not necessarily opposed to Canadian industrialization. Nevertheless, it is clear that the imperatives of national self-interest as well as pressure from her own industrial capitalists would lead her to reject Canadian attempts to become the workshop of the Empire. The Labour Party in particular opposed British preferences on manufactured imports and revoked them when they held power during 1923 and 1924.

An excellent illustration of the attitude of the British state toward the pretensions of Canadian manufacturers can be found in the rebuffs they received when seeking orders from the purchasing agents of the colonial administrations. Not surprisingly, an informal code seems to have dictated that contracts were to be given whenever possible to firms located in Great Britain. Trade and Commerce compiled a thick dossier dealing with the frustrations encountered by Canadian companies who tried to bypass this rule by arguing that they, too, were "British."[39] P.C. Larkin, Canada's High Commissioner in London, attempted to assist Canadian industrialists in this matter, only to conclude it was hopeless. He wrote:

Table Nine
Canadian Trade with Selected Areas of the
British Empire, 1920-1939 ($ million)

	Imports to Canada		Exports from Canada	
	1920-29	*1930-39*	*1920-29*	*1930-39*
Australia	28	77	164	193
British Africa	14	71	105	138
New Zealand	48	46	128	98
Great Britain	1,069	1,197	3,870	2,834

SOURCE: Canada, *Trade of Canada*, 1939, vol. 1.

if anyone imagines that the people here who control Indian affairs will allow a contract for as much as a nail which they can obtain in this country to go to Canada they are mistaken and Mr. Butler [president, Canadian Car and Foundry] is quite right when he says "that the policy of inter-Empire trade is a myth in which our Mother Country has no real sympathy." She certainly has no sympathy with contracts being given out of this country which can be executed here. . . . I have no doubt that every contract given out by India that will be made impossible for us to tender for will be made so.[40]

Like Britain, when the white Dominions embraced the principle of imperial preference, it was with their own economic self-interests fixed firmly in sight. Following Canada's 1898 lead, they unilaterally extended tariff concessions to Britain in the early years of this century. Like Canada, they held hopes of eventually persuading her to grant them reciprocal privileges on their agricultural exports. Because Britain absorbed the bulk of these goods, it made economic sense to create goodwill by doing all that was politically feasible to encourage the sale of British goods in their domestic markets.

In contrast, the economic incentive for granting the same preference to Canadian manufacturers was simply not there. Not only did Canada accept a very minor portion of the trade of the other white Dominions (as she needed few of their products), but all were in a deficit position in their trade with Canada, as we can see in Table Nine. Significantly, these deficits were swollen by the import of precisely those commodities in which Canadian industries sought favoured treatment.

Decisively, these other Dominions were eager to initiate their own import substitution industrialization in the products Canada was exporting. And, they hoped to begin as soon as their internal markets had grown to the point where they could support such enterprises. Canadian politicians had been given notice of the temporary nature of Canada's intermediary role as early as 1893. During that year, our first Minister of Trade and Commerce, Mackenzie Bowell, had journeyed to Australia to investigate trade prospects in that country. On his return, he wrote that the Australians were

> day by day growing strongly protectionist. . . . When I was met with the argument that they were putting on such high duties in order to enable their people to manufacture such articles as we could send them, I simply replied that they were quite justified, but until they were in a position to supply their own wants we wanted to sell to them instead of having the Yankees do so. To this they made no objection. [41]

When the Australians eventually conceded a preference to Canada in 1925, it was on the clear understanding that its benefits would last only as long as it took them to organize domestic production. In bringing forward the preference legislation, the Australian Minister of Trade and Customs observed that Canada was now being granted concessions on imports worth some 18 million pounds,

> of which motor-chassis account for more than half . . . unfortunately [they] are not at present made in Australia . . . Canada's trade in motor chassis with this country, until we begin to make motor chassis for ourselves, should be looked upon with favour by all those who believe in inter-imperial trade. [42]

As a first step in undertaking the complete local assembly of imported vehicles, the Australians had adjusted their tariff four years previously to induce the manufacture of auto bodies in that country.

The success of this venture was observed with great interest in South Africa. By 1925, its government was ready to adopt a similar course of action. It discontinued its preference on completed vehicles and lowered its tariff on chassis imported to be fitted under bodies built in South Africa. Some were eager for even stronger measures to induce local assembly, but the government counselled that patience could be profitable. The South African Minister of Finance spoke to his legislature of negotiations with a foreign manufacturer (probably Ford) interested in import substitution:

> The representatives of a firm, which came here some time ago to establish a motor car assembling station, pointed out to us that they were very anxious to increase their operations, but whereas they sell 30,000 cars in Australia, here they sell only 4,000. We import only

15,000 cars of all makes per year, so any firm which desires to establish assembling stations here will have to spend a lot of money. While we are not going as far as Australia has gone, we will see how things go and perhaps we may revise our policy later on.[43]

Progress in ISI proceeded far more rapidly in the Dominions than almost anyone had expected. By the mid-1920s, a number of U.S. automakers had warehouse-assembly branch plants in operation in these countries. Many products previously imported from Canada were now manufactured locally with predictably negative effects on Canadian trade. As a consequence, Canada slipped from second place in world automobile production during the 1920s to fifth in the early 1930s.[44] This ISI-related decline in export sales was an important contributor to the industry's disastrous collapse during the Great Depression. In 1932, it was only working to approximately 15 per cent of its capacity.[45] Although export sales were again to pick up after 1933, they never approached their earlier peak (see Table Seven). Average sales in the years before World War Two were only two-thirds of those of the previous decade's boom between 1923 and 1929. As well, the industry did not progress very far up the technological ladder. Almost 90 per cent of its exports in 1938 were complete vehicles, while parts still dominated imports.

While demand in the Dominions for "made-in-Canada" vehicles remained relatively strong in the late 1930s, the reprieve could only be temporary. There, in the midst of worldwide depression, ISI was proceeding with remarkable vigour. After the early bust years of the decade, substantial growth was experienced in the manufacturing sectors of New Zealand, South Africa, and Australia. New Zealand recorded a 50 per cent increase in production from 1928 to 1938; South Africa, 75 per cent. Between 1929 and 1937, the Australian volume of manufacturing rose by 40 per cent. By way of comparison, in these same years, Canadian manufacturing suffered a decline of some 8 per cent.[46]

State Policy and Branch-Plant Exports

How did Canadian political leaders react to the flaws we have discovered in imperial import substitution? In general, as we witnessed at the beginning of the chapter, they remained optimistic that the CMA could deliver on its pledge to use this strategy to build a "permanent" base for Canadian industrial exports. Trade and Commerce Minister J. Malcolm came as close as anyone to being a critic. He believed that Canada was destined to become the world's second largest exporter of manufactures. Still, he blasted the warehouse-assembly nature of much Empire production as not being "of very much consequence to Canada."[47] Not surprisingly,

then, Malcolm was a strong supporter of the 1926 domestic drawback legislation which, it will be recalled, gave tariff rebates to manufacturers who
could produce vehicles with at least 50 per cent Canadian content.

Malcolm's predecessor in Trade and Commerce had taken a somewhat
less aggressive stance. In 1924, T.A. Low had received a delegation of the
Canadian presidents of Ford, General Motors, and Willys-Overland.
These important industrialists were dismayed over rumours that the
Dominions were preparing to raise their Canadian content requirements
to 75 per cent. Low's assistance was requested in lobbying for a reduction
to "some amount not exceeding 50 per cent." They also wanted the most
lenient possible interpretation of what constituted "raw materials" for the
purposes of determining Canadian content so that they could remain free
to import a large portion of their parts from the U.S. In assuring these
manufacturers of his "very best" efforts in pursuing "the interests of your
industry in this connection," Low appears to have found nothing objec-
tionable in their approach from the standpoint of the national interest.[48]

Malcolm's successor, H.H. Stevens, also became involved in attempting to ease the Empire content difficulties of the automobile manufacturers. In 1930, the colonial administration of Trinidad issued a new
regulation that required all civil servants who obtained government car
loans to purchase vehicles "entirely the product of the British Empire." In
effect, this meant that only products of Great Britain were eligible. The
trade commissioner in the field warned his department that the regulation
was a "menace to the sale of Canadian cars" because it might lead to the
cancellation of private orders from patriotic British residents of the territory. Stevens hotly protested to the British that the requirement was
"unfair." "It is obviously impossible for us to state that our cars are 100 per
cent British manufacture," he commented; "the cars manufactured in
Canada run from fifty to eighty per cent British manufacture." Stevens's
intervention was rewarded by a lowered 50 per cent rule. However, even
this was not sufficient to satisfy all the Canadian suppliers. The trade commissioner reported "a great deal of disappointment that the figure has
been set so high."[49]

These two examples serve to highlight a more general issue. Instead of
attempting to lower content quotas on behalf of the manufacturers, to
what extent could the Canadian state have used them as a lever to coerce
the branch plants to undertake more processing in this country? It would
appear that this policy option was never seriously entertained. The effectiveness of the one move undertaken in this field, the domestic drawback
regulation, is questionable. Its Canadian content quota was set at a rather
low 50 per cent, it was not applied to re-exports, and it came much too late
to quiet Empire criticism.

The rhetoric of the Conservative Party during this period suggested that they would seek a better standard of performance from the manufacturers. Bennett was certainly aware of the content problem. In 1928, he declared that:

> with decreasing exports we are assembling [automobile] parts to a greater extent than ever before. That means less work for Canadians – less manufacturing and an increasing tendency towards the assembling of parts. Now what is the aim of the Conservative Party? It is to endeavour to make this country economically independent. . . . If we are obliged always to go abroad for all our machinery, what will happen supposing, in a moment of caprice, that foreign supply is cut off?[50]

When their turn to govern came in the early years of the Depression, however, the Conservative industrial strategy was revealed as nothing more original or challenging than jacking up the tariff. This experiment, of course, was always in favour with the ISI manufacturers, whether branch plant or Canadian-owned.

As for the Liberals, high tariffs held few attractions. It will be recalled, however, that they coupled lower automotive tariffs in the 1920s with drawbacks for manufacturers who could build 50 per cent Canadian cars. This helped cement King's low-tariff farm and Progressive Party support.[51] But there were also political costs. The protests of the automotive industry and its workers, which included a brief closure of a General Motors plant and a rally of 3,000 workers in Ottawa, forced King to modify some aspects of the legislation. Automakers were particularly irked by the Canadian content provisions, although they reluctantly learned to live with them. Only the Canadian auto parts manufacturers and Ford, which sensed a competitive advantage because of its unusually high domestic content, would have been likely to support a Liberal move to increase content quotas.[52]

Faced with this hostile reaction from one industrial sector, the Liberals would naturally be wary of ever offering the drawback incentive in others. In addition, their general laissez-faire orientation would have made the more drastic step of regulating a higher Canadian content unthinkable, save in the most terrible of circumstances. When all was considered, the political difficulties that would have resulted from probing these questions too deeply were far outweighed by the potential advantages of emphasizing the government's role in what was, on the surface, apparent export progress on the part of the manufacturers.

Besides, apart from the content question, King's administration was not a great believer in the ability of the manufacturing interest, with imperial preference or not, to deliver any extensive benefits to the nation through its export trade. Instead, they looked for succour to the sale of

Table Ten
Dominion Imports from Canada and the United States,
1920-1939 (per cent of total)

	Australia*		New Zealand		South Africa	
	U.S.	Canada	U.S.	Canada	U.S.	Canada
1920-24	22	3	16	5	15	3
1925-29	24	3	18	8	16	3
1930-34	16	4	15	6	14	3
1935-39	16	7	12	8	18	4

*Fiscal years.
SOURCES: Australia, Bureau of Census and Statistics, *Year Book*; New Zealand, Department of Statistics, *Year Book*; Union of South Africa, Union Office of Census and Statistics, *Year Book*, various years.

Canada's abundant resources in its "natural" market, the United States. So it was that King delivered this comment on Bennett's attempt to help Canadian industry to "blast" its way into world markets:

> If the tariff can be used as an instrument of national policy by raising duties to help the manufacturing industry of this country, why might it not also be used as an instrument of national policy to help the great primary, basic industries of the country in their production by lowering the duties? . . . what is most needed is a tariff which will help us export commodities, rather than a tariff that will help to prohibit importations.[53]

Through trade agreements with the U.S. in 1935 and 1938, King was to prove as good as his word. In exchange for American concessions on Canadian resources, the tariff door was once again propped open for the freer entry of U.S. industrial products.

For our purposes, more problematic than either the tariff or content issues was the whole notion of relying on the branch plants to motor the export strategy of Canadian manufacturing. After all, what was being created here was not a manufacturing sector capable of standing on its own technological feet and developing a line of products competitive in world markets. Rather, the strategy's success was predicated on U.S. firms being willing and able to transfer a certain portion of their foreign business to Canada. While many U.S. firms in the interwar period saw it to be in their interest to do so, many more did not. Table Ten demonstrates that even in the case of the coveted white Dominion markets, imperial preference was not a sufficient incentive to divert the lion's share of U.S. trade to Canada. In the crucial period of the 1925-29 economic boom, U.S. sales were running at more than twice Canada's level in New Zealand, five times Canada's average in South Africa, and eight times greater in Australia. Although some moderate closure of this gap was experienced during the Depression, particularly in Australia, this was to hold no long-term significance.

The trade commissioners were often far more clear-headed on this issue than were their political masters. Because these were men of practical field experience, they tended to recognize the dangers of remaining dependent on the branch plants to furnish Canada with its industrial export strategy. For example, in late 1919, one trade commissioner told the Windsor Chamber of Commerce that

> American firms establishing in Canada secure the advantages of free sites, taxation exemption, cheap power and good laws. Many such branches are established over here and in other parts of the Dominion for the purpose of doing export trade within the British empire. However, in many cases the selling organization is in the United States, and there is no authority in Canada to do an export trade within the empire.[54]

Over the years, the trade commissioners were to report many instances of export blocking on the part of U.S. firms in commodities as diverse as automobiles and bedsteads.[55]

Yet another snag in relying on the branch plants to produce Canada's manufactured exports also worried the trade commissioners. As we have already indicated in the case of the automakers, even when U.S. firms did choose Canada as their entrepôt to the Empire, such decisions were vulnerable to being rescinded later and production shifted elsewhere. When such a shift in production was contemplated, it would appear that Canadian branch plants frequently requested the advice and assistance of the trade commissioner stationed at the prospective site. This posed a thorny dilemma. To what extent should Trade and Commerce carry out its mandate for overseas service to Canadian industrial capital in these cases, when it knew that it might be damaging to the long-term interests of Canadian trade? The department compromised. Trade commissioners were instructed to avoid "encouraging" such migrations "because it has not been considered that Canada can spare the export of capital for this purpose." All assistance short of official approval, however, seems to have been rendered. One widely experienced Trade and Commerce official noted that "we have, of course, given the best advice possible as to labour conditions, raw materials, factory regulations and the like, and have tried to avoid any precise advice."[56]

On occasion, the trade commissioners appear also to have believed it a normal part of their duties to act as a lobby for the branch plants with the governments of the countries where they were posted. This was particularly true of the Canadian content controversy. In 1926, the agent in New Zealand wrote his branch director in Ottawa of his activities in this regard:

> I am enclosing herewith two clippings which appeared in the Wellington papers recently, relating to the annual meeting of the New Zealand Association of British Manufacturers, from which you will see that . . . a direct insinuation was made that Canada is now controlled economically by the United States, so far as the motor industry is concerned. . . . I think you will agree with me that this is . . . a matter for continual work to overcome whatever prejudices may be created. . . . I may say that an effort has been made in a very informal way to counteract any impressions which may have been left in the minds of the Cabinet Ministers concerned. . . .[57]

The Director of the Commercial Intelligence Branch was favourably impressed with this trade commissioner's initiative and replied approvingly:

> I think you would do well to endeavour to overcome, in every way you can, any prejudices which may exist in New Zealand against purchasing from Canadian plants . . . associated with American interests. In our efforts to increase the export trade of Canada, we cannot leave out of the picture branch industries of American firms.[58]

Conclusion

In the interwar period, our discussion reflects for the first time the growing importance of the branch-plant industrial sector. By way of contrast to the earlier era in which Canadian-owned industry was dominant, a coherent export strategy was developed by a number of important branch plants – import substitution for the Empire. These enterprises transferred some of their export business from their U.S. operations to take advantage of the preferential tariffs that Canada enjoyed in Great Britain and the white Dominions.

We have seen that this strategy, while it may have served the short-term interests of the U.S. firms in question, did little to develop the long-term export potential of Canadian industry. It was superficial, temporary, and incomplete. Under it, Canadian manufactured exports were often merely the products of warehouse-assembly processing. The strategy was doomed to early collapse because of a number of ideological and economic barriers in its intended markets. As well, the other Dominions manifested a growing determination to begin their own ISI as soon as their domestic markets grew large enough to support economic production. Finally, a significant number of U.S. firms did not participate in this strategy. They forbade exports by their Canadian subsidiaries because they found it more profitable to centre foreign trade in the parent operation.

The collapse of the imperial import substitution strategy in this period marks the beginning of the modern era in Canada's inability to export finished manufactures. From this point, the branch-plant pattern of a fragmented domestic market filled with small, uneconomic producers incapable of being internationally competitive, even if their parents were to permit them export freedom, became firmly established. Canadians, with the exception of iron and steel production, retained ownership of only those industrial sectors that were to decline in world trade.

Despite the extremely high stakes, the state failed to act decisively during this period to put Canadian industry in a less vulnerable position. Although problems with the branch-plant structure were recognized by the political elite, they were not judged to be fundamental. King, for example, in concert with what we shall discover in Chapter 6 to be the economic orthodoxy of his era, believed that Canada was inevitably progressing from a resource export stage to a stage in which manufactured exports would be dominant. Accordingly, little in the way of remedy was offered except a rather limp device to encourage the production of the 50 per cent Canadian car.

Chapter Six

Branch Plants: Blocked Exports

~~~~~~

Remarkable. Although an overworked word, it serves to capture the flavour of Canada's economic expansion in the three decades that began with World War Two. From 1938 to 1968, Canada's gross national expenditure rose by five times, the value of manufacturing output by six times, and the net value of capital stock invested in manufacturing by over four times (all figures adjusted to compensate for inflation). [1]

Equally impressive was the tremendous swelling in the capital stock of direct foreign investment in Canada during the post-Depression era. Two central economic sectors, manufacturing and mining, moved from a position of majority Canadian ownership to majority foreign ownership with two-fifths foreign control at the beginning of this period and three-fifths at its conclusion. In the two decades after the war alone, the book value of foreign investment increased sevenfold. Table Eleven shows foreign investment in Canada at its early 1970s peak.

Taken as a whole, then, this period was marked both by striking advances in industrial activity and by foreign control of the firms responsible for carrying it out. What was the relationship between the two phenomena? As we examine this era, we must never lose sight of the fact that those with political and economic power in Canada generally believed that foreign investment had *caused* this economic growth. In 1968, the Ontario Minister of Trade and Development submitted with forthright crudeness that "we'd still be chasing Indians if it were not for foreign investment." [2] It is a short step from this kind of identification of foreign investment as the force behind economic growth to a conviction that the promotion of foreign direct investment would produce even more economic growth, which, in turn, would pay large electoral dividends to the government or political party able to associate itself most closely with it. Those few outside the centres of state power who worried about the long-term consequences of foreign economic domination were accused of attacking

Table Eleven
Foreign Control of Canadian Manufacturing,
1971 (per cent of total)

	Assets	*Sales*
Food	46	34
Beverages	31	32
Tobacco products	85	78
Rubber products	93	91
Leather products	23	21
Textile mills	54	51
Knitting mills	22	16
Clothing industries	12	9
Wood industries	31	24
Furniture industries	19	16
Paper and allied industries	46	43
Printing, publishing, and allied	11	11
Primary metals	41	37
Metal fabricating	42	43
Machinery	75	77
Transport equipment	82	91
Electrical products	67	65
Non-metallic mineral products	62	51
Petroleum and coal products	99	99
Chemicals and chemical products	79	81
Miscellaneous manufacturing	50	51
Total manufacturing	59	57

SOURCES: Statistics Canada, *Annual Report*, 1972; Corporations and Labour Unions Returns Act, Part I, Corporations, March, 1975.

the standard of living of ordinary Canadians and/or of trying to turn Canada into a northern "banana republic."

The logic behind this kind of rhetoric is hard to comprehend. By far the greatest portion of the foreign investment splurge was generated within Canada. Only one-quarter of the 1946-60 expansion in foreign-controlled enterprises was funded from foreign sources.[3] During the succeeding two decades, this portion fell to under one-fifth. To a significant extent, the existing pre-war complement of branch plants, especially in the growth consumer industries of the manufacturing sector, simply expanded in step with the remarkably strong post-war domestic economy. Funding came mainly from retained earnings on operating profits made in Canada, loans from Canadian financial institutions and investors, and investment incentives built into the tax system. It is important to note, however, that the advantage of access to the relatively small share of imported foreign capital Canada used must be balanced against the inevitable return of dividends to foreign parents. During the 1970s, this return flow reached levels twice as great as the value of new foreign capital entering Canada.

The mistaken opinions of our political leaders in this instance would be of little consequence if foreign investment had affected Canada's ability to export manufactures in a positive or even a benign manner. As will become apparent, this was not the case. Rather, the branch-plant economy reinforced and further institutionalized the inward-looking nature of the earlier import substitution model of Canadian industrialization. As can be seen from Table Eleven, foreign investment was concentrated in just those key modern manufacturing sectors like chemicals, machinery, transport, and electrical goods that led the post-1950 export charges of other industrial countries. During this period, Canadian manufacturing settled into its role as a regional site, much like California, the U.S North-east, and the Middle West for the location of American industry. Politics, in the form of the Canadian tariff, created the necessary conditions for the northward transfer of a share of U.S. production.

Barriers to Canadian subsidiary exports came in two main forms: administrative and technological. These limitations often were based in a conception of the Canadian market as part of the U.S. company's domestic operations. According to this view, the subsidiary had been allocated its territory within North America and exports were the province of the *international* division of the U.S. head office. Yet, even if Canadian branch plants had been given complete export freedom, few were in a good position to make anything of it. C.P. Kindleberger reminds us that "a new good . . . is likely to expand exports to the extent that other countries are unable initially to produce it but want to consume it."[4] Unfortunately, Canadian subsidiaries lacked the technological punch to generate internationally marketable innovations. Highly dependent on their parents for imports of machinery, processes, and patents, the technological capabilities of the typical branch plant were slight. They frequently extended no further than inconsequential modifications of the parent's line of products to meet the peculiarities of Canadian taste.

"Chronic" Technological Dependence

The tripwires of the import substitution for the Empire export strategy were discussed in the last chapter. One of the most important of these, it will be recalled, was the well-publicized desire of the other Dominions to initiate their own ISI process for the U.S. goods being shipped from Canadian factories during the 1920s and 1930s.

Nevertheless, those who understood the ultimate implications of this trend were less concerned than they might have been. L.D. Wilgress, then director of Canada's trade commissioner service, told the 1939 annual meeting of the CMA that the country would continue to have many advantages in exporting manufactures to the "less-developed" agricultural countries now beginning their own secondary industries. The branch plants would save the day for Canadian trade. It was logical, Wilgress reasoned, for U.S. investors to assign "a share" of their export business to their Canadian subsidiaries because of the small size of our domestic market. "Although greatly assisted by preferential tariffs," he observed, "it is a natural tendency based on sound business practice."

Hence, in the course of time, "North American skill" and Canada's contiguous position to "the greatest and most progressive manufacturing country in the world" would allow us to move up the technological ladder. Rather than the consumer goods on which the modest export successes of the 1920s had been based, Canada's branch plants would now ship capital or producer goods such as machinery.

> . . . all the time these countries may be building up new manufacturing industries we shall not be standing still, but will be developing new export industries, the products of which will be shipped abroad in place of those no longer required in our principal markets because of the development of home industries. In other words, the process is one of constant change. Export opportunities for some products in certain markets may gradually be reduced but new openings will be created for other products. [5]

Wilgress's logic was actually very sound if applied to an industrial structure with a mature capital goods industry. As we already know, this was something Canada had never developed. Following their ISI pattern, Canadian manufacturers had for the most part left their technological base in the hands of others. We could hardly expect to export what we could not produce for ourselves. Worse, lacking a potent capital goods industry, from where was the stimulative impetus for the creation of new exportable products to come?

If there was ever any room for doubt in this matter, World War Two dispelled it completely. Ironically, on the eve of the war, the president of the CMA had suggested that Canada was basically self-sufficient in machinery and "not depending too greatly on external sources for supplies which might be cut off by a war."[6] This was indeed a balloon begging to be popped. As a 1947 government report recorded, pre-war Canada lacked "an integrated heavy industry" and exhibited a "high degree of dependence upon American and British sources for heavy equipment, tools, and machinery, specialized materials and parts." Consequently, when the war came, "much of the machinery and equipment" for defence production "had to be imported" and a new Canadian machine tool industry "virtually created."[7]

In his authoritative history of the 1939-45 Canadian war effort, C.P. Stacey concluded that "Canadian industry generally was based upon American production methods, standards and techniques, and was dependent upon American imports of machinery, spare parts, subassemblies and components."[8] This observation was nowhere more true than in the capital goods industry. There, the situation was so desperate that it became the infant ward of the federal state. Through the Department of Munitions and Supply and various Crown corporations, the government centralized the purchasing, warehousing, and distribution of the nation's production machinery. Such matters as deciding on priorities for acquisition, reallocating machines between factories, and loaning equipment to manufacturers were all in the province of these agencies. So, too, were the design and engineering of new machinery and the supervision of production in new and existing machine tool factories in Canada.[9]

All of this unprecedented state control may have rendered the technological answers to Canada's wartime manufacturing headaches, but the changes it wrought were not sufficiently radical to provide for a long-term solution. No sooner did production fall back into private hands than the nation was in the midst of a capital investment splurge. While consumer goods industries were compensating for undermaintenance during the Depression and war years, new resource extraction projects were opening for business. Incredibly, two-thirds of the necessary machinery and equipment put in place for this investment in 1948 were imported, as were three-quarters of the machine tools. In that year as well, Canada was the world's largest importer of machinery, equipment, and parts, bringing in a total in excess of the combined value of American and British imports of these commodities.[10]

These massive imports of capital goods contributed in no small way to Canada's post-war foreign exchange crisis. In 1947, Alex Skelton, a principal adviser to C.D. Howe (who, as Minister of Munitions and Supply, Reconstruction, and then Trade and Commerce, dominated federal economic policy-making between 1940 and 1957), provided his boss with a strikingly clear exposition of Canada's quandary:

Canadian manufacturing industry in general, and in particular Canadian branch plants modelled on the parent U.S. industry, consume a proportion of U.S. raw materials, semi-processed materials, tools, equipment and services in every unit they produce currently. If in addition, a capital expansion programme is being undertaken (as at present) this involves additional U.S. "content" (materials, services and capital charges). [11]

Skelton took care to distinguish between the "abnormal" causes of Canadian foreign exchange difficulties related to post-war dislocations and the "chronic" problems that stemmed from foreign direct investment. "Temporary expedients" would suffice for the "abnormal" predicament, but the "chronic" problems required "some fundamental adjustments." However, "the necessities of the moment may help in getting them started." In Skelton's mind, the needed "fundamental adjustments" would have weaned Canadian manufacturers from "simply accepting the convenient model of U.S. industry which is naturally based on U.S. raw materials." Pressure would have been placed on the branch plants to increase Canadian production content or to "develop specialized production in Canada for export to U.S. domestic or export markets as an offset to the Canadian industry's imports from the U.S.A."

Even though he averred agreement "in general" with Skelton's analysis, the policy solution of Howe and the Liberals leaned more in the direction of a "temporary expedient." [12] In November, 1947, the Emergency Exchange Conservation Act placed prohibitions and quotas on imports of consumer goods and demanded the licensing of imports of capital goods. [13] By this means, Howe supposed that the assembly character of Canadian industrial production could be rounded into a more complete process. The restrictions, Howe pronounced, "had the very decided effect of stimulating the manufacture of components which had previously been imported, not because they could not have been made just as well in Canada, but because it was easier to import them than it was to organize their production in this country." In this regard, the intent of the legislation was very similar to the 1920s attempt to upgrade the Canadian content of automobiles. Indeed, within the capital goods sector, automobiles and trucks were the primary targets for component replacement by domestic production. The other principal ingredient in the capital goods program appears to have been the deferral of investments for commercial, office, service, and amusement purposes. [14]

In short, virtually nothing was being done about the "chronic" nature of the problem. As Table Twelve demonstrates, capital goods for the resource and manufacturing sectors flooded across the border before, during, and after the import control program was withdrawn in 1950. The most that might be suggested is that the domestic content of Canadian production was modestly augmented after 1951. But, unfortunately, that was all that seems to have been desired. Shortly after the Emergency

Table Twelve
Canadian Imports of Machinery and Imports Classified
According to Purpose, 1946-1960 (per cent of total imports)

Year	Machinery*	Value Ranked against Other Import Groups**	Consumer Goods***	Producer Materials and Equipment****
1946	6	I	18	45
1947	7	I	24	47
1948	8	I	21	50
1949	7	I	25	48
1950	7	I	26	51
1951	8	I	23	49
1952	9	I	24	45
1953	9	I	26	43
1954	9	I	24	43
1955	9	I	25	44
1956	11	I	25	46
1957	11	I	24	46
1958	10	I	26	43
1959	10	I	29	44
1960	10	I	29	44

*Excludes household and agriculture.
**Rank adjusted from 1946 to 1949 in concert with post-1950 DBS practice of separating refined and crude petroleum.
***Includes farm and road transport equipment but excludes food.
****Excludes farm and construction equipment.
SOURCES: Computed from Canada, Dominion Bureau of Statistics, *Trade of Canada*, vol. 1; *Canada Year Book*, various years.

Exchange Conservation Act was proclaimed, Howe signalled the manufacturers that he did not want them to rush into the production of capital goods that could not be "produced competitively in Canada under normal conditions."[15] He apparently felt that Canadian ISI manufacturing could be deepened by greater domestic production of components only if foreign machinery and technology continued to be used to equip our factories. To illustrate, he objected to a proposed 10 per cent excise tax on U.S. capital goods imports because Canadians could not supply such machinery. A tax would simply increase costs and discourage needed capital investment without checking imports.[16]

Table Thirteen

Machinery Trade by Major Machinery Producing Countries, 1973

Country	Percentage of Domestic Requirements Imported	Percentage of Production Exported
United States	10	17
Japan	10	24
Federal Germany	34	63
Great Britain	34	50
France	50	45
Sweden	50	54
Canada	60	30
Canada (1978)	66	40

SOURCE: Canada, Employment and Immigration, Task Force on Labour Market Development, Technical Study 28, Peat Marwick and Partners, "The Medium-Term Employment Outlook: The Canadian Equipment and Machinery Industry," July, 1981, Exhibit II.

Without the necessary "fundamental adjustments" in the 1940s and 1950s, it should not be surprising that Canada remained heavily dependent on foreign suppliers of capital goods through the 1960s and 1970s. In fact, at the end of the 1970s, Canada was still the world's largest machinery importer on a per capita basis.[17] Canada's comparatively anemic performance in this keystone sector for technological innovation is portrayed in Table Thirteen.

Besides the import dependence of the capital goods sector during this period, there were other clear indications of the extent of the technological barriers to generating exportable innovations in Canada. Contemporary studies of multinational firm behaviour had documented their preference for concentrating their research activities in their home countries. Innovations developed in foreign parent locales were subsequently protected by local patents in host countries like Canada. Such patents played the dual function of impeding local technological advance through imitation and adaptation and ensuring a monopoly position for the foreign firm in the local market. This monopoly position allowed the multinational to engage in a number of restrictive business practices, including limitation of export sales.[18]

Many studies of this era confirmed that the general pattern of multinational firm marketing and product development policies just described was widely reproduced in Canadian industry. Researchers drew a direct line between Canada bearing the highest levels of foreign ownership of its manufacturing sector of any developed nation and its status as the technologically weakest of the industrialized countries. In the early 1970s, it was found that approximately 95 per cent of patents issued in Canada were registered to foreign owners, mostly U.S. residents. Further, of twenty-five countries examined in a government report, Canada stood first in the percentage of foreign-owned patents and last in the percentage of domestically owned patents.[19] Other authors during this period observed that U.S. firms had established Canadian subsidiaries as a way of spreading over a somewhat wider customer base some of the staggering expenses of modern research and development activities in high-technology manufactures. As a consequence, Canada had been left with a "fragmented and inefficient" branch-plant structure holding little "technological depth" and without "the size and sophistication needed to be competitive on world markets."[20]

A 1971 study of fifty Canadian subsidiaries also discovered a strong relationship between the branch-plant economy and the erection of technological barriers to manufactured exports. In general, it reported, the research facilities of the branch plants tended to be more directly related to product adaptation for the Canadian market than to innovation for export markets. In instances where the branch plants came up with innovations demonstrating export promise, parent head offices made decisions on whether production would remain in Canada, would be shared with another international division, or would be "pulled back" to the parent corporation. "In no case," it was affirmed, "did we find a Canadian subsidiary that felt it had the freedom to enter foreign markets at will with a product which it thought could be produced in Canada and competitively exported."[21]

The federal government response to branch-plant technological dependence was to attempt to fill Canada's innovative vacuum by giving financial support to a wide range of research and development (R&D) programs. In fact, during this era the Canadian government carried out a larger proportion of national R&D activities, many with direct industrial applications, than was true for any other major industrial country. Yet, as Table Fourteen demonstrates, even massive government spending could not offer a long-term solution to this structural problem. As one mid-1970s study put it, "broad brush" programs of state assistance for industrial R&D were not highly effective because "most of the high technology and manufacturing sectors of the Canadian economy are dominated by foreign ownership, but only certain types of subsidiaries have any real potential for innovation leading to greater exports and domestic employment."[22]

**Table Fourteen
Business Enterprise Expenditure on
Research and Development as a percentage
of Industrial Domestic Product, 1967 and 1975**

	1967	*1975*
United States	2.5	1.9
Great Britain	2.0	1.7
Sweden	1.2	1.7
Germany	1.3	1.6
France	-	1.4
Japan	0.8	1.2
Canada	0.7	0.6

SOURCE: Statistics Canada, *Annual Review of Science Statistics*, 1979, p. 23.

Administered Markets

Reliance on borrowed foreign technology, as discussed in Chapter Two, does not by itself preclude the evolution of a more independent technological base capable of sustaining world competitive manufacturing. What is required is a commitment from industry to assimilate, adapt, and innovate on the base of the technology it initially borrowed. In our survey of the half-century before World War Two, we could discover no zeal for this endeavour on the part of the great majority of Canadian manufacturers. Observers of the time often concluded that our industrialists either were unenterprising or were mesmerized by the domestic market. We have intimated that more formal administrative barriers written into licensing agreements or genetically encoded in the subsidiary-parent relationship may have provided a better explanation for Canada's early silence in world markets. When we reach the post-war epoch, however, there is little room for further doubt. In keeping with the by then dominant presence of direct foreign investment in the economy, eyewitnesses after World War Two began to record more clearly the restricted nature of Canadian production.

This era in Canadian trade was rung in with public alarms from the 1945 publication of *Canada and International Cartels*. Undertaken by the Combines Investigation Commission as the war was winding down, it was a remarkable study of export blocking. Three hundred manufacturing and trading companies had been surveyed to determine the effects of foreign ownership, patent and licence agreements, or other cartel arrangements on their international trade. The report distinguished three levels at which export restrictions had been placed on Canadian firms – licensee, branch plant, and international cartel. A number of instances were uncovered in which Canadian licensees were forbidden to export. The following company statement was cited as a typical example:

> We have confined our manufacturing and distribution of the various items of [deleted] equipment, produced under the patents and licences which we hold, to the Dominion of Canada because those patents and licences confer rights exercisable only within this country. . . . To the extent that any article we manufacture is patented our export of it to a foreign country would expose us to infringement proceedings at the instance of a patent-holder or licensee in that country.[23]

Not surprisingly, cases in which foreign branch plants had been left free to determine their own export policies were "relatively rare."[24] Generally, it was concluded, export policies were formulated to maximize the sales potential of the parent firms.

The most revealing data dealt with international cartels. These, according to the report, were formed through agreements between U.S. and European manufacturers to split world markets between themselves. Canada, for the purposes of such agreements, was considered as part of the U.S. market. If production was established in Canada it was on the condition that no attempt be made to export. One such cartel arrangement investigated by the Commission involved the chemical firm CIL (Canadian Industries Limited, jointly controlled by the U.S. DuPont and the British ICI, Imperial Chemical Industrial Limited). CIL, the evidence indicated, was viewed by its controlling partners as nothing more than their beast of burden in the Canadian market. Lammont DuPont, president of DuPont between 1926 and 1940, was quoted as stating that

> We regard CIL as the vehicle of industrial effort for ICI and DuPont in Canada. . . . The theory back of the CIL operation, so far as ICI and DuPont are concerned, is expressed in the old saying "Canada for Canadians" meaning – the industrial operations of the partners in Canada are intended to be conducted through CIL. CIL was not set up to do anything else and has, we believe, never been considered so. If the above is correct, it seems to us to follow directly and as a matter of course that CIL shall stay in Canada and not spread out into other countries, either by laying down plants, exporting their products or

licensing under their processes, unless both ICI and DuPont believe it is advantageous to so spread out and then only to the extent and for the time and under the conditions that ICI and DuPont agree upon.

This policy, it was disclosed, meant that CIL had to resist "considerable pressure" from the Canadian government to develop its export trade and could not take advantage of tariff preferences in areas like the British West Indies and Australia. [25]

This report by the Combines Investigation Commission was the last published by the government to be so explicit on the subject of export blocking. And, naturally enough, the branch plants themselves were not about to proclaim from the rooftops their policies in an affair so potentially sensitive to Canadian national sensibilities. Yet, although unfortunately out of the reach of the general public, alarming evidence of the administrative barriers to Canada's manufactured exports grew after 1945 in the files of Trade and Commerce.

Departmental awareness of the serious structural restraints on the trade of Canadian subsidiaries built steadily toward a crescendo in the first two decades following World War Two. Directly after the German surrender, a meeting of the trade commissioner service was held to discuss the "absence" of an "overall" Canadian trade policy in respect to foreign enterprises. This division advised its deputy minister of its concern in this matter.

Fear was expressed that some of the larger industrial organizations or agricultural groups are making their own export policies without consideration being given to the best interests of the country as a whole. A representative of an important Canadian company controlled from the U.S.A. manufacturing primary materials recently expressed the opinion that Canada should concentrate on the production of these raw materials and that his company was adopting the policy of in general discouraging the manufacture of finished goods from their raw material in Canada. Examples have come to the attention of the Department where parent companies abroad have restricted the freedom to export of their controlled branch industries in Canada. [26]

More and more such "examples" were to surface in subsequent years. Indeed, in the post-war period, Trade and Commerce correspondence became very matter-of-fact on the export-blocking question. Take, for example, this reply to an overseas officer from a director of the Export Division on his department's failure to unearth a Canadian supplier for a potential foreign order. "I am not particularly surprised at the attitude of the manufacturers as most of the firms are branches of American houses and are not too interested in shipping from Canada," he said. [27] Or witness this response by a commodity officer in the Export Division to a complaint that a specific branch plant could not export. This firm, he noted,

> is controlled by its parent company in the United States as far as exports are concerned. . . . There are dozens of firms in the same category. They are established to manufacture for the Canadian market. There are also dozens of Canadian firms which are licensed to manufacture for the Canadian market only. The only way to solve this problem is for Canadian manufacturers to design and make competitive substitutes which can be exported. The above situation has existed in the industrial equipment industry since almost the time of Confederation and is a widely known fact in the engineering business. [28]

Trade and Commerce was frequently to find itself embarrassed and compromised by these circumstances. Many subsidiaries were in the habit of passing along foreign inquiries generated by the Canadian trade commissioners to their parent operations, who then pursued the order. The department appears to have responded by attempting to keep a record of the export policies of Canadian branch plants. But this system often broke down, much to the annoyance of the trade commissioners in the field. [29] In one particularly notable incident, the executive vice-president of a U.S. subsidiary explained to a trade commissioner who was soliciting orders on his behalf that his firm, after all, was not interested in exporting. Confusion had arisen from the unauthorized attendance of a company officer at a 1960 Trade and Commerce export trade promotion conference in Ottawa.

> I am sorry to admit that the whole situation is a complete surprise to me. Apparently when the invitation to attend the Conference was sent to [us] it was received by a junior member of our company and he took it upon himself to determine who should attend and what should be discussed. For this I apologize. So that you may set your records straight [this subsidiary] is a marketing group set up to sell all the products of the [U.S. parent]. . . . Any questions on policies regarding foreign export must be cleared with [our parent] at the following [New York] address. [30]

By 1957, departmental concern had grown to the point where Professor A.G. Huson from the Faculty of Business Administration at the University of Western Ontario was commissioned to do a special study on export blocking. Working with a survey sample of fifty foreign-owned subsidiaries, Huson determined that:

less than half have appointed Canadian export managers, less than one in four can be said to be developing Canadian export experience, only one in five have separate export organizations, and one in ten have their own independent foreign representative. Only one in three claim freedom to compete with their parent; only one in four, a voice in their company's export policy; and three-quarters declare that their exports are strictly controlled by the parent.[31]

It is reasonable to suppose that these figures roughly squared with the daily field experience of Trade and Commerce officers. Six years later, Huson's conclusions were cited in a background document prepared for a meeting of trade commissioners. As well, in their conference report, the trade commissioners repeated that "probably 75% of the [subsidiary] companies have their exports strictly controlled by the parent."[32]

Unseen by the public, a miniature storm of activity gathered around this question through the late 1950s and early 1960s. In 1958, Trade and Commerce and External Affairs jointly agreed to approach U.S. parent companies in an effort to get them to relax export controls on their Canadian subsidiaries. "Few executives will deny," it was noted, "that U.S. control of secondary industry in Canada has a tendency to reduce prospects of export business for the subsidiary company, particularly of any exports to the U.S. market, unless a conscious effort is made in that direction." Still, these approaches should not be so aggressive as to leave any doubt "in the mind of U.S. executives about Canada's continuing interest in U.S. investment in Canada, and the continuing need for capital for future development."[33]

From this point, the topic of export barriers imposed by direct foreign investment in Canada emerged on at least five occasions in six years during formal, high-level departmental meetings – in 1958, twice in 1960, and again in 1962 and 1963. Until the last of these meetings, discussion always centred on how best to "exploit all opportunities for the education of the parent corporation in the Canadian point of view."[34] The education process, however, was slow, frustrating, and often checkmated. One trade commissioner, who called on a large number of parent companies in Chicago, listed the obstacles placed in his path:

Some firms frankly designated the Canadian market as a domestic market in which they were not interested in export. Some had revised the organization of the Canadian company to fit in with their overall designs, reduced costs, and automatically cut out possibilities of export. Some stated that they were very desirous of expanding their Canadian operation through exports in order to make their Canadian firm pay, but felt that the high cost of parts and components which they had to bring into Canada, plus the smallness of the

Canadian market, rendered Canadian products non-competitive. They pointed out that the very factor which encouraged them to enter Canada, i.e. the Canadian tariff, militated against the possibility of export. Some considered it advantageous to maintain the export offices in the United States, but it was evident quite often that the U.S. export office was not too conscious of the operation of the Canadian subsidiary.[35]

The account of another trade commissioner leaves us with a very clear sense of the curious mixture of humility, timidity, and missionary zeal with which the problem was tackled:

... my own modest efforts during the time I have been in New York have revealed how tortuous and difficult it can be to influence parent company policies. At the outset, one normally requires an entree to the company for other reasons, in order to establish the contacts that eventually make it possible to allude to parent company policies without causing resentment. Some frustration results when, in many instances, one learns that Canadian subsidiaries are considered part of the parent company's domestic operations and *not* part of their international division. For example, about two years ago we established a contact with the head of the purchasing department of [a Canadian parent in New York state].... This resulted in establishing a contact with the Senior Vice President in the International Division. Better than half a day was spent in the International Division, only to learn that the Canadian subsidiary is considered part of their domestic operation, and that only overseas plants reported to the International Division. Eventually, contact was established with a Senior Vice President in the domestic operations, who seemed to feel there was some merit in permitting their Canadian plants to seek markets in Commonwealth countries. However, he informed me that this would have to be a decision of the Financial Vice President and Treasurer, who would have to be convinced that the parent company's profits could be enhanced by diverting some exports from Canada. I lunched with the Treasurer, and while he seemed sympathetic, he advised me that this would be a matter of major policy requiring a decision of the Chairman of the Board and the Board of Directors itself. He promised to discuss it with the Chairman, and we are hopeful that, ultimately, some change in this large corporation's policies may be developed.[36]

Faced with responses like these, it is no wonder that doubts began to emerge on the adequacy of education alone. These doubts were to appear full blown in the subsidiary export session of the 1963 trade commissioners' conference in Ottawa. "It is becoming increasingly evident that contact between departmental officers in Ottawa and abroad with parents and subsidiaries alike could not possibly cover all the subsidiaries located in Canada, even after a long period of years," this group concluded in its final report.

These middle-ranked officers, well seasoned by service in the export trenches, fully ventilated their many frustrations with the branch-plant *modus operandi*. "It was generally accepted that if any worthwhile improvement in Canada's export trade is to be achieved, subsidiaries of foreign organizations must play a more active role," they bluntly concluded. The situation required "a system of meaningful incentives and perhaps legislation." Their critique of foreign direct investment in Canadian industry was thorough and sophisticated; their recommended policy instruments were interventionist to the point of legislative regulation.

> In too many instances the subsidiary is established as a branch office to supply merely another sector of the North American market and to take advantage of the abundance of natural resources in Canada – thus to become an obedient satellite and not a competitor in world markets. Such an attitude has interfered with product development and research, with diversification of products and markets, with growth and operation of plants at a higher rate of capacity, and with the development of a more flexible and self-sufficient industry. . . . Experiences of the past reveal that the piecemeal, uncoordinated approach, particularly in the absence of legislation or specific policy aimed at the root of the problem, can have at best only limited success in achieving the [subsidiary export participation] objective.

Additional and augmented tax breaks and government export services were among the incentives reviewed by the conference. The legislative mechanisms that received attention ranged from regulatory licensing to export quotas, all with a view to "provide a certain degree of export autonomy to existing as well as newly established Canadian subsidiaries." Not unmindful of the "immediate adverse reaction" such legislation might provoke, the trade commissioners nevertheless advised their political masters to proceed.

> Contact with subsidiaries and parents in the past and the experiences of other countries would suggest that foreign firms are not deterred by legislation which does not prevent a profitable return on investment. Undue anxiety and thus reluctance to consider any form of legislation dealing with foreign subsidiaries seems unwarranted.

Finally, the conference agreed that a new survey be conducted to further assess export autonomy among the branch plants. This was to be followed by "high priority" approaches to key firms.[37]

A thorough critique of foreign restraints on Canadian trade had become deeply imbued in important segments of Trade and Commerce by the mid-1960s. So much was this the case that when a prominent individual with a special interest in export promotion was preparing a speech on the topic "Canadian Businessmen – Are They Meeting the Challenge?" he approached the department for ideas and background information, and then as a response he was fired this missive by a clearly vexed division chief:

> The biggest problem facing the Department in its endeavours to expand Canada's exports rests in the fact that the major capital and industrial plant equipment manufacturers in Canada are controlled by foreign capital. . . . The foreign subsidiary companies . . . have the largest manufacturing complexes in Canada and, as a consequence, the financial resources to permit sales on an international basis. . . . Canadian companies in certain industries have been found to be less than keen when asked to consider doing further processing in Canada on certain raw materials. . . . This in turn leads to the question [of] foreign control of our larger industries and the effect on their Canadian subsidiaries' export policies. Many of these primary producers have plants abroad which fabricate goods for the world market from Canadian raw materials. The Canadian company in certain cases is limited to the Canadian market or, at most the Canadian and Commonwealth markets. In many cases the Canadian company is unable to quote on export enquiries directly but must get the foreign parent companies' permission which is not always granted. [38]

A 1977 memorandum from an Assistant Deputy Minister (ADM) in the then Department of Industry, Trade and Commerce (ITC) confirmed that the issue of export blocking was as salient in the 1970s as it had been in the previous two decades. [39] Citing evidence from "a multitude of sources," including interviews with senior executives, departmental contacts, Statistics Canada data, and private studies, this memorandum pointed to "considerable evidence" that Canadian branch plants were "not aggressively seeking export opportunities abroad. Because of corporate policy, many firms are either unwilling or unable to pursue projects abroad. . . ."

Appended to this report was a joint ITC-Export Development Corporation (EDC) study of the export practices of five branch-plant capital equipment manufacturers. As we observed at many earlier points in our inquiry, this industry group is of critical importance in international trade because it can provide the technological leadership for the creation of new exportable innovations in other sectors. The authors of this mid-1970s study took care to point out that although their findings applied specifically to the five surveyed companies, they were "general enough in nature to apply to a broad range of foreign-owned subsidiaries in Canada."

Established to "penetrate and secure the Canadian domestic market," most of the surveyed firms had "significant limitations on freedom to initiate exports." The study submitted they had "little or no export marketing strategy, per se, but export on an opportunity basis usually as an extension to the market of their domestic lines." Basic decision-making on international marketing "is almost always centred outside of Canada and rationalization of the parent firm's objectives takes precedence over those of any branch plant or host country." The formation of Canadian export consortia had been frustrated because even if one firm "had freedom to export, usually one or more of the partners would have limitations put on them by their parents and the bidding attempt on any tender would eventually abort." Still, one factor that could sometimes persuade these subsidiaries to export was access to EDC or Canadian International Development Agency (CIDA) financing. On the other hand:

> We have evidence that four of these firms (all with capacity in their plants) recently referred export business obtained by Canadian engineers to their parents or related foreign companies because EDC or CIDA financing was not required. The Export Manager of the fifth firm pleaded with us to put pressure on his company so that he in turn could press his parent for export freedom because without EDC or CIDA financing he had none.

The ITC bureaucrats of the International Financing Branch were clearly frustrated by the flabbiness of the only two policy tools they had been given to fight the administrative barriers to Canadian industrial export trade encoded in the structure of branch-plant production – exhortation and subsidies. They expressed their conviction that

> the answer lies not in increasing ITC resources devoted to this activity, but in the readiness of the Canadian export community to pursue the business. In discussions with the companies, many reasons are given for the absence of Canadian interest in multilaterally financed projects but most excuses are related to our alleged uncompetitiveness in world markets. Yet these same companies, when pursuing EDC financed business, are very vocal about their international competitiveness and only emphasize the need for competitive government financing.

Accordingly, this ADM recommended, as had his predecessors in the 1960s, that direct action should be taken against offending foreign firms.

Subsidiaries, he proposed, should be cut out of CIDA projects and ITC and EDC support programs unless they could demonstrate that they had export freedom.

"Baying at the Moon"

When the trade commissioners advised against "undue anxiety" in confronting the branch-plant barriers to Canadian export, they were to prove themselves far bolder than their political leaders. Virtually without exception, the elected officials ignored, misunderstood, or even deliberately obscured the issue. Wedded to the promotion of foreign investment as an instrument of economic growth, they were generally loath to rock the boat they hoped would keep them electorally afloat.

In some senses, C.D. Howe can be seen as the archetypal figure here. Understanding as he did the surface dimensions of the problem, he would have been delighted to enlist the voluntary co-operation of the branch plants in correcting it. Still, he simply did not consider the issue of sufficient importance to challenge their considerable economic and political power directly. Consider the previously discussed Emergency Exchange Conservation Act of 1947. Among Howe's principal objectives in bringing forward this legislation was to improve the nation's foreign exchange crisis not only by restricting imports but also by stimulating the export of Canadian resource *and* manufactured products. To this end, Howe's officials came up with a complex scheme to allow industries to import more if they increased their foreign sales in tandem. In an editorial entitled "Why we can't go on as 2nd class Americans," the *Financial Post* applauded Howe's initiative. "Both branch plants and a good many Canadian plants which have working agreements with U.S. firms have their activities regulated by assorted agreements on marketing, exports, pricing and so on," this business journal observed. "But if Canada is to go forward aggressively to full mature development, some way must be found of escaping our position of economic colonialism and of letting Canada have her full share of North American industry."[40]

In the longer run, Howe hoped a reciprocity treaty with the Americans would introduce more manufactured exports from Canada into the U.S. market. Prime Minister King scuttled the whole idea, although we will see in the next chapter it was in keeping with the free trade economic orthodoxy of the federal civil service elite in this era. Not only did King feel that such a program would be politically dangerous, but he viewed Howe's notion of selling manufactures to the U.S. as "absurd."[41]

King was right in this. Without a frontal attack on both the technological and administrative restraints outlined in this chapter, no general progress in exporting industrial goods could realistically be expected. More knowledgeable on this question than most of their successors were to prove themselves, Howe's opponents of the day taunted him with the feeble nature of his attempted reform. Concluding that branch-plant behaviour could not be altered "merely by reasoning with them, or by any sort of inducement which has no teeth behind it," the CCF referred pointedly to the lessons on export blocking of *Canada and International Cartels.* [42] But it was J.M. Macdonald, president of the Dominion Progressive Conservative Association, who really belled the cat. He told Howe that "he might as well go bay at the moon" as get the subsidiaries to "change their whole way of doing things."

> I have talked to people in business who assure me that certain things are indeed possible. United States subsidiaries will be able to manufacture some things, some parts, and send them across the line, but I am assured that it cannot amount to much in a short time. It is reversing the trend; it is contrary to the policy that brought people here who set up industries in Canada, and the minister will have quite a time. [43]

As predicted, Howe's plan to persuade branch plants to export to the U.S. soon fizzled and died. Yet, in the boom conditions of the 1950s, the Liberals saw little point in pursuing the matter. Massive resource exports were filling the gap. As Howe mused in 1954 when he admitted that Canadian manufacturers were finding it "increasingly difficult" to compete on world markets, this "should provide no particular cause for alarm."

> Canada does not lack for export opportunities and it is not necessary or even desirable for Canadian producers to be able to compete in world markets in all lines of merchandise. In our principal staple export items, Canadian producers are highly competitive the world over. So long as this is the case there is little basically wrong with our foreign trade position. [44]

Yet, Howe had not dismissed the problem. Nor was he afraid to raise it again when it suited him. Perhaps prompted by evidence of export blocking presented at the hearings of the Royal Commission on Canada's Economic Prospects, Howe made a pitch for improved export performance from the branch plants in 1956 speeches in Milwaukee and Chicago. He complained:

> Too often our trade representatives abroad turn up export opportunities for a subsidiary operating in Canada only to find that the United States parent does not permit the export business to be done from the Canadian plant. Mind you we do not object to doing

occasional export promotion for United States corporations but you will agree that it is rather difficult to justify the expense to the Canadian taxpayer. Once again I recognize that there are problems. But I do plead for a careful re-examination of export policies affecting branch plants. . . . I am not suggesting that U.S. corporations should act contrary to their interests. I am suggesting that they may be overlooking a good bet by not allowing their Canadian plants to take on more export business.[45]

His remarks were consistent with his entire approach to the issue – co-operation, not coercion. In fact, it could well be argued that by speaking out Howe was attempting to forestall more drastic measures on the part of future Canadian governments. To illustrate, he drew the attention of his audience to the "rigid laws" restricting foreign investment in many countries. "There are no such laws in Canada. I hope there never will be," Howe affirmed. Nevertheless, he warned the U.S. businessmen that they must learn to "reckon" with the "pride" and "nationalism" of Canadians.

If Howe was reluctant to take the bit between his teeth here, at least he was straightforward about it. This is more than can be said for most who succeeded him at the locus of national economic policy-making. In general, politicians on both sides of the House of Commons maintained silence on the issue or minimized its importance. Their fire was saved for the far less meaningful problem of extraterritoriality – the application of U.S. law to American-owned subsidiaries in Canada to prevent them from accepting export orders from Communist countries like Cuba or China. Crying all the while that their rivals were surrendering Canadian sovereignty, the major parties used the issue of extraterritoriality as a convenient partisan club with which to hit each other when they were exiled to the Opposition benches. Meanwhile, it was (little or no) export business as usual for most Canadian factories.

The Conservatives had made some noises before being elected in 1957 that they were concerned about the more general problem.[46] Nevertheless, G. Churchill, their Trade and Commerce Minister, when asked about the matter in the House, lulled the members to sleep. "This is a problem which is constantly under review," he assured everyone, "and by the process of education and persuasion we are finding that more and more companies are moving in the right direction."[47] Churchill's successor, George Hees, also found it expedient to duck direct questions on the issue.[48] Still, we have seen that, under the Conservatives, some Trade and Commerce bureaucrats refined a critique of foreign restraints on Canadian export trade.

When they returned to office in 1963, it would appear that the Liberals put a cap on these reform-minded civil servants. This was not what a casual observer of the Liberal re-entry might have initially expected. The Finance Minister, Walter Gordon, delivered a budget speech that U.S. investors found highly inflammatory. He called for a larger measure of Canadian ownership in the economy and greater controls over foreign direct investment. Export blocking was one area Gordon specifically singled out for corrective action: "Export markets should be sought actively wherever they may be found, and should not be limited out of regard for the interests of parent or associated companies abroad."[49]

But Gordon was not Minister of Trade and Commerce. That job belonged to Mitchell Sharp, a former deputy minister in the department under C.D. Howe and Gordon's nemesis in cabinet. Years later, Gordon was to refer with considerable understatement to Sharp's "lukewarm attitude on the independence issue."[50] Among Sharp's first business in his department was the scuttling of the trade commissioners' plans for a comprehensive survey of the export policies of U.S. parents.[51] It will be recalled that this had been by far the mildest of the recommendations on subsidiary exports to emerge from their 1963 conference. Sharp denied killing the survey, but went on record a year later with an intriguing definition of the national interest in this affair. He was opposed to asking the branch-plant automakers if it was the "stated policy" of their parents to forbid exports outside of the Commonwealth. "I do not believe it would be in the public interest to give such general answers," he pronounced. "I feel they only confuse the issue."[52]

Gordon did not and could not survive the angry storm his budget attack on foreign investment whipped up both in the business community and in the Liberal Party. His promise of subsidiary export reform went with him. This, as well as other problems with branch-plant performance, was now to be "addressed," and almost as speedily "resolved," by a set of guidelines for "good corporate behaviour" announced by the Liberals in 1966. Among the goals established was the "maximum development of market opportunities in other countries as well as Canada." Scarcely eight months later, the then Minister of Trade and Commerce, R. Winters, left the highly misleading impression that this thorny problem could be permanently resolved by such a superficial device. He paid tribute to the

> encouraging response as regards the development of export markets
> . . . indicative of a growing participation by foreign-owned subsidiaries in markets abroad. I have been especially encouraged by the number of companies advising of their plans to give increased attention to foreign market opportunities, including those venturing into the export field for the first time.[53]

Astonishingly, less than three years after a senior officer in Trade and Commerce had concluded that "foreign capital" was the "biggest problem facing the department in its endeavours to expand Canada's exports," Winters, either misled or deliberately misleading, made even more extravagant claims by asserting that

> ... nothing uncovered so far by the Department or any independent researchers would indicate that there is any validity to the charge that foreign ownership per se acts against our national interests. . . . For example, some have argued that foreign subsidiaries do less than their share of exporting – a claim which, if widely proven, would be of very serious concern to me, as Minister of Trade and Commerce. Some companies do have their sales policies determined at head office and do not export from Canada. But the majority of subsidiaries do export now and some of the remainder indicate that they intend to do so. The statistics we now have are the best proof of their performance. We will continue to encourage the few stragglers as indeed we do for Canadian-owned companies. [54]

Writing a decade later in a confidential memorandum, a senior bureaucrat in Industry, Trade and Commerce dismissed the Winters "good corporate behaviour" export and procurement guidelines for foreign subsidiaries. In contrast to the glowingly optimistic reports that Winters himself had given on the success of these guidelines, this high official judged that "although eleven years of records exist, there is little evidence that [they have] had the desired effect in altering company policies." [55]

Buy Canadian

We will leave the last word to the manufacturers. How did they view their position in world markets as the modern era of branch-plant dominance got under way? Remarkably, and risking some oversimplification, we find the same divisions around Canadian industrial strategy emerge here as we discovered in the earliest period of our industrialization. On the one side, led now by the foreign subsidiaries, stood the overwhelming majority oriented toward ISI and the domestic market; on the other, a small minority lectured their compatriots on the virtues of developing internationally competitive specializations.

Chronicled in the last chapter was the withering away of Canada's Empire markets and with them the promise of a "permanent" basis for Canada's manufactured exports. During the 1940s and early 1950s, the demands of wartime production, combined with post-war dollar currency restrictions in Britain and the Dominions, destroyed most of what was still left of this trade. The majority of the branch plants had nowhere to turn but inward. With import replacement as their *raison d'être*, they carried with renewed vigour the turn-of-the-century banner "Canadian goods for Canadian people." Positive factors, in this instance, were those elements, like the tariff and immigration, that protected and extended the domestic market. Things that could threaten it, like freer trade and import competition, were opposed.

Exports, as they disposed of surplus production, were not in themselves bad. But home demand always came first. One CMA president, who apparently took exports more seriously than many, ventured so far as to say after the war that "Canada must produce first for Canada's needs but that in itself will not spell prosperity – a surplus must be produced for foreign markets before full employment can be reached."[56]

For a pesky minority, however, "surplus" export wasn't good enough. This group peppered the export sessions of CMA meetings with their quite different approach. To illustrate, one manufacturer summarized in a brief sentence the basis of an outward-oriented world specialization. "In our small Canadian population, the orders are comparatively small," he observed, "but in the export business there is no limit to the size of orders you may get, which would then cut down your costs and improve your export relations." In this regard, the presentation made by a Coleman Lamp and Stove official to the CMA was especially noteworthy. Pulling no punches, he lectured those "who feel satisfied with your smug little business at home, you who long years ago abandoned the pioneer spirit, who decry every little setback or depression which occurs here or across the line in the United States." During the Depression years of 1933 to 1938, he boasted, his company had tripled its overall sales. An export drive that increased the value of exports more than tenfold had made this possible. "Methods were improved and costs and selling prices were lowered as a direct result of the additional export volume," he related. This heightened efficiency allowed for even greater Canadian market penetration.[57]

Some of these outward-oriented industrialists were alive to the relationship between an independent technological base and the capacity to generate exportable innovations. T.L. Moffat, a household appliance manufacturer whose export objective was 40 to 50 per cent of turnover, wrote Trade and Commerce of the need for "vastly increased" government assistance for "research and engineering." In setting forth his case, Moffat paralleled many of the arguments presented in this book.

It is important that Canadian manufacturers carry out a larger fraction of research and development work in this country rather than continue to import technical information. Of course it is realized that we cannot become leaders in all lines but there is no reason in the world why Canada, with the backing of an extensive research program, cannot attain a pre-eminent position in many products. . . . Two countries which have achieved outstanding success as a result of coordinated research are Sweden and Switzerland; notwithstanding many trade restrictions prevailing today, people everywhere specify and prefer Swedish electrical apparatus in many cases – chiefly because many of the products they turn out are superior. . . . Sweden has a comparatively small domestic market, yet Swedish competition in many items is felt in numerous foreign markets.[58]

The greater mass of manufacturers took offence at criticisms, direct or implied, of their export failings. "It is all very well," sniffed one CMA president (who also happened to head a subsidiary), to advocate large-scale international trade, but

our commercial relations should be guided always by the consideration of what is being made in Canada or what can be made in Canada. We should maintain such protective measures as will ensure the greatest possible volume of articles being made in Canada. We should extend our international trade by exchanging our products for articles which are not made in Canada or cannot be made in Canada.[59]

Yet another branch-plant manager and CMA activist was to rail against the "illogical and misleading" opinion of many "experts" that export trade was to be the "provider of full employment, the fountainhead of prosperity and the panacea of all ills" in the post-war era.

I am enunciating no new theory when I assert that export trade cannot possibly survive except by artificial aids (and in these I include letting the home trade subsidize it) without a flourishing home trade. . . . Therefore let us first enlarge our home trade by a larger population, by higher standards of living, made possible by lower production costs.[60]

Indeed, increasing the size of the home market through immigration was to prove a popular notion among the industrialists after the war. A 1947 survey of CMA members by *Industrial Canada* on "obstacles in the way of building up Canada as a strong industrial nation" returned Canada's lack of population as its most frequent response.[61]

The assumptions of this inward-oriented faction culminated in the period's one major campaign by the manufacturers to gain greater public acceptance for their brand of industrial strategy. Spurred by the economic downturn of the late 1950s, its "Buy Canadian" theme revived a crusade mounted periodically by the CMA since the early 1900s. Predictably, in none of its four points, on which "our very survival as a nation" was held to depend, was there any mention of exports. Import substitution was everything.

> The first is to invest in the development of our own industries. The second is to process more and more of our own raw materials. The third is to enforce a realistic tariff policy reflecting our hopes for our country's future. The fourth is to consume our own manufactured products.[62]

The target here, of course, was the consumer. Guilt was the major weapon as the manufacturers set out to establish the purchase of their products as an "economic commandment." The CMA president instructed his members that

> we've got to show that buying "Made-in-Canada" will bring prosperity to the family of the consumer to whom we are speaking.... We have got to satisfy the Canadian woman in particular that, unless she buys the goods made by Canadians, other Canadian wives will not have the money with which to buy the goods made by her husband or, for that matter, any Canadian worker. We have got to establish in the minds of all consumers that their individual well being ... is indivisible from that of manufacturing industry. ... [63]

On the basis of our analysis, this approach seems absurd and even dishonest. As Table Twelve illustrated, imports of producer goods, notably machinery, equipment, and components, far outweighed imports of consumer goods in Canadian trade throughout this era. This, we have pointed out, reflects the relatively weak backward linkages inherent in subsidiary production. Not surprisingly, the branch plants were among the most enthusiastic promoters of "Buy Canadian": "It is vital to the future growth and independence of this nation that we reduce our imports of manufactured goods," declared the president of Canadian General Electric. At least one U.S. firm went so far as to cite the campaign as a factor in its decision to establish a new branch plant in Canada.[64]

Judging the "Buy Canadian" venture as a great success, the CMA was to keep it running for many years to come. In 1962, it received substantial support from the Ontario government, which launched its own $500,000 campaign to encourage citizens of the nation's industrial heartland to shop Canadian. The text of a saturation media blitz read, "if each of us in Ontario diverted an additional $2 a week from imported to domestic goods ... [this] should create 60,000 new jobs." The Minister of Economics and Development told Ontarians that government and industry could do little, that it was up to the individual to do his best in reducing imports. "Government policies can only be translated into facts through the actions of individuals," he asserted. "We believe it is up to the individual to do everything in his power to work for a trade surplus."[65] He did not make it clear, however, how an individual Ontarian should act if he or she wished to create additional employment by prodding the manufacturers to create an export trade for Canada.

Conclusion

Great transformations occurred in the period from the Second World War to the mid-1970s. Canadian industry, now dominated by foreign capital, entered a more mature phase of development. Still, this maturity can withstand no more than a surface inspection. After nearly a century of steady growth, very little progress had yet been made by Canadian manufacturing in bringing a respectable portion of its products to a level where they would be able to stand on their own in world markets.

As well, the familiar elements of ISI appear in a more modern guise. Although we must acknowledge the existence of exceptional firms (for whom another study needs to be written), the mass of Canadian manufacturers in this period proved themselves no less fascinated with "occupying" the home market than they did in the era of the National Policy. Technological dependence, whether measured through imports of capital goods or patents and R&D, scarcely abated. And Canadian industry, bound by the administrative barriers to export trade imposed by its foreign owners, found itself no more willing than ever to use this borrowed knowledge to assimilate, adapt, and innovate toward world competitiveness. Trade and Commerce records confirm that where patents and licences had first prevented the exports of Canadian-owned firms, after the Great Depression of the 1930s directives from branch-plant head offices in New York and Chicago became the most formidable obstacle to Canadian manufactured exports.

The state in this era is characterized by a divided outlook on these problems. Its Trade and Commerce bureaucratic arm, charged with the stimulation of Canadian exports, showed signs of becoming steadily more exasperated with the export blocking it identified as a structural feature of branch-plant manufacturing. At the same time, the political arm of the state, which depends for its electoral health on a growing economy, appeared prepared to wink at these costs of foreign direct investment as long as the wider economic benefits promised by continental integration seemed secure. Uninformed and misinformed, the public lacked access to the information they would have needed to make their weight felt in this matter.

Chapter Seven

Continental Rationalization: An Additional Worker for Nothing

~~~~~~

Choice has been a recurring theme throughout this book. We have witnessed, from the 1870s to the 1970s, Canada's political and economic elites arriving at policy and investment decisions that together established an overall direction for the evolution of our manufacturing sector. Contrary to those who posit various economic/environmental or political/social quasi-determinisms to explain Canadian industrial development, we have stressed the impact of choices made in the face of other options available to the policy-makers.

This approach especially informs our examination of the post-National Policy era in which modern Canadian manufacturing was founded. For that period, we chronicled the selection, both conscious and by accretion, of an industrial strategy with striking similarities to ISI. This path was neither imposed externally by British statesmen and capitalists nor delegated in any crude or direct fashion to some group of their Canadian proxies. That being said, the economic, political, and cultural constraints related to Canada's position within the British Empire proved extremely influential in the ultimate decision to place maximum emphasis on staples extraction, and the power brokers of Canadian economic policy remained satisfied with an industrialism whose horizons were bounded by the domestic market.

Once implanted, this ISI strategy conditioned future Canadian industrial expansion. Individual Canadian manufacturers who tried to deviate from the norm and establish a more independent, export-oriented direction for their firms risked both their capital and their sanity. How was the necessary back-up innovative network of support to be generated within an industrial sector that persistently exhibited extreme forms of technological dependence? And where was venture capital to be borrowed when the banks were accustomed to the safe returns guaranteed by the association of most Canadian manufacturers with already proven foreign firms and product lines?

Politicians, faced with the growing dominance of the branch plants as the twentieth century progressed, also found problematic the policy options that would have altered the rules of the ISI road. The cost of challenges on specific performance questions like R&D and export blocking would have to be weighed against the unknown value of possible gains in an overall situation that most judged already good. Further, as they were now powerful economic citizens, the branch plants had the ability to punish or reward politicians. This could be done directly through campaign funding or by the provision of directorships and other favours on retirement. More significant, however, and far more subtle was the way in which the branch plants could now collectively manipulate the levers of economic expansion or contraction. Politicians were understandably loath to disturb the investment "climate" on which their electoral fortunes depended.

In setting out these economic and political barriers to the reform of ISI, we must be careful not to slip into a static and deterministic account that precludes change. Indeed, this chapter will establish that in recent decades significant changes to the mode of Canadian industrial production have been catalyzed by worldwide upheavals in trade in investment associated with the gradual retreat of U.S. economic power and investment, the competitive rise of European, Japanese, and NIC manufacturing, and the liberalization of both world and North American tariffs under the trading regime of the General Agreement on Tariffs and Trade (GATT). With an economic structure highly exposed to the international political economy, Canadian decision-makers have had to adjust themselves to a transformed external environment. Indeed, this chapter documents a significant reconstruction of the pattern of Canadian industrial production. Canadian manufacturing has moved from the branch-plant ISI model described in Chapter 6, to the continentally rationalized production regime that will provide a focus for our discussion here.

As was the case with ISI, continental rationalization was not externally imposed on Canadian manufacturing in a crude or direct fashion by powerful international political or economic forces. Rather, in the context of international economic restructuring, domestic *ideas* about the realistic, the possible, and the profitable furnished the logic underlying Canadian choices within both the state apparatus and privately owned firms. As R. Whitaker has wisely noted, perceptions of "objective economic interests" must be given due weight in understanding such behaviour. Choice, he cautions, resides not only in the particular economic structures thrown up by particular geographic factors, historical timing, technological levels, and world market conditions, but also in the peculiarity and uniqueness of particular cultural mixes – national experiences – which prestructure the perceptions by classes and individuals of the objective economic factors.[1]

Policy Options: Nationalists and Continentalists

Choice requires options or alternative possibilities. On questions related to Canadian trade and industrial policy, two bitterly contending schools of thought monopolized national debate from the 1950s to the present. Both schools rooted themselves in a critique of the export and R&D shortcomings of Canadian ISI branch-plant industrialization. Both schools generally assumed that Canada should continue to benefit from its close ties to the U.S. economy. Divisions were sharpest on the issue of how these ties could best be managed to address the performance failures of Canadian manufacturers. Active protagonists in this debate could be readily discovered among Canada's political, bureaucratic, economic, and intellectual elites. During the 1970s and early 1980s, for example, the public struggle between continentalists and nationalists was personified in the opposing orientations of two federal government research agencies, the Economic Council of Canada and the Science Council of Canada.[2]

The continentalist school favoured the elimination of trade and investment barriers between Canada and the United States. The unhindered play of continental market forces, according to this view, would maximize Canadian prosperity through rewarding productivity and the efficient use of resources. Canada-U.S. free trade would force Canadian branch-plant manufacturing to become more internationally competitive through *rationalizing* its production along continental lines. The nationalist school, suspicious that market-driven decisions would shortchange Canada, promoted greater domestic control over the pace and extent of continental integration. Foreign investment, according to this view, prevented Canada from reaching its considerable economic potential. As far as Canadian branch-plant manufacturing was concerned, nationalists wanted it *deepened* through employing a state-directed industrial strategy to promote Canadian-owned enterprises and to coerce a better deal from American investors in Canada on R&D performance and export freedom.

While the state interventionist nationalists were able to claim fleeting victories in this struggle, the neo-liberal continentalists won most of the important battles. Three factors account for the sway of the continentalist position over both the economic and state elites in Canada. First, in advocating for Canada a basically unrestricted movement of trade and investment, the continentalist school echoed comfortably the everyday orthodoxy of business culture as well as the academic lessons of liberal economic theory taught to civil service managers in most universities. The nationalist school, in direct contrast, was identified with illiberal state intervention on a massive scale. To illustrate, as early as 1946, a Trade and Commerce official had summed up the subsidiary export-blocking problem by observing that "apart from an educational program which the government is now carrying out, nothing can be done short of taking plants over from private industry, a move which is out of the question."[3] In a similar vein, Jean Chrétien, when he was ITC Minister in the mid-1970s, rejected the policy direction of a nationalist industrial strategy. "We are not a communist state or a socialist state where everything is controlled by the government," he averred.[4]

Second, the continentalist school was able to claim that its approach was more up-to-date and relevant to an international production regime undergoing renewal. A renovated world economic order featured the breakdown of national trade and investment barriers, increasingly internationalized industrial production, and the growth of liberalized trading rules under the GATT and regional trading blocs. With an emphasis on adjusting to, rather than resisting, international restructuring, continentalist policies like Canada-U.S. free trade were argued to be necessary and realistic while nationalist policies that would hold back investors from modernizing Canadian industries were said to be anachronistic and doctrinaire.

Finally, and perhaps decisively, by applauding the role of foreign investment in Canadian development, continentalism could attach itself very compatibly to the growing political and economic power of the branch plants. As it would have required directly confronting the power of foreign firms and their governments, a nationalist industrial strategy had to have been rated extremely hazardous. We saw, in Chapter 6, how the political elites of the 1960s had so little appetite for a public scrap with the branch plants over export blocking that they withheld from the public the detailed evidence that their officials had gathered on the subject over many years. One minister, it will be recalled, even went so far as to declare that the release of such information would not be in the "public interest." It was much the same story when the bureaucrats' evidence of export blocking eventually surfaced in the early 1980s. Gerald Regan, Minister of State for International Trade, stated flatly that it would not be in "the best interests of Canada for achieving development and investment to have an absolute and over-all rule" to force branch plants to export from Canada to world markets.[5]

It has been the task of this book to decipher, for each era, a dominant pattern from the many decisions, small and large, made by firms, politicians, and state bureaucrats that have lent character to the development of Canadian industrialism. We have referred to this pattern as an industrial strategy or industrial policy. It is in this light that we can discern the incremental implementation of a reformist industrial policy during the two decades of Liberal rule that began in 1963 (punctuated only by the 1979 Clark government). Dominated by the neo-liberal continentalist vision, the policy of continental rationalization pursued under the Pearson and Trudeau governments nevertheless incorporated strands of state interventionist nationalism from time to time. We can think of this policy as reformist because it was directed toward overhauling the fundamentals of Canada's industrial sector so as to protect the traditional Canadian regional share of continental manufacturing from a changing international production regime. Continental rationalization was also an industrial policy that sought to remedy some of the more glaring performance problems of ISI branch-plant production without confronting directly the foreign owners of these factories.

The auto industry was the focal point of industrial reform. Autos were the definitive centrepiece of industrial modernity with high public visibility and important employment consequences. Liberal interest in reorganizing the Canadian auto sector was manifested as early as the exchange crisis of 1947 when it was singled out in a radio speech by Finance Minister D.C. Abbott under the heading of "Better Balance in Branch Plants Operations Needed."

> We have always wished to encourage development of U.S. branch plants, but in the face of our exchange problem today we suffer from the disadvantage that these plants are heavy importers of parts and materials which must be paid for in U.S. dollars. . . . It should be possible . . . for the Canadian automobile industry . . . to produce automobile parts or models for sale in U.S. dollars to balance the large purchases of components and materials which they make in the United States.[6]

These concerns about the auto industry's negative drag on the Canadian balance of payments were to resurface in the early 1960s. Also highlighted were the fears surrounding the restructuring of international manufacturing production that had been raised in the 1961 Bladen Royal Commission on the Automotive Industry. With remarkable foresight, V.W. Bladen warned Canadians to focus greater attention on the rising tide of foreign industrial competition.

> Everywhere I went in England and in Europe, I saw automotive production facilities being expanded or expansion being planned.

These plans are not geared just to expanding domestic markets in these countries, they are based on the expectation of continued and expanding exports. It is clear that the world market is going to be intensely competitive in the present decade. Canadian policy must be determined now in full recognition of the present plans for European expansion.[7]

The problem, Bladen said, was that the existing structure of Canadian ISI automotive production could never achieve the economies of scale that would be required to meet the newly jacked-up level of international competition. "The technology of the industry demands more and more expensive and specialized machinery. This requires ever increasing volume before the full economies can be achieved," he noted. Constrained to purchase "costly high-speed, single purpose machinery, the capacity of which, in many cases, is in excess of the requirements of the Canadian market," Canada-based manufacturers were at an increasing international disadvantage and would inevitably lose ground to more efficient producers.[8] Employment would shrink with the application of new labour-saving technology unless a way were found to secure "an increasing share of production in an expanding market." Bladen rejected as answers to the "long-run need to adjust to the changing world market" both free trade, because it would lead to a "socially irresponsible . . . drastic contraction" of the industry, and increased tariff protection, because it would lead to the "misallocation of resources" and "politically intolerable" consumer prices.[9] He favoured instead a politically managed integration of North American automotive production based on freer trade in motor vehicles. Bladen acknowledged that a continental rationalization strategy ran counter to "nationalistic sentiments" but declared:

I do not believe that the interdependence which stems from trade is a threat to national independence. I also believe that trade which increases our wealth and industrial strength can contribute to the development of our cultural and political independence.[10]

Tariff Liberalization and Industrial Restructuring

Bladen's analysis of the changing character of international manufacturing production, his critique of Canadian ISI automotive production, and his recommended direction for public policy changes were taken up in the 1965 Canada-U.S. Auto Pact. C.M. "Bud" Drury, the responsible Liberal minister, explained that "no matter how carefully the Canadian vehicle and parts producers managed their businesses, no matter how diligently they took advantage of the latest technologies, they faced higher costs than those of their competitors outside Canada." Imports were flooding the Canadian market. For Canada to hold on to a respectable share of North American production, the ISI model would have to be jettisoned in favour of one organized around the rationalization of continental production. As Drury put it, "the problems of short runs, variety, high costs and the rapidly expanding trade imbalance could best be countered by gaining access for Canadian products to the much larger total North American automotive market." However, the rationalization of North American automotive production was not to be based simply on the market logic of free trade, but was also to incorporate the political logic of balancing the interests of weak and strong that underpinned the "special relationship" between Ottawa and Washington. "For the first time in the history of our trade relations with the United States," Drury boasted of the Canadian production share guarantees in the Auto Pact, "we have an arrangement which recognizes that the differences in size, financial strength and in the relative development of our industries require special provisions to ensure that Canada, in fact as well as in theory, derives real and reciprocal benefits from trade agreements between the two countries."[11]

A second important policy initiative linked to industrial reform in the continental rationalization mould was Canada's adherence to the GATT regime. Canada had signed on to the GATT in 1947. A nation as dependent as Canada on world trade, W.L.M. King had reminded Canadians, could not stand outside an international movement designed to expand world trade. In so saying, King rehearsed arguments that remain standard fare in Canadian political debate.

> For Canada the conclusion of the General Agreement is of particular importance. Nearly a third of our national income is derived from external trade. We stand to gain much from the re-establishment of multilateral trade on a broad basis. The alternative to multilateral trade is bilateralism and barter deals. Canada would be one of the heaviest losers from the contraction of world trade which would follow from the general adoption of a policy of special deals between pairs of countries.[12]

While Canada adhered to freer trade multilateralism in principle, it continued to shield its manufacturing sector from the full force of deep tariff cuts up to and including the 1960s Kennedy Round of the GATT. However, the 1970s Tokyo Round negotiations produced a marked reorientation of Canada's protectionist position and a significant erosion of the tariff walls that had previously fostered Canadian ISI.[13] Allan MacEachen, who as Deputy Prime Minister and Privy Council President in 1978 was in charge of Canada's Tokyo Round negotiations, stressed, as had King, how "essential" a "satisfactory world trading environment" was for Canada as a "major trading country." Canada, being trade dependent, could not stand outside the new international trading order. Following the logic of neo-liberal continentalism, however, MacEachen saw not simply necessity but virtue in freer trade. As in the Auto Pact model, ISI manufacturing could be beneficially restructured, he believed, through greater exposure to international competition.

> Our objectives in these negotiations must be considered an important element in our efforts to promote the efficient development of Canadian industry and to gain broader export opportunities for our manufacturers. . . . improved access abroad should allow us not only to increase exports and export earnings but to achieve the longer production runs and increased productivity that are needed in many cases for Canadians to compete more effectively both in world markets and our own. . . . on the import side, while lower tariffs will obviously involve greater competition from abroad for Canadian producers, they should also, by reducing the costs of imported raw materials and other production inputs, strengthen the competitive position of our own manufacturers as well as bring lower prices or costs to consumers. [14]

The vision of some policy-makers extended further still. Continental rationalization of the Canadian manufacturing sector under the GATT regime was seen by them to be only a way station on the journey to full Canada-U.S. free trade. After canvassing Canadian business opinion from 1975 to 1977, the Senate Committee on Foreign Affairs forcefully restated and updated the industrial diagnosis first advanced in the 1961 Bladen Royal Commission on the Automotive Industry. Intensifying international competition, the Committee members observed, was threatening to drown traditional Canadian ISI production under a flood of products from Europe, Japan, and the NICs of Asia and Latin America, as well as from the United States. Canadian manufacturers were lagging ever further behind the "new low-wage, growth centres" of the NICs and the "scale and specialization" of the advanced OECD countries. Falling rates of Canadian tariff protection following the implementation of the upcoming Tokyo Round of GATT tariff liberalization could address Canada's competitive problems by bringing "about some rationalization of the presently fragmented Canadian industry." Since American manufacturing already enjoyed "a much higher degree of specialization" than Canadian manufacturing, Canadian productivity improvements from rationalization could grow at a relatively faster rate than those of the United States for "the next several decades." On the other hand, in an increasingly competitive international environment, a failure to adhere to the liberalized GATT regime would bring unacceptable political and economic costs.

In a protected environment the technical competence of Canadian industry would diminish farther, isolated as it would be from the necessity of competitive performance. With little import competition, incentives for better productivity rates, superior technology or increased efficiency would be lacking . . . the Canadian standard of living would decline with Canadians facing higher prices, reduced incomes and a restricted choice of goods. Such a course would be costly and harmful to Canada.[15]

Everything depended on achieving production economies of scale far greater than possible when confined to the Canadian market. Canada-U.S. sectoral trade agreements across industries like chemicals and steel modeled on the 1965 Auto Pact pattern would have been desirable supplements to the GATT but were no longer obtainable, the Committee concluded. The Auto Pact was based on the "unique characteristics" of continental automotive production, namely the parent-subsidiary relationship of a "very small number of companies and the [ir] clearly identifiable product." It was "doubtful" that the United States would ever again agree to managed continental trade built on production safeguards designed "to maintain a fair and equitable share of production" for Canada.[16] Yet, "without unimpeded access to the United States market, it will be difficult – even with government encouragement – to rationalize industrial production and for Canada to become more competitive." Worse, the Committee reasoned with remarkable foresight, as tariff barriers fell with the GATT Tokyo Round liberalization, protectionist pressure would likely shift to the erection of non-tariff barriers:

Canada may find itself increasingly squeezed out of the U.S. market. Only a blanket exemption for Canada, which should be negotiated as part of a free trade arrangement, could avoid this risk, and reverse the trend for U.S. companies to close their Canadian subsidiaries and for Canadian companies to move southward.[17]

Canada's manufacturers were also slowly coming to terms with the changing external environment. Hand in hand with policy movements toward tariff liberalization and continental rationalization came a fundamental change in the traditionally fanatical obsession of Canadian manufacturers with "fully occupying our home market." As we observed in Chapter 6, through the 1940s, 1950s, and early 1960s, industrialists publicly promoted those elements, like the tariff and immigration, that protected and extended the domestic market, and opposed freer trade and import competition. Nevertheless, recognizing that the global trend was now away from protectionism and toward greater competition in international trade, they gave grudging support to the 1967 Kennedy Round of the GATT as long as the federal government provided "adjustment assistance" to firms that suffered from the new trade regime. At the same time, they held to their customary position that "existing custom duty rates in this country are barely adequate to provide the necessary climate in which Canadian industry can flourish and grow."[18]

After the staged process of gradually lowering tariffs in the Kennedy Round had got under way without bringing devastating consequences, and when manufacturers began to assess favourably the Auto Pact as a possible model for the organization of production in their own industries, there was less ambiguity about and more real enthusiasm for further Canada-U.S. tariff reductions.[19] For example, a 1972 mail poll by *Industrial Canada,* the organ of the Canadian Manufacturers' Association, found that two of its responding readers answered "yes" to the question "Should Canada be working toward a North American Common Market?" for every one who answered "no." Some of the respondents noted the need to meet the trading challenge posed by the European Community. Others simply recorded their view that manufacturing production in the two countries was already inextricably coupled. For example, the director of long-range planning and organization for IBM (Canada) argued that "geography and the allocation of markets and resources have in fact created a North American economic community. Formal recognition of this fact in a treaty between Canada and the U.S. would be especially beneficial to our country. It would ensure a special status for Canadian exporters in U.S. markets and trade policy."[20]

By the end of the 1970s, the manufacturers had absorbed further staged tariff reductions, experienced the full force of the international trade dislocations noted earlier, and still had the Tokyo GATT reductions to look forward to in the 1980s. Accordingly, the CMA found it an appropriate moment to canvass its members more completely on Canada-U.S. free trade. When asked in 1980 to assess the net impact on their firms from such an arrangement, approximately two-thirds estimated that it would either have no effect on business or would lead to expansion while only one-third felt it would result in contraction.[21] Just five years later, the Macdonald Royal Commission suggested that as few as 20 per cent foresaw contraction.[22]

In this context, it is not especially surprising that the traditionally protectionist Canadian Manufacturers' Association came out strongly in the mid-1980s in favour of Canada-U.S. free trade. Insight into the logic that propelled this attitudinal revolution can be found in the testimony of R. Phillips, president of IPSCO, a Regina steel producer, before the special House of Commons-Senate Joint Committee examining the issue of Canada-U.S. free trade in the summer of 1985. "I do not think there is an entrepreneur in Canada," he argued, "that cannot adjust [to free trade] over a period of ten years, because we are used to making all sorts of changes in our markets more often than every ten years."[23]

Dollar Devaluation and Industrial Restructuring

The first major prong in Liberal industrial strategy, then, was tariff liberalization. The second was currency devaluation. Devaluation was employed as an instrument for easing the transition between ISI tariff protectionism and GATT tariff liberalization and had three related effects on the structure of Canada's international trade in manufactures. The first was to supply a measure of protection for domestic industries in the context of the fall in Canadian tariff barriers that accompanied the Kennedy and Tokyo Rounds of the GATT. The second was to stimulate trade by lowering the cost of Canadian industrial exports (and/or increase the profitability of Canadian exporters) in the same context of falling tariff barriers in the markets of Canada's principal trading partners. To illustrate, the 1978 report of the Senate Committee on Foreign Affairs elucidated in a remarkably clear fashion these first two of the three relationships between liberalized trade and Canadian currency devaluation.

> An exchange rate differential can provide a more general and efficient protection than the tariff, one which also encourages adjustment to changing economic conditions and opportunities. The 15 per cent depreciation of the Canadian dollar vis-à-vis the U.S. dollar in the past two years represents a greater measure of protection than most Canadian tariffs now offer and in addition provides a form of subsidy to Canadian exports to the United States larger than most U.S. tariffs now in place.[24]

Third, devaluation positioned Canada, over time and in certain key sectors, as a relatively low-wage production locale within the continental economy. During the period studied in this chapter, tariff liberalization was progressively creating the conditions necessary for the rationalization of continental production. To be a viable strategy as international competition intensified, however, continental rationalization had to give producers greater freedom in following the criteria of economic profitability to decide where in North America they would locate their production facilities. Most Canadian locales were relatively uncompetitive in regard to direct proximity to major North American markets or transportation networks. As we know from Chapter 6, Canada could certainly never hope to sell itself as a North American growth node for the research and development of new products or processes. There remained one bright spot in assessing the continuing suitability of Canadian plant locations as tariff barriers fell – wages. Traditionally, Canadians were accustomed to a

Figure 1
Value of the Canadian Dollar in Relation to the U.S. Dollar,
1969-1993

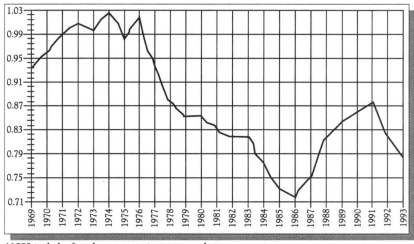

*1993 includes first three economic quarters only.
SOURCE: Calculated from *Bank of Canada Review*, various years.

somewhat lower standard of living than that enjoyed by Americans. This had always been justified as the price necessary to maintain a separate economic and political nationality in a relatively sparsely populated northern country. Currency devaluation, as we will soon discover, became a public policy device to lock many Canadians into a relatively lower standard of living than workers doing similar jobs elsewhere in the American economy.

From the early 1970s, Liberal policy-makers began to worry that the rising earnings of Canadian workers relative to American workers could sink their plans to restructure Canada's industrial production along continental lines. John Turner, Finance Minister in 1972, warned that the Canadian ISI manufacturing sector was "the most exposed and the most vulnerable to the challenge of change and international competition" and urgently required renovation "to promote the development of Canadian manufacturing industries that are fully capable of meeting and surpassing competition from other countries." He observed that Canadian unit costs of production, in which wages were a principal component, had been rising more rapidly than those in the United States. A then rising value for the Canadian dollar in relation to the U.S. dollar further compounded the relative production cost problem. Turner's answer was indirect. Instead of attacking Canadian compensation levels or the value of the dollar head on, he chose to cut substantially Canadian corporate taxes on manufacturing.

Firms were to use their tax savings "to get out and hustle, to grow, to compete, and to build jobs for Canadians." Through tax reform, Turner hoped to give restructuring firms enough fiscal room "to finance new research and development, to finance an expansion of productive capacity, to introduce new product lines and to finance the development of new cost-reducing methods."[25]

By the mid-1970s, the Liberals were less certain that they could win the relative cost battle through indirect means. Where Canada had enjoyed a surplus in both its automotive and merchandise trade with the U.S. in 1970, these sectors were recording significant deficits by 1975. In the run-up to the imposition of mandatory income controls in the fall of 1975, Turner warned that Canadians had "been building serious cost increases into our economy which threaten to erode the competitive position of our industries both at home and abroad." The major cause of these cost increases, Turner argued, was

> the accelerating rise of wages and salaries, which account for some 70 per cent of our total national income. It is quite true that the rate of wage and salary increases in Canada has been exceeded in many industrial countries overseas. But we can never forget that the United States is our major competitor and our major market, buying and selling some 65 per cent of all the goods we export and import. And it is in relation to the United States that our competitive position is being most seriously undermined.

By trying to leapfrog American wages, Canadian workers were threatening "to price our goods out of world markets and to lessen the capacity of our business firms to expand their operations."[26]

In introducing the 1975 anti-inflation incomes policy legislation, Finance Minister Donald Macdonald indicated that a devaluation of the Canadian dollar had been considered, and rejected, as an alternative to wage controls. Currency devaluation would, he claimed, only bring temporary relief to the competitive position of the manufacturing sector because it would fuel inflation elsewhere in the economy and lower business confidence. In the end,

> continuous cost and price increases, coupled with constant erosion of our currency, offer no practical basis for a healthy and dynamic future economy. Such a course would intensify savings erosion, engulf money markets and hinder both the yield on new corporate investments and housing starts.[27]

By late 1976, however, Macdonald was cautiously setting out the case for a devaluation of the Canadian dollar. While still worrying about accelerating inflation, he observed that devaluation would both stimulate exports, by improving "the competitive position of Canadian goods and services being sold to foreign customers," and offer "a degree of protection" to Canadian producers in the domestic market.[28] The wider theoretical case for devaluation was later advanced within a 1978 study by the Senate Committee on Foreign Affairs. Here, it was submitted that devaluation "largely compensated for the relative increase in unit labour costs in Canada relative to the United States, between 1970 and 1977," which had weakened Canadian competitiveness. This rise in Canadian unit labour costs was attributed to relatively low levels of productivity in the old ISI production regime coupled with spiralling Canadian wages. According to the Committee, compensation in Canadian manufacturing grew faster during the early years of the 1970s than in American manufacturing to the point where, by mid-1975, Canadian wages in this sector surpassed those in the United States.[29]

Traditionally, "most Canadians accepted that their wage and salary rates would be at least marginally lower than in the United States." This view was breached by the Auto Pact. The productivity gains following in its wake encouraged Canadian workers to hold out for wage parity with American workers. Wage parity in the auto sector might have been manageable, the Senate Committee noted, but "stimulated by the buoyant economic conditions of the early 1970s, workers in industries other than the auto industry, and especially in the public sector, began pressing for wage increases to match the auto workers, even where there were no comparable productivity gains." Devaluation was a substitute, then, for general wage restraint. "In general, Canadian productivity rates cannot support parity with the United States," the Committee reasoned. "If unit labour costs are to be competitive with U.S. industry, a substantial differential in the exchange rate of the dollar will be essential for many years."[30]

If workers attempted to recover the losses suffered to their standard of living as a result of devaluation, the Committee warned, Canada's newly established competitive advantage would disappear. "This benefit from the exchange rate depreciation is a one-time gain," it held. "Moreover, it will only be effective as long as salary and wage increases do not attempt to recoup the actual fall in Canadian living standards which the exchange rate decline reflects." In the context of an overall industrial strategy now built on the twin towers of tariff liberalization and dollar devaluation, the Committee saw yet another advantage to the speedy negotiation of a Canada-U.S. free trade agreement. "Bilateral free trade," it claimed, "should now be perceived as a discipline to hold Canadian wage rates in line."[31]

By early 1978, the Liberal government sounded far more confident that the benefits of devaluation outweighed any possible dangers. Jean Chrétien, as Minister of Finance, argued that "the dollar, *adjusted to its real value,* favours exports. We have seen this happen during 1977, when the

Canadian commercial surplus has gone from $1 billion to $3 billion."[32] Now convinced that devaluation was the answer, Chrétien revisited the concerns of his predecessors with relative Canada-U.S. production costs.

> There are a lot of advantages of having a depreciated dollar at this time because in many areas we had lost our competitive position. Canadians were paying themselves more than our main competitors. Take the pulp and paper industry that I have in my own riding and I say to my own electors that they were asking too much, $1.75 more than their competitors in the United States. It is the same in the textile and so on, but the depreciation of the dollar has brought back our competitive position in many fields.[33]

ITC Minister Jack Horner theorized that Canada would always need a favourable exchange rate differential against the U.S. dollar.

> . . . Canada should have a 90-cent dollar all the time – all the time, because we have a different climate to do business in. We have a cold, Arctic climate. It costs more to heat the factories in Canada than it does in the United States, therefore, the energy bill being what it is today, we need an advantage. Our transportation system is not naturally as good as that of the United States. . . . We have not got that natural advantage so we need a 90-cent dollar all of the time.[34]

Jean Chrétien heralded the economic benefits for both export promotion and import protection produced by devaluation.

> When I look at the advantages of a devalued currency, I have to report that the industrial sector of this country, which was in bad shape some years ago is now gaining the benefit. Many sectors are operating at full capacity . . . like the pulp and paper and wood industry. . . . The industries that have to compete in the Canadian market . . . are operating almost at full capacity too, because the devalued Canadian dollar has made Canadian goods more competitive, not only in terms of exports but in terms of the Canadian market.[35]

Speaking more than a decade later, in 1991, Chrétien once again confirmed the purposive nature of the Trudeau government's devaluations: "the dollar went down when we were there because in Canada the paper mills were closed down, the mines were closed down, and it was the instrument I used to bring Canada back to a competitive position."[36]

The radical scope of this program of devaluation, recorded in Figure One, can scarcely be exaggerated. Between 1976 and 1986, nearly thirty per cent was lopped from the value of the Canadian dollar relative to the U.S. dollar. The stimulative effects of these dollar devaluations are recorded in the Canada-U.S. trade accounts of the last two decades.

Canada's average annual merchandise trade surplus with the United States was nearly eleven times greater between 1982 and 1992 than it was between 1973 and 1981. In automotive trade, 1973 through 1981 were deficit years for Canada, yet from 1982 to 1992 Canada recorded annual surpluses. The fire sale on relative Canadian labour rates that the devalued dollar has produced has been graphically portrayed by Buzz Hargrove, president of the Canadian Auto Workers. In his testimony before a Commons committee in February of 1993, Hargrove noted that Canadians "enjoy vis-à-vis the U.S. about $9 an hour labour cost advantage in the auto industry, a major advantage. For every four workers it costs the industry, whether it be Japanese transplants or American industry to hire in the United States, they can hire five in Canada, an additional worker for nothing."[37]

Nationalist Moments in Liberal Industrial Policy

Notwithstanding the clear dominance of continentalist thinking in the critical choices relating to industrial policy made during this period, the nationalist school continued to offer critiques of, and alternatives to, the incremental elaboration of a continentally rationalized industrial regime. During the Pearson years, a Task Force on the Structure of Canadian Industry, commissioned by nationalist cabinet minister Walter Gordon, suggested that "the Canadian public interest would be directly served by new national policies which recognize the need for a stronger government presence to countervail the power of multi-national firms and, on occasion, foreign government power exercised over these firms."[38] Prepared for yet another nationalist Liberal cabinet minister, Herb Gray, the 1972 Gray Report recommended a number of specific policy instruments to review and regulate the performance failures of both existing and new foreign-owned enterprises in Canada. A number of serious branch-plant performance problems were identified by the Gray Report, including export blocking. Citing a 1969 ITC survey of nearly 1,000 foreign subsidiaries *with a declared export interest* operating in Canada, it reported that 58 per cent of U.S. branch plants and 43 per cent of other foreign subsidiaries were faced with export restrictions imposed by their parent companies.[39]

Following directly from the Gray Report was the 1973 creation of the Foreign Investment Review Agency (FIRA) to screen new direct foreign investment in Canada as well as foreign takeovers of established Canadian companies. FIRA was never much more than an exercise in symbolic politics. Remaining outside of its review process was the bulk of existing foreign investment in Canadian manufacturing. These are the very subsidiaries whose technological dependence and administratively blocked exports had created the competitive trade problems for Canada that this volume has documented. And, while it was a symbol so relatively ineffectual that it could not galvanize strong support from a nationalist constituency, FIRA was vested at the same time with great negative power by the continentalists. It crystallized their deepest fears that the nationalists might find a way to employ this instrument to seize from them the policy initiative.[40]

On a wider front, the first tentative initiatives taken in the direction of a nationalist industrial strategy by the central Priorities and Planning Committee of the Trudeau cabinet in the early 1970s were thwarted systematically by the bureaucratic elites within Finance and Industry, Trade and Commerce. ITC, according to one insider, responded "to the form of the [industrial strategy] demands while ignoring their content" by launching an elaborate consultation process whereby various manufacturing sectors could inform the department of the areas in which they felt public-sector activities could assist industrial development.[41] In this manner, the department deflected a potentially menacing policy direction into its own familiar turf – export and product innovation subsidies. Predictably, when asked, the manufacturers told ITC that their ideal industrial strategy would feature more lavish and better co-ordinated spending and tax incentive programs and fewer public restraints on their activities.[42]

Even as senior economic bureaucrats and the business community were sandbagging a nationalist industrial strategy, the public was increasingly identifying itself with the ideas of the nationalist school. In 1956, 68 per cent of Canadians believed U.S. investment had been good for Canada, but by 1978 only 30 per cent held this opinion. In 1978, as well, over one-half of Canadians supported buying back majority control of U.S. companies operating in Canada even when loaded with the intimidating qualification that this "might mean a big reduction in our standard of living."[43] This emerging nationalist public sentiment received its first electoral test in 1980. Desperate for Ontario seats, the Liberals promised an industrial strategy for Canada and implied a tougher line on the control of foreign investment.

For the shot in the arm his industrial strategy plank gave the successful Liberal campaign in Ontario, nationalist Herb Gray was rewarded with the ITC portfolio following the election. He promptly signalled the manufacturers that it would be unrealistic to expect the continuation of a "hands-off" industrial development policy. "The time has come," he said, "for Canada to learn from the examples of others' successes."[44] The views of the nationalist ITC bureaucrats recorded in Chapter 6 had finally found expression at the political centre.

Shortly thereafter, Gray presented a remarkable document to the Trudeau cabinet: remarkable because of its three radical challenges to the industrial policy of continental rationalization that the Liberals had been incrementally implementing since the 1960s. First, it contended that the branch-plant economy presented serious structural barriers, both administrative and technological, to the realization of Canadian industrial potential. Second, these structural barriers, it claimed, could never be corrected simply through government exhortations and public expenditure programs. Finally, it suggested that the government would have to begin to monitor branch-plant performance with an eye to framing "regulatory mechanisms" to "ensure that MNEs [multinational enterprises] perform to world standards in terms of innovation and export freedom." As for the current federal policy instrument in this field, the Foreign Investment Review Act, since it did "not pertain to most of the activities of MNEs now operating in this country," it was held to be an "inadequate tool to fully address" the problem.[45]

Gray's cabinet paper threatened to give the continentalist school's bogeyman, FIRA, its first real teeth. In the wake of the dramatic late 1980 announcement of a nationalist policy initiative by the Liberals in the resource domain, the National Energy Policy (NEP), rumours began to circulate in Ottawa that Gray was planning the "NEPing" of several manufacturing sectors. Not surprisingly, Gray's analysis caused a sensation in upper-level Ottawa. It was not very long before word began to leak out that he was having difficulty in selling his ideas to cabinet. The efforts of Economic Development Minister and Senator H.A. Olson to "moderate" Gray's impact by introducing a rival document for cabinet discussion were an open secret.[46] It took nearly eighteen months after Gray's initial presentation to cabinet for a much briefer industrial policy statement to be introduced as a supplement to the November, 1981, Liberal federal budget.

Put simply, Gray and other nationalist Liberals lost the fight in the Trudeau cabinet. Entitled *Economic Development for Canada in the 1980s,* the budget statement stood the project of a nationalist industrial strategy on its head and reaffirmed the long-term policy investment of the Liberals in continental rationalization. It communicated three simple messages to Canadian capital. First, during the 1980s, leading investment opportunities would be in resource exploitation, not industrialization. Second, as economic development would be resource-led by a projected $440 billion in potential megaprojects, Canadian industry could discover its niche through orienting itself to the domestic market to fill the need for manufactured inputs generated by all this activity. Finally, foreign investors were reassured that the Liberal government had no intention of monitoring or controlling foreign investment, outside of the energy sector, in a more rigorous manner.[47]

Speaking subsequently, Senator Olson confirmed the turn toward economic orthodoxy and even selective ISI taken by the Trudeau government after its brief, post-1980 election, flirtation with a nationalist industrial strategy. Our preoccupation with "moving away from being hewers of wood and drawers of water is all behind us," he opined. "We're not going to process every one of our natural resources into the final product." Protectionism was dead and the harsh realities of industrial restructuring were upon us.

> From here on, the national Government will invest its capital in areas of prospective growth, in the future. . . . We're going to stop propping up mature industries that will never be competitive in this generation, like textiles, clothing, footware and a number of others.[48]

Why did the nationalists lose and the continentalists get *Economic Development for Canada*? Just as there were precise partisan political reasons for the emergence of the nationalist industrial strategy option in 1980, so, too, we must look toward the specific political configuration of the Liberal cabinet in 1981 for our explanation. In late 1981, the Trudeau cabinet was desperate to show some hopeful policy direction in a period of intense economic dislocation, desirous of breaking partisan ground in the western provinces that would have had the lion's share of the megaprojects promised in the statement, exhausted by its labours in the constitutional and energy fields, and afraid of any further confrontations with U.S. business interests and the Reagan presidency. On this latter point, it must be remembered that many successful Canadian industries, branch plant and otherwise, were now well on the path toward continental rationalization and openly hostile to the interventionist premises of a nationalist industrial strategy. Visions of continental integration and freer trade with the U.S. danced in their heads, not a regime of governmental regulation designed to force them to create specialized, internationally competitive products and firms.

And so, after a brief moment in the sun, the ideas of the nationalist wing of the 1980 Trudeau cabinet were pushed into the policy basement. Gray himself was exiled to the post of Treasury Board President, well out of the way of trade and industrial policy. Talk of industrial strategy was replaced with talk of sectoral trade agreements with the United States in such areas as specialty steel, urban transportation equipment, petrochemicals, textiles, and clothing. Sectoral trade agreements, it was calculated, would replicate within other industrial spheres Canada's Auto Pact successes and would thereby make Canadian manufacturing "more competitive in the world as a whole."[49]

Canada-U.S Free Trade: Institutionalizing the GATT

From the vantage point of the early 1980s, it seemed clear that the Auto Pact and the GATT regime had proven to be very effective instruments in liberalizing trade between Canada and the United States. When the staged reductions of the Tokyo Round were finally completed in 1987, it was anticipated that some 80 per cent of Canadian exports would enter the U.S. duty free and some 95 per cent would be subject to tariffs of 5 per cent or less. On the other side, 65 per cent of U.S. industrial exports would enter Canada duty free and 91 per cent with rates of 5 per cent or less. This prompted the Senate Committee on Foreign Affairs to proclaim triumphantly that "a de facto free trade area" between the U.S. and Canada would then exist in respect to tariffs.[50]

And so, the Mulroney Conservative government startled many observers when it announced in the fall of 1985 that it was seeking bilateral free trade negotiations with the Americans. With the impending approach of "de facto" Canada-U.S. free trade with respect to tariffs under the GATT, what could have induced the Tories to re-politicize what has historically been a very explosive issue in Canadian politics?[51] As we shall see, a unique conjuncture of three circumstances prompted this initiative.

The first of these circumstances was rooted in the continuing struggle between the continentalists and nationalists. Since at least the 1960s, both schools had been offering formula solutions for the chronic ills of Canada's manufacturing sector – the continentalists prescribed free trade while the nationalists pumped for an industrial strategy. In this struggle, neither side had as yet been able to realize fully its vision or to sweep its rival from the field. Nonetheless, the continentalists had seen things go mostly their way until the 1980 election. The temporary ascendency of the nationalists with the introduction of the National Energy Policy and bold talk of "NEPing" other manufacturing sectors deeply traumatized the continentalist school. Even though Gray's industrial strategy eventually ran aground in the Trudeau cabinet, they became determined not to be caught off guard again. The early capsize of the successor Liberal megaproject gambit in the wake of the severe economic recession of 1982 and the collapse of oil prices opened the door to an intense round of evangelizing through the ranks of the business community by the continentalist school on behalf of free trade.[52] The continentalists were determined to seize the opportunity presented by the policy reversals of their foes and the economic distemper of the early 1980s to press home a Canada-U.S. free trade agreement that would consolidate and institutionalize their hegemony.

Much relief for Canada's chronic economic infirmities was promised to the general business community in the campaign that marked the lead up to the Canada-U.S. free trade negotiations, but few specifics beyond the brand name of the patent elixir were actually ever given. As a result, confusion over the meaning and impact of freer trade with the U.S. was as commonly expressed among some business groups as was certainty that it would offer solutions to high unemployment and rising prices as well as low productivity and weak markets. Take, for example, this "we have to do something" response by J. Geldart, president of the Atlantic Provinces Chamber of Commerce, to a question from a 1985 Commons-Senate Committee as to whether her organization had enough information to support its "general feeling in favour" of freer trade.

> Can we afford to wait? I think that is another thing we have to look at. I believe we have to do something. Is it going to take 50 years? Someone told me today that it might take 50 years to figure out what the ramifications of this are going to be to Atlantic Canada and for it to get ready. We have to do something . . . I think that is what our resolution [favouring free trade] reflects – the general desire and will to get on with the business of selling more to bigger markets. And we see New England as the big market.[53]

A second factor convinced the Mulroney Conservatives to give continental free trade an early priority within their policy agenda. They believed it would offer them partisan advantage. To begin, it was an issue that held strong appeal for two important strands within the party – the traditional western free trade electorate and the neo-conservative right, especially from Quebec, who favoured it both because free trade smacked of free enterprise and because an agreement would bring Canada closer to Reagan's America. As well, business interests important to the party strongly impressed upon the Tories their need for such an agreement. The active support of business groups mobilized by the campaign for free trade was eventually to prove a decisive factor in the 1988 re-election of Mulroney's Conservatives. But Canada-U.S. free trade was also an issue that the 1985 Tories believed could be sold to the public as a demonstration of their "decisiveness and consistency" in formulating an "economic renewal program." Conservative Party polling indicated, according to a document leaked from the Prime Minister's Office, that:

> The majority of Canadians do not understand fully what is meant by the terms free trade, freer trade or enhanced trade. The popular interpretation of free trade appears to be keyed to the word "free." It is something for nothing – a short cut – to economic prosperity. It is bigger markets for Canadian products, more jobs, more of everything. It is, as Terrence Wills of the Gazette puts it, having your cake

and eating it too. . . . But are respondents really thinking when they express their opinions on free trade? Gregg suggests not, calling the free trade issue a "non-brainer". . . .[54]

In spite of the "significant risks" that they acknowledged in politically managing the free trade issue, Tory strategists determined that from a partisan perspective, after an undistinguished first year in office and an extremely rocky path littered with bank failures and rancid tuna to cross at the beginning of their second, the policy leadership and initiative they could showcase to the public by being seen to seize the moment to enter free trade negotiations with the U.S. made it worth the gamble.

To this point, we have examined two factors that propelled Canada-U.S. free trade to the head of the first-term political agenda of the Mulroney government. Both of these invoked free trade as a symbol: for business, as a symbol of their hopes for a quick and painless solution to Canada's economic ills; for the Tories, as a partisan symbol to unite the party faithful and to demonstrate to the voting public their economic management skills. The third factor was grounded far more in the concrete realm of commerce. By the early 1980s, Canada's economic elites had become worried about the continuing security and stability of the new continentally rationalized trading environment that had been growing up under the already extensive trade liberalization between the two countries, as well as by the radical devaluation of the Canadian dollar.

Witness after witness from the Canadian business establishment appearing in the summer of 1985 before a special House of Commons-Senate Committee targeted United States *non-tariff barriers* as the real subject of any future Canada-U.S. trade negotiations. "Tariffs are already very low on Canadian steel products entering the U.S.A.," observed J.D. Allen, president and chief executive officer of Stelco, "in fact, it is not the tariff but rather the increase in non-tariff measures that affects the flow of steel."[55] R. Booth, chairman of the CMA Trade Policy Committee, submitted:

> Whether one is talking about trade enhancement, free trade, and so on is not irrelevant, but is a side issue. Essentially, what we are urging is an effort to remove the non-tariff barriers. We acknowledge your point that indeed tariffs are coming down and, by 1988, will be virtually eliminated on the majority of goods. So it is essentially the non-tariff barriers which are the issue.[56]

F. Petrie, president of the Canadian Export Association, made much the same point in observing that "trade between Canada and the United States is not regulated as much as it has been in the past by the tariff. It is really the non-tariff barriers that are the main villains, so to speak, in our access to the United States."[57] Finally, J. Hale, vice-president of the Canadian Organization of Small Business, related that "cosb's experience in assisting members with trade-related issues has underlined the fact that non-tariff barriers are often a far more significant obstacle to smaller companies entering the U.S. market than are formal tariffs or import quotas."[58]

The concern here with non-tariff barriers was not simply an abstract one relating to a relatively small amount of lost potential business. Rather, the Canadian economic establishment feared that the weighty investments, actual and anticipated, that they had already made in continentalizing production might be rendered unprofitable by the vagaries of the U.S. political process. A. Powis, chairman of the Task Force on International Trade of the Business Council on National Issues, pointed to a massive current U.S. trade deficit as the most significant factor in promoting the American use and threatened use of non-tariff barriers and suggested that "just in our own self-defence, we had better get in behind those things." He went on to declare:

> . . . most of their anger, in fact, almost all of their anger, is directed toward the Japanese, Brazilians, or Europeans. Nobody seems to be particularly mad at Canada, in spite of the fact that we are the second largest contributor to their trade deficit. But the dangers, I think are very real. All you have to do is spend a few days down in Washington to realize how real they are. We are facing a threat right now of legislated lumber quotas, tariffs and whatever, which could absolutely devastate whole sectors of this country.[59]

J.D. Allen of Stelco related how his company was caught unprepared for this "threat" and how surprised and disappointed they were to discover themselves considered a "foreign" firm when they had previously thought of themselves as partners with U.S. manufacturers in a struggle to keep "the North American product competitive."

> Our shipments travel daily by truck and rail across our joint border, whereas imports from the rest of the world tend to be boatloads being brought in by trading companies. . . . In essence we are just like U.S. steel suppliers. It was quite a surprise, then, to find ourselves in early 1984 being painted with the same brush as offshore suppliers, and potentially headed for quotas that were directed at the rise of unfairly traded imports from offshore into the U.S. We had never really planned for such a dilemma.[60]

At the mid-point of the 1980s, then, in pressing for free trade negotiations with the U.S., as their immediate and urgent objective Canada's economic elite sought relief from the nightmare of having the southward flow of their products halted by a soon-to-be-erected wall of non-tariff barriers. H.E. Demone, vice-president of National Sea Products, argued that impending 1986 U.S. Congressional elections dictated a promptly organized Canadian trade initiative.

> A year from now the mid-term U.S. elections will certainly be under way, at least the campaign. The American legislators will come under pressure from their constituents for increased protectionism. With the current structure of the Canadian fishing industry, the threat of countervail action by American interests will be of ever increasing concern. If such an action against fresh or frozen fish were ever to be successful, it would put the long-term viability of the entire industry in jeopardy. [61]

Some business leaders were convinced that if Canada simply declared its intent to begin negotiations, they would gain safe harbour for their exports for some years to come. D. Morton, president and chief executive officer of Alcan, took this view:

> We believe that a clear commitment by Canada to enter into negotiations with the U.S. to explore the issues for freer trade would have the effect of delaying or maybe even exempting Canada from the effects of actions that by many people's standards now appear to be inevitable in the U.S. in the coming period. And even though the negotiations may take months and the implementation may take years, the fact that they are started and the intent would be an immense barrier against such action against us. [62]

While some counselled the tactical use of free trade negotiations as a short-term defensive measure, others were more concerned with stabilizing and extending their existing investment in continental integration. For example, R. Varah, director of commercial development for Dofasco, decried the "air of uncertainty" that had resulted from the U.S. use of non-tariff barriers:

> ... one does not go ahead and make any long-term investments, or even short-term investments when that kind of cloud is hanging over one's industry and its access to the U.S. market. So one might say that it [free trade] would be more appropriate for secure access rather than more access. [63]

R. Cyr, chairman of the Canada-United States Advisory Committee of the Canadian Chamber of Commerce, put the same argument rhetorically. "What companies will be willing to invest in Canada if this atmosphere of uncertainty and constant harassment of our exports continues?" he asked, "What jobs will be created without investment?" [64] The submission of the

Canadian Export Association also underlined the importance of a Canada-U.S. trade treaty in creating an attractive investment climate. "To plan effectively and to invest with confidence, many Canadian industries need assurance of access to the United States market," it noted, and "stability is the key consideration here."[65]

In the end, the Tories were unable to deliver to Canadian business its principal objective – secure access to the American market. Although the Americans were willing to remove the remaining tariffs between the two countries in the 1987 Canada-U.S. Free Trade Agreement (FTA), they refused to renounce their recourse to imposing non-tariff barriers against Canadian goods. Chapter 19 of the FTA permitted both countries to retain their domestic anti-dumping and countervailing duty laws, although appeals on whether these laws have been properly applied could be made to bi-national review panels. Although lacking an independent enforcement mechanism, these panels' decisions were nonetheless agreed to be "binding on the Parties." To discourage either country from simply writing new laws designed to overturn panel decisions they did not like, both parties agreed that any such legislative changes must be consistent with GATT codes on dumping and subsidies. In article 1907, Canada and the United States gave themselves five years to work out a mutually acceptable definition of subsidies and unfair trading practices.[66]

Many of the most controversial of the FTA sections did not actually address tariff matters directly. Chapters on resources, energy, and investment were designed to make the Canadian federal state nationalist-proof by precluding any future government from reprising the 1980 Trudeau nationalist outburst. As one Tory cabinet minister boasted to Calgary oil executives, the FTA's energy provisions were "insurance against your own government" to prevent the re-introduction of a National Energy Policy.[67]

The Canada-U.S. Free Trade Agreement, in relation to tariff barriers, did little more than incrementally build on the "de facto free trade area" between Canada and the U.S. that had already been constructed under the GATT and the Auto Pact.[68] Accordingly, it could never have lived up to the wildly exaggerated claims of paradise or perdition that came from its supporters and detractors. Just the same, the 1988 "free trade election" was a raucous brawl by partisan political forces carrying once more into the fray the tattered 1960s banners of the nationalists and continentalists. The Liberals, hoping to replay their 1980 electoral success, fell back once more on their populist nationalist wing. One of their most effective television advertisements purported to show the FTA negotiators taking an eraser to the Canada-U.S. border on a map of North America. For its part, business strongly supported the Tories, not because the FTA delivered secure access to the U.S. market (as it did not), but because they feared that the defeat of the Mulroney Conservatives would again open the door to nationalist state intervention.

Free Trade and Continental Rationalization: The Ledger

The economic evidence forcefully supports the view that the FTA did not play a decisive role in the progress of the continental rationalization of North American industrial production. Rather than being the cataclysmic economic event of popular lore, it was little more than a marker on a much longer road.

Proponents of the FTA have argued that the greater access to the American market it supposedly provides has spurred greater efficiency and competitiveness on the part of Canadian manufacturers and, consequently, greater penetration of the U.S. market. It is indeed true that Canadian industries now hold a somewhat larger portion of the combined Canada-U.S. market for manufactures than they did at the beginning of the 1980s, expanding their share of the total from 6.6 per cent in 1981-83 to 7.3 per cent in 1989-91.[69] However, this gain cannot be explained principally in terms of the Free Trade Agreement but must be placed in its larger global context. Liberalized trading rules under the Tokyo Round of the GATT and the globalization of international production added up to significant losses for American manufacturers in their own marketplace during the 1980s. Canada's take in these American losses between 1981-83 and 1989-91 was actually very modest, only approximately 15 per cent of total U.S. losses. Further, the rise in Canada's combined market share over this period can more logically be attributed to pre-FTA dollar devaluation policies, the 1965 Canada-U.S. Auto Pact, and increased access under GATT agreements negotiated in the 1960s and 1970s.

Table Fifteen underlines the very reserved nature of Canadian gains in the U.S. market for manufactures during the 1980s. Without the benefit of the FTA, Mexico, the EC, Japan, and five of the most important Asian NICs all increased their share of the U.S. market at a significantly higher rate than Canada between 1981-83 and 1989-91. In addition, Table Fifteen shows that Canada's share of total imports of manufactures into the U.S. market actually declined somewhat relative to that of other importers; from 19.9 per cent in 1981-83 to 18 per cent in 1989-91.

On the other side, opponents of the Free Trade Agreement have argued that it has resulted in the loss of hundreds of thousands of Canadian jobs because of increased U.S. penetration of the Canadian market and the repatriation of branch-plant production to U.S. plants. In fact, during the 1980s, the U.S. share of the Canadian market in manufactures rose *before*

Table Fifteen
Producer Country Share of
United States Market in Manufactures

	Import Market Share			Total Market Share		
	1981-83	*1985-87*	*1989-91*	*1981-83*	*1985-87*	*1989-91*
Canada	19.9	17.6	18.0	1.9	2.3	2.6
Mexico	3.0	3.5	5.1	0.3	0.5	0.7
EC	20.6	21.5	19.6	1.9	2.9	2.9
Japan	21.5	24.6	22.0	2.0	3.3	3.2
Asia NICs★	13.0	15.1	14.6	1.2	2.0	2.1

★Includes Korea, Hong Kong, Taiwan, Singapore, and China.
SOURCE: Statistics Canada, *Trade Patterns: Canada-United States, The Manufacturing Industries 1981-1991*, March, 1993, Table 7.2, p. 34.

the ratification of the FTA, not after. The U.S. share rose from 24.5 per cent in the 1981-83 period to 27.4 per cent in 1985-87 and remained at exactly the same level of 27.4 per cent in 1989-91. Table Sixteen shows that certain of Canada's manufacturing sectors, including textiles, clothing, and furniture, did suffer significant import penetration during the 1980s. However, the FTA alone cannot bear the burden for these losses. As we earlier argued, liberalized trading rules under the Tokyo Round of the GATT and trends toward the globalization of international production must also be factored into our considerations. As well, Table Sixteen demonstrates that in certain leading manufacturing sectors, notably machinery, transport equipment, and chemicals, the loss of market share was considerably greater during the 1970s than in the 1980s.

The economic record verifies, then, that the FTA cannot carry the weight of the arguments of either its proponents or opponents. Factors with a longer shelf life, such as trade liberalization under the Auto Pact and the GATT and state-fashioned devaluations of the Canadian dollar, have greater explanatory power. It is very clear that Canadian production has been spatially re-oriented through many incremental steps taken during the last quarter-century. Nevertheless, the economic evidence also plainly indicates that the Canadian production system has simply been *reshuffled* rather than *transmuted* insofar as our factories continue to be organized in accordance with continental marketing strategies established in U.S. head offices rather than becoming highly efficient and technologically advanced

Table Sixteen
Imports as a Per Cent of the Domestic Market

	1965-70	*1979*	*1989-91*
Food and beverages	7	10	13
Tobacco	1	2	2
Rubber and plastics	16	23	35
Leather	18	34	60
Textiles	23	29	45
Knitting mills	16	31	27
Clothing	6	13	30
Wood products	9	14	12
Furniture and fixtures	5	13	29
Paper and allied	8	10	20
Printing and publishing	14	16	14
Primary metals	25	35	41
Fabricated metal	12	15	24
Machinery	65	75	74
Transport equipment	51	72	74
Electrical and electronic	24	40	68
Non-metallic mineral products	15	19	27
Petroleum and coal products	11	3	12
Chemicals	11	35	34
Other manufacturing	50	55	67

SOURCES: Senate, Standing Committee on Foreign Affairs, *Proceedings*, December 9, 1980, pp. 14:26, 14:28; and Statistics Canada, *Trade Patterns: Canada-United States 1981-1991*, Table 7.1.1.

plants capable of autonomously generating world-competitive products.[70] Under the continentally rationalized Auto Pact model, managerial authority, research and development, and export marketing all typically remain the prerogatives of U.S. parent firms.[71] Too frequently, the principal reason U.S. manufacturers remain in Canada is to take advantage of workers carrying state-subsidized social benefits and paid in relatively cheap Canadian dollars. American firms also stay to fly their corporate colours in a valuable and distinctive regional market.[72]

As Table Seventeen demonstrates, growth in manufacturing production in the United States and other OECD countries during the 1980s far

Table Seventeen
Average Annual Growth Rates in
Manufacturing Production, 1980-1990

Japan	4.4
U.S.	3.4
OECD total	2.9
Germany	2.2
Canada	1.8
Sweden	1.6

SOURCE: OECD, *Industrial Policy in OECD Countries*, Annual Review, 1992, Table 12.

outstripped that experienced in Canadian industry. Canada continued to encounter reverses on the international trade front as well. Chapter 1, it will be recalled, showed that Canada's finished exports as a proportion of total exports were significantly below the norm for other rich industrialized countries in 1990. In fact, between 1980 and 1992, Canada suffered a cumulative trade deficit in fully manufactured end products of a staggering $311 billion.

The relative decline of Canadian industrial competitiveness during the last two decades is efficiently captured in Table Eighteen, where OECD market penetration in turnkey industrial sectors is documented. Japan made striking advances across all sectors between 1970 and 1990, mainly at the expense of the United States share of the OECD market. Germany and Sweden either held their own or shouldered slight declines in some sectors. Canada, in contrast, suffered the dramatic deterioration of between one-quarter and one-third of its OECD market share across all of these leading sectors.

Chapter 6 recorded the technological barriers to Canadian manufactured exports that prevented Canadian firms of the 1950s to the mid-1970s from developing the technological punch necessary to generate internationally marketable innovations. As no reforms of substance were undertaken during the post-World War Two period to address these structural problems, it should be no surprise to find that Canadian industry is still a technological laggard. A comparison of Table Nineteen with Table Fourteen in Chapter 6 shows that Canada's lowly position in industrial R&D is the same in the 1990s as it was in the 1960s. And the prospects for improvement in the immediate future are grim. As Table Twenty shows, the somewhat better than average growth rates in Canadian industrial R&D

Table Eighteen
Export Market Shares of Total OECD Market
by Type of Industry, 1970-1990

		Total Manufacturing	*High Technology*	*Science-based*	*Medium Technology*
Japan	1970	9.7	12.0	6.1	7.6
	1980	11.7	15.3	6.6	12.4
	1990	12.8	19.1	12.2	14.5
U.S.	1970	17.8	28.3	34.5	19.6
	1980	15.7	25.1	32.1	16.6
	1990	14.8	23.7	26.7	13.2
Germany	1970	16.6	16.1	14.6	20.8
	1980	16.8	15.9	14.7	19.7
	1990	17.5	14.6	14.3	21.1
Sweden	1970	3.3	2.4	1.8	2.7
	1980	2.7	2.3	1.6	2.4
	1990	2.5	2.1	1.8	2.2
Canada	1970	6.4	3.6	3.7	8.0
	1980	4.2	2.0	2.0	4.4
	1990	4.4	2.6	2.3	5.0

SOURCE: OECD, *Industrial Policy in OECD Countries*, Annual Review, 1992, Table 49.

of the late 1970s and early 1980s tailed off dramatically in the late 1980s. Entering the 1990s, only approximately 1,700 of more than 40,000 Canadian manufacturing firms were engaged in R&D activity. Further, a 1989 Statistics Canada survey discovered that fewer than half of the manufacturing companies responding had implemented one or more of twenty-two "leading" manufacturing technologies.[73]

Following the case made in Chapter 6, foreign ownership of Canadian industry, as well as the historically specialized regional role that Canadian industry has played within continental production, largely accounts for the contemporary deficiencies of industrial R&D in Canada. Take, for

Table Nineteen
Business Enterprise Expenditure on
R&D as a Percentage of GDP, 1991

Japan	2.15
U.S.	1.92
Germany	1.76
Sweden	1.61
EC	1.23
Canada	0.78

SOURCE: OECD, *Main Science and Technology Indicators*, 1, 1993, Table 25.

example, the automotive sector, where Canadian branch plants taking advantage of the devalued dollar have specialized in labour-intensive assembly work while design and engineering work have remained with U.S. parents. The results of this spatial division of labour are illustrated in Table Twenty-One. Although automotive exports currently make up nearly one-quarter of Canada's total exports, Canadian R&D in motor vehicles is only an insignificant portion of what we already know to be a relatively puny national R&D effort.

Prospects for the development of a potent Canadian capital goods sector capable of carrying on its creative shoulders the development of technologically innovative manufactured exports seem no closer now than they were during the immediate post-World War Two period. Canada's share of world machinery trade fell from 1.3 per cent of world exports in 1978 to .07 per cent in 1989. In addition, Canada's trade deficit in machinery increased 31 per cent in real terms between 1978 and 1989. In the machinery sector as well, the negative effects of foreign ownership and an unbalanced continental division of labour in R&D are evident.[74] A 1991 federal government report on Canada's industrial competitiveness set out the negative effects of high levels of foreign ownership in the industrial equipment manufacturing sector in the following manner.

As a matter of corporate policy, these foreign subsidiaries in Canada tend to purchase their equipment from the same supplier as their foreign parent company, usually a non-Canadian one. This truncates an already limited Canadian market. Furthermore, as a matter of corporate policy, these foreign subsidiaries can act as a single-source supplier, but the major part of their product lines are supplemented

Table Twenty
Average Annual Growth Rate in
R&D Expenditures in Industry

	1975-81	*1981-85*	*1985-90*
Japan	8.2	11.2	8.0
U.S.	5.2	8.6	1.0
Germany	6.1	5.2	3.4
Sweden	5.1	10.1	0
EC	4.8	5.0	4.5
Canada	10.6	8.9	2.4

SOURCE: OECD, *Industrial Policy in OECD Countries,* Annual Review, 1992, Table 27.

by production from the parent firm. Accordingly, the subsidiaries expend little effort expanding production in this country. Canadian manufacturers are limited to providing the specialized products that they produce and, consequently, are unable to offer one-stop shopping. . . . Canadian subsidiaries of foreign-owned companies obtain sophisticated technologies from their parents and consequently conduct little or no R&D in Canada. . . . The type of R&D performed by subsidiaries operating in Canada tends to be development or adaptation of the parent companies' technology to Canadian market conditions.[75]

A 1991 analysis of the Canadian economy prepared for the Mulroney government and the Business Council on National Issues by U.S. economist Michael Porter reached a similar diagnosis of the shortcomings of Canada's machinery sector in relation to international competitiveness.

Machinery industries are a sign of healthy economic upgrading. They give a country's core industries quicker access to and more control over fast-changing process technologies. Superiority in machinery and related and supporting industries can help to sustain competitive advantage in primary goods. Primary goods producers can often work closely with machinery firms located in their home country to upgrade and improve productivity. This relationship tends to be more difficult to build with foreign suppliers. In short,

Table Twenty-one
R&D in Motor Vehicles as a Percentage
of Total Industrial R&D, 1990

Japan	13.7
U.S.	11.0
Germany	16.4
Sweden	15.7
Canada	1.9

SOURCE: OECD, *Industrial Policy in OECD Countries*, Annual Review, 1992,
Table 31.

with few competitive machinery industries, many Canadian businesses are deprived of the dynamic interactions that foster process innovation and upgrading.[76]

Industrial Policy under Mulroney

Following the long-standing approach of their predecessors in Ottawa, the Conservatives did little during their 1984-93 tenure in government to address directly the structural limitations of Canadian manufacturing that we have just reviewed. To be sure, the Tories fancied themselves as great policy innovators. They came into office promising to rejuvenate Canada's industrial sector by freeing policy space for the market to do its job of creating wealth. In practice, "opening Canada for business" meant deregulation, privatization, and dismantling interventionist nationalist instruments like the NEP and FIRA.[77] It also meant institutionalizing liberalized trade in the form of the FTA. The Canada-U.S. FTA was soon extended into NAFTA (North American Free Trade Agreement) by incorporating Mexico into the original Canada-U.S. framework. Deeply mired in economic recession as the Mulroney era drew to a close, the Tories launched a "prosperity initiative" in late 1991 to convince Canadians of the need to improve their economy's international competitiveness. "Yes, we can" was the pathetically puerile slogan of the accompanying $4.5 million public advertising campaign.[78]

Whatever the partisan heat that surrounded these Tory initiatives, they actually broke very little new policy ground. As this chapter records, the NEP and FIRA were creatures of quite specific nationalist political moments in a usually reliably continentalist Trudeau cabinet. With the

November, 1981, publication of *Economic Development for Canada,* the Liberal continentalist ship had righted itself. The FTA did little more than incrementally build on the "de facto free trade area" between Canada and the U.S. already constructed by the Liberals under the GATT and the Auto Pact. Finally, the Tories' "prosperity initiative" campaign was a 1990s incarnation of what this volume has shown to be a long tradition of empty government economic crusades against inappropriate targets. It has always been politically easier to exhort Canadians and Canadian businesses to improve their individual behaviours than to face squarely problems deeply rooted in the structures of the national economy.

On one critical issue relating to industrial policy, the Conservatives struck out on their own. Attacking directly one of the twin prongs of continental rationalization, they revalued upward the Canadian dollar. As Figure One demonstrates, during their first two years of office the Tories followed the Liberal course and continued to allow the value of the Canadian dollar to decline gradually relative to the U.S. dollar. Between 1986 and 1991, however, they yanked up the dollar by approximately 20 per cent – from 72 cents U.S. to 87 cents U.S.

A turnabout this drastic demands an explanation. It provoked screams of betrayal from the same business community that had played a decisive role in the 1988 re-election of the Conservatives. Making the FTA look bad, it led rapidly to a flood of disinvestment decisions by U.S. and Canadian firms. Currency revaluation also contributed to the length and the depth of the crippling recession that plagued the final years of the Mulroney government.

One explanation for the unanticipated rise in the value of the Canadian dollar held the Americans responsible. According to a widely circulated – and hotly denied – Ottawa rumour, U.S. negotiators had demanded and received a secret codicil to the FTA binding Canada to keep the Canadian dollar between 85 and 90 cents U.S. during the first three years of the treaty's implementation.[79] In fact, to understand this policy choice made by the Tories, one need look no further than the previously announced policy preferences and often stated ideological predispositions of the central economic thinkers in the Mulroney government. Precisely the same logic the Conservatives had deployed to argue against Liberal devaluations in the late 1970s and the early 1980s was methodically and stubbornly applied to the economic situation they faced a decade later.

As Finance Minister in the 1979 Clark government, John Crosbie allowed that while a dollar devalued at that point to about 85 cents U.S. had stimulated Canada's exports, this did not offset the negative economic effects of the inflationary cost of imports of capital goods and food from the U.S.[80] Prior to the 1979 election and again just before his government fell at the end of that year, Joe Clark suggested that the "appropriate

range for the value of the Canadian dollar" was 88 to 92 cents.[81] Crosbie
later confirmed the Tory preference for this somewhat higher level for the
Canadian dollar, enshrining it in the venerable context of the policy legacy
of John Diefenbaker.

> Instead of a weakening Canadian dollar, with the resources this
> country has, the Canadian dollar should be a burgeoning dollar. If
> we had economic sanity and economic sound policies we would have
> a burgeoning dollar. It would not be worth only 83 cents or 84 cents,
> it would be back to the level of the old "Diefendollar" the 92.5-cent
> dollar. . . . The "Diefendollar" at 92.5 cents looks pretty good to
> Canadians today.[82]

It was Michael Wilson who articulated most clearly the logic of the
Conservatives on the dollar during the early 1980s. Wilson held steadfastly
against what he believed to be the soft, government interventionist option
of devaluation because it could offer nothing more than a temporary and
inflationary respite from the country's problems with its international
competitiveness. Much better, in his view, would be the application of a
strong dose of market reality that in time would get the economic fundamentals in order and thereby provide for a more permanent corrective
remedy. Countries with strong economies had low inflation and strong
currencies. "Those countries which have strong currencies have lower
interest rates," Wilson argued. "If we have a strong Canadian dollar, we
will have lower inflation. Every economist will agree on that."[83]

Following the analytical string of monetarist economic orthodoxy, Wilson claimed that currency devaluations put a national economy on an
inflationary treadmill. Subsequent to a currency devaluation, inflation
results from more expensive imports, from overheating the economy with
export demand, and from rising wage demands from workers trying to
take advantage of the export boom or to recapture a portion of their living
standard that they had lost to the devaluation. In time, devaluation-
induced inflation would erode any competitive advantage gained from the
initial devaluation and create built-in demands for yet another round of
devaluation. Wilson articulated this view in 1982.

> Some people have said let the dollar drop. Some people have said let
> the dollar go and do not worry about the inflationary aspects of doing
> that. I say that is the wrong way to go. That is the easy way out. It
> might shield us from those problems for one or two years, but then
> we will be back to where we started unless we introduce fundamental
> policies that will get us back on the rails again. . . . We should intro-
> duce some policies to restore the level of confidence in the country
> that will encourage Canadians and foreigners to bring back that

money which they took out over the past year or year and a half. We can then revive our dollar, giving us the flexibility to drop interest rates to the level they should be.[84]

The problem of international competitiveness, then, could best be addressed by attracting new foreign investment. In Trudeau's Canada of the early 1980s, the confidence of foreign investors could only be boosted by cutting back on inflationary government spending, introducing investment incentives for the private sector, and, above all, scrapping the NEP and FIRA, Wilson surmised.[85]

In spite of his assuming the post of Finance Minister, it would have been very awkward for Wilson to follow through immediately after the Conservative's 1984 election victory on his ideas about strengthening the value of the Canadian dollar. He had been politically sandbagged on this issue by his Prime Minister prior to the election. When asked for his preference between a lower dollar and higher interest rates, Mulroney said he would allow the dollar to drop.[86] Within days, John Crosbie was faced with the embarrassing task of reversing Tory policy on the dollar in the Commons by asserting that "in the present situation, the only possible alternatives are to have a lower Canadian dollar or higher interest rates. We opt for a lower Canadian dollar, and not higher interest rates which will ruin economic growth in this country."[87]

The Mulroney government did allow the dollar to continue to fall during 1985 and 1986. From that point the dollar began its gradual ascent, first reaching 80 cents U.S. in early 1988. At that juncture, Wilson claimed an early victory for Tory economic policies and restated his 1982 argument that strong economies possessed strong currencies:

the strength in the Canadian dollar will be a reflection of the strength of the Canadian economy. . . . We have introduced a number of measures over the last three and a half years that are improving [Canada's] competitive position. It is one of the key reasons why we have seen the strength in the Canadian dollar.[88]

With the dollar trading around 86 cents U.S. in December of 1989, and under severe attack from his critics, Wilson again reached back to the ideas he first articulated in the early 1980s. The Canadian economy, running "at full capacity" since 1986, was overheating, he declared. Canada was in danger of climbing on the same inflationary treadmill experienced during the final Trudeau years.

We have seen the effects of this in price inflation, in wage inflation, and we are seeing it in monetary aggregates. The bank loans are growing at 12 per cent per annum. . . . These are all signs that this country's economy must slow down some. If it does not slow down, if we do not see a control of inflation, we are going to get back to the 13 per cent inflation rate we had back in 1981.[89]

Inflationary pressures were once more increasing Canadian unit labour costs in manufacturing relative to American unit labour costs, thereby "seriously eroding our ability to compete internationally."

> Since the fourth quarter of 1986, manufacturing unit labour costs have climbed almost 10% relative to labour costs in the United States and Germany and about 20% relative to Japanese labour costs. The pressures have been building rapidly. The rate of increase in Canada's unit labour cost has doubled in the past two years. Remember that these underlying labour costs . . . account for 60% of total business costs.

Relatively lower returns to labour had been key to Canada's maintaining a respectable regional share of North American manufacturing in the context of continental rationalization. Wilson's analysis of wage levels and Canada's competitive position reflected this underlying structural reality. As he understood it:

> Above all, we must all fight inflation by reducing underlying cost pressures that push up prices. The greatest of these pressures by far is wage costs. There has never been a sustained reduction in Canadian inflation in the absence of moderation in wage cost growth.

But Wilson, as we already know, had already forcefully placed himself on the record in opposition to the Trudeau Liberal policy of fixing the price of Canadian labour relative to American labour with a cheap dollar. And so, with his more orthodox approach, wage inflation would have to be squeezed out of the economy through monetary and fiscal means. Higher interest rates and a stronger dollar would "moderate the pace of demand" in the economy – bring market discipline through an economic downturn. More workers chasing fewer jobs would mean less wage inflation. On this basis alone, Wilson judged, could Canadian competitiveness be more permanently guaranteed. Before interest rates or the dollar could be lowered, "we have to see the underlying cost pressures in the economy turning down. If we do not see those turning down, we are just going to be feeding the problem and making it far more serious . . . ." Economic symptoms had to be separated from economic causes, Wilson reasoned.

> For a number of months many people have been saying the problem is high interest rates and a high Canadian dollar. Those are the symptoms of the problem. The causes of the problem are the

underlying competitive pressures. The more people can change their focus from the symptoms to the cause, the closer we can come to a resolution of the problem. . . .[90]

Wilson's monetarist orthodoxy here cut very little ice with business and business economists. They began from the simple calculation that the higher the value of the dollar, the lower the ability of Canadian manufacturers to compete effectively in the North American market. Profits and production were both being ravaged, they complained. Business had backed the Conservative campaign to ratify the FTA, never thinking that the dollar might subsequently be radically appreciated by their partisan allies.[91] The Tories were flirting with an economic crisis. In the early formative years of the FTA, Canada was losing ground, perhaps permanently, as a preferred North American production site. Corporate Canada complained that for the sake of an economic theory prescribing high interest rates and a high dollar, the locational advantages gained by Canada through past currency devaluations had been voluntarily surrendered. To illustrate, R. Phillips, president of IPSCO, opined that "it's shot the hell out of the manufacturing economy of Canada. Just look around in Southern Ontario at the closed plants." R. Le Hir, general director of the Association of Quebec Manufacturers, declared that "our country is going down the drain."[92]

Witness after witness appearing before Commons committees in 1990 insisted that the appropriate value for Canada's dollar was at or below 80 cents U.S. For example, Carl Beigie, chief economist at McLean, McCarthy, fixed the "purchasing power parity" of our dollar at 78 cents U.S. Wilson's strict monetarism had put the policy cart before the productivity horse in a way that threatened the future growth and even viability of Canadian manufacturing, Beigie contended.

> I would love to see Canada build up, as in my judgement the Free Trade Agreement . . . will do – Canada's relative productivity performance. Then we can justify a high value for the Canadian dollar. But by putting the dollar up before we can hopefully get the productivity up, for one reason because we do not get the capital investment because the interest rates are too high, what we are essentially doing is encouraging a lot of decisions to potentially close down Canadian operations because at current exchange rates it is too expensive to operate them, or not to expand Canadian operations until such time as the currency comes to a more appropriate level. The timing on that could be quite long, and I think this is not being given serious enough attention in this country.[93]

L. Thibault, president of the Canadian Manufacturers' Association, counselled a "75¢ to 80¢ range" for the dollar. Tory fiscal policy, said Thibault, could be compared to driving a car with one foot on the gas and the other on the brake. He, too, predicted a bleak future for Canadian plant locations because of the Tory currency revaluation. Most CMA members had calculated that U.S. locales were now lower cost than Canadian sites.

> We recently did a survey of our members and found that about half of the companies responding have carefully compared the overall cost and tax levels in Canada relative to the United States. Of those companies that did the comparison, 75% report that U.S. costs, in their views, of manufacturing are lower than those in Canada. Now if this situation is allowed to continue, we are in danger of permanently undermining our ability to be able to produce in Canada.[94]

L.J. Taylor, president of the Canadian Exporters' Association, favoured a Canadian dollar valued between 78 cents and 80 cents U.S. A dollar above 86 cents U.S. acted as a "self-imposed tariff of at least 10% on our sales in the United States and as much as 15% on our sales elsewhere around the world."[95] Fully 80 per cent of Canadian Exporters' Association members surveyed in 1990 reported that the appreciation of the Canadian dollar had hurt their exports. Over one-half said that the harm was "serious" or "very serious" and that they had lost exports over the previous year as a result.[96] Taylor warned the Commons committee that "once markets are lost it is very difficult if not impossible to regain them. Exports have been stagnant for well over a year, so the problem is becoming serious, even disastrous in its impact."[97]

Many business leaders caustically pointed to the negative relationship between the upward revaluation of the Canadian dollar and the FTA. For example, R. Woodbridge, president of the Canadian Advanced Technology Association, explained that while pre-FTA tariffs were an inconsequential barrier to Canadian firms selling in the American market, the appreciated Canadian dollar was a major headache.

> ... the high-tech sector got, out of the Free Trade Agreement ... primarily a reduction of U.S. tariff rates that ranged between 4% and 7% on about one-quarter of the products we exported into the U.S. Since the free trade agreement has come into being we have replaced that little tariff barrier, which was not really trade diverting at all, with a 14% to 17% tariff of our own making in the [appreciation] of the Canadian dollar. So essentially what is happening is that we are

managing the national economy in a way that negates the benefit of the Free Trade Agreement.[98]

P. Koenderman, president and chief executive officer of Babcock and Wilcox Canada, explained how his branch plant's support for the FTA had blown up as a direct result of the Tory revaluation of the Canadian dollar. His remarks reflect what many other business people were experiencing and thinking in the economically depressed waning years of Progressive Conservative government.

> During the days of the free trade debate in Canada we were very enthusiastic supporters of such an agreement. We were, within our corporation within North America, the low-cost producer, and compared to our U.S. sister manufacturing organizations we stood to benefit greatly from a free trade agreement in that more work would be shifted to Canada. . . .
>
> Given the appreciation of the Canadian dollar relative to the U.S. and other currencies, the situation today is very much different, in that within our company we are now the high-cost producer within North America and we are struggling to remain competitive. It is a very, very serious situation. We are virtually cut off from work that we would get from our parent company in the U.S. . . . within our corporation we are sensing a great loss in Canada as a good place to do business and make major investments. This perception, rightly or wrongly, has a very significant effect on day-to-day decisions, and causes steady erosion of our support in terms of future business prospects. I do not think we would be much unlike similar companies structured the same way we are.[99]

Conclusion

The contemporary period of global economic restructuring, with its origins in the 1960s and gathering real momentum during the 1970s and 1980s, provoked a dramatic upheaval in Canadian manufacturing. Two rival industrial strategies, centred in the nationalist and continentalist schools, provided the logical context for the policy choices that were made by Canada's economic and political elites during this era. This chapter records that from the beginning the continentalists were dominant. Although the nationalists did have some fleeting policy victories, they never managed to transcend their association with notions of state interventionism and economic protectionism. This inability put them out of step with the renovations taking place in the increasingly liberalized international economic environment and isolated them from Canada's dominant economic decision-makers.

The primacy of the continentalist position was reflected in the incremental evolution of a reformist Liberal industrial policy under the Pearson and Trudeau governments. This industrial policy of continental rationalization sought to overhaul Canadian branch-plant manufacturing so as to maintain Canada's established regional share within continental manufacturing. It developed along two fronts. Tariff liberalization under the Auto Pact and the GATT was meant to lengthen Canadian production lines by gaining access to American markets and so bring them closer to international standards of competitiveness. Dollar devaluation was meant to ease the transition between ISI tariff protectionism and GATT tariff liberalization and to provide a continuing rationale for investment in relatively low-wage Canadian manufacturing locales.

Although the Mulroney Conservatives fancied themselves as great economic policy innovators, their emblematic 1987 Canada-U.S. Free Trade Agreement simply built upon the already imposing liberalized trade edifice constructed by the Liberals under the Auto Pact and the GATT. Recognizing the writing on the wall of the world economy for the traditional branch-plant production regime, the historically protectionist Canadian manufacturing class had been adjusting to continental rationalization for a decade or more before the signing of the FTA and numbered themselves among the FTA's principal champions. However, continental rationalization has not led to the creation of a world-competitive Canadian manufacturing sector because continental production has been reshuffled rather than transformed. Overall, the Canadian industrial production system continues to be technologically debilitated and administratively truncated to fulfil goals established by American head offices. The persisting fundamental weaknesses within Canadian manufacturing were strikingly illuminated by the economic chaos resulting from the ideologically driven decision of the Tories to revalue the Canadian dollar upwards between 1987 and 1992.

Chapter Eight

Conclusion: NAFTA and Beyond

Business and the Mulroney government never reconciled their sharp differences over the dollar. Their public squabble over its value did not subside until the dollar, likely dancing in no small measure to the rhythm of the federal electoral cycle, began in late 1992 a steep descent to well below 80 cents U.S. Business and the Conservatives were able, nevertheless, to patch up their currency quarrel long enough to present a united front favouring the extension of the FTA to include Mexico – the North American Free Trade Agreement.[1] A survey of CMA members during 1990 showed that an overwhelming 88 per cent favoured Canadian participation in the NAFTA negotiations.[2]

As had been the case with the Canada-U.S. Free Trade Agreement, many of NAFTA's tariff issues were themselves of little immediate practical consequence. During the 1980s, Mexico had abandoned its highly nationalist investment and trade policies, revitalized its *maquiladoras* free trade zones, loosened its restrictive foreign investment regulations, and signed the GATT.[3] By the end of that decade, and as a result of these reforms, Canadian (and U.S.) markets were already very open to Mexican manufacturers. As CMA President L. Thibault explained, Canadian "manufacturers . . . see Mexico obviously as a competitor, but you know they are [in the Canadian market] now. There is nothing preventing Mexican products basically from coming into Canada now. The tariff levels are relatively insignificant."[4] In spite of this open access, Mexico and Canada, sharing an economic centre of gravity in the United States, played only peripheral roles in each other's markets. Like Canada, most of Mexico's trade in manufactures is in the form of intra-corporate transfers between U.S. parent firms and their subsidiaries.[5] And so, in 1990, Mexico was the destination of less than half a per cent of Canadian exports and the source of somewhat over 1 per cent of Canadian imports.[6] Thomas d'Aquino, president of the Business Council on National Issues, explained that the greatest challenge posed by Mexico to Canadian manufacturers was not actually within the Canadian market itself but came from

> ... the increased competitiveness of Mexican-produced goods in the United States market. Mexico's strengthened competitive position will increase the pressure on the number of Canadian manufacturing industries that sell heavily in the United States. But it is important to recognize that Canadian manufacturers and exporters will face greater competition with or without a NAFTA.[7]

If Mexican trade was piddling to Canada, and trade was anyway relatively open under the GATT, what can account for the clamorous championing of NAFTA by Canadian business? There were some immediate economic concerns and objectives. These were most frequently addressed through the "hub and spoke" analogy, where fears were raised that the U.S. would become a directing hub connected through many separate free trade deals to subordinate national spokes like Canada and Mexico. This kind of arrangement, it was argued, would have a strongly detrimental impact on Canada as a preferred location site within North American manufacturing. Gerald Regan, former Trudeau Minister of International Trade, explained how the hub and spoke would work against Canadian plant locations.

> The point is if a company in Germany were intending to service the entire North American market from a plant on this continent, and the United States had free access for product manufactured in that country, but Canada had it only with the United States, it would be one more argument in favour of siting your plant in the U.S. rather than in Canada.[8]

Corporate leaders also believed that there would be strategic advantages to the FTA industries in transferring some of their labour-intensive production to a low-wage Third World country like Mexico rather than to a NIC. This was because the FTA capital controlled, and would therefore directly benefit from, most of the backward and forward economic linkages within an expanding Mexican industrial structure, while a NIC had the potential to grow into an economic competitor. The CMA's Thibault set out clearly the logic of this position:

> ... if we are going to have to rationalize production with highly labour-intensive kinds of activities that cannot be sustained in our high cost environment, it makes a lot more sense for these activities to go on in Mexico than in Taiwan or South Korea, because one of the interesting aspects of Mexico is that 75% of their imports are from North America. So to the extent that they prosper and grow,

the feedback to the American and Canadian industrial economies is much, much greater, and so the system starts to benefit from that integration.[9]   .

NAFTA was further viewed by Canadian business in the strategic light of matching the successful manufacturing model of the advanced industrial countries of the European Community. Through incorporating under their industrial leadership the labour and markets of less-developed and underdeveloped countries, the EC countries were jacking up their international competitiveness. In response, Thibault suggested, the FTA partners needed to project their own concept of "what we are trying to achieve over 10 years or 20 years" – a regional development "vision" capable of energizing North American economic growth in "the way the Europeans are doing with their own economy."

> Much as the Europeans find that the combination of factors they have with high-technology, highly developed economies like·Germany and France and so on, and the less developed economies in Southern Europe and, of course, eastern Europe now tacked on to that, which provides essentially undeveloped countries but with a tremendous skill and pool of labour, that combination of factors of production . . . is enormously exciting and powerful in terms of potential and future economic growth. When we do some thinking about it I think we will probably conclude that we can do something similar in North America.[10]

Finally, corporate Canada hoped that in signing on to NAFTA, this country might get one step closer to being able to repair the major hole left by the negotiators of the FTA. As previously discussed, because under the Free Trade Agreement the U.S. could still apply its anti-dumping and countervailing duty laws, Canadian producers remained vulnerable to American non-tariff barriers. And NAFTA delivered no substantial improvements on the unsatisfactory trade dispute mechanisms set out in Chapter 19 of the FTA. Nevertheless, since Canada was one of the NAFTA signatories, it was now in a position where it could continue to press for meaningful improvements to the trade regime. Membership has its privileges, business observed. This was precisely the point made by T. d'Aquino, speaking in 1992 for the influential Business Council on National Issues. "Trade agreements are not static things, written in stone, but dynamic things," he observed. "As one sees with the European Community, the Treaty of Rome, EFTA [European Free Trade Agreement], and many other agreements, they are constantly evolving." Perhaps not surprisingly, d'Aquino had a shopping list of specific improvements to

NAFTA that he wanted Canada to use its membership leverage to pursue. "Replacing existing national anti-dumping laws by a common set of competition anti-trust standards" and "some form of explicit subsidy code" were the featured items on this list.[11]

How did Canada's public debate over the ratification of NAFTA compare to the mid-1980s brawl over the Canada-U.S. agreement? In short, the positions of both sides in the FTA struggle, as discussed in the previous chapter, were more appropriate to the 1950s and 1960s than to the 1980s. In those earlier decades, Canadian industry was based on an import substitution that had successfully transferred northward a share of U.S. production which, although truncated, was roughly proportional to Canada's population. At that time it made sense to question whether Canadian branch-plant manufacturing was to be *deepened,* using a state-sponsored industrial strategy to pry an even better share of continental production from American capital, or *rationalized* along continental lines through instituting Canada-U.S. free trade. By the mid-1980s, the Auto Pact and the GATT process of tariff reduction had left Canadian production deeply committed to the latter strategy. No amount of puffing or panting by either side could alter that reality, and in the end the "debate" was more about the organization of political partisanship than economics.

The public debate over the terms of NAFTA, as it was defined in Canadian politics between 1989 and 1993, reprised before a fatigued and cynical public many of the hackneyed arguments first put forward during the FTA squabble. Both sides predictably claimed that Canada's post-FTA economic record confirmed the correctness of the arguments they had advanced during 1988.[12] The record presented here would suggest that both sides were simply compounding confusion. The modest statistical progress toward continental rationalization, which the Tories and corporate Canada trumpeted as "success," was merely the continuation of a long process that began with the Auto Pact and was further nurtured by the GATT. By the same token, the alarming de-industrialization of Canada's last few years can be laid in part at the door of the same GATT regime that FTA critics so often offer as a sainted alternative, but this recent de-industrialization was mostly due to the ideologically driven, idiosyncratic, monetary policy pursued by the Tories and the Bank of Canada between 1987 and 1992. The high-interest, high-dollar policy of this period destabilized one of the twin prongs of the post-World War Two Canadian industrial strategy of continental rationalization, the successor to tariff-induced import substitution. Continental rationalization, as has been documented here, had been predicated on a series of deep currency devaluations to make Canada a relatively low-wage production zone within certain key sectors of the American economy.

A new dimension was introduced in the debate over NAFTA, however, and it is well worth our consideration. While the mid-1980s FTA debate was about institutionalizing the terms of incorporation of the Canadian region within the American economy, the 1990s NAFTA debate was centred on institutionalizing the terms of entry of a Third World social formation into a First World political economy. And, beyond Mexico, article 2204 of NAFTA provides for an accession clause under which other underdeveloped countries in Latin America can be admitted to the club.

As we recounted in Chapter 1, since its European colonization and the dispossession of the Native peoples on its territories, Canada has been organized as an economic (and cultural) region of the world hegemonic power and has, as a consequence, enjoyed a position near the top of the international hierarchy of wealth. The terms of the Canadian debate over NAFTA were consistent with the reproduction of this privileged position in the world economic order. It was in this frame that the Canadian NAFTA protagonists sought ways *to regulate* the entry of Mexican labour into our economy consistent with the interests of the Canadian social forces that animated them. Put crudely, capital's objective has been to constitute Mexico as sort of a low-wage Bantustan within the continental economy where labour can be annexed at Third World rates for specific parts of the continental production process. From the perspective of meeting the challenges posed by intensifying regional trading bloc competition, capital's strategy could actually be in the long-term interest of Canada-U.S. labour insofar as it might be able to protect their favoured geo-strategic position in the international political economy. However, organized labour's answer has been in the short term: either raise the return to Mexican labour to rates comparable to ours (an impossible condition) or abandon the project. In other words, employ regulatory mechanisms that will prevent FTA labour from having to compete directly with Mexicans. Bob White, president of the Canadian Labour Congress, delivered labour's uncompromising position on this issue to a House of Commons committee in early 1993:

> NAFTA will lock us into a completely integrated economic space with Mexico, which has extremely low wages, extremely low labour, social and environmental standards compared to Canada, and, indeed, to the United States. . . . the fundamental purpose of the agreement is to allow. . . . mainly U.S.-based transnational corporations to pursue an international competitiveness strategy based upon low wages, denial of labour and democratic rights, and disregard for environmental standards. . . . the inclusion of Mexico in the FTA would further increase pressures upon Canadians to accept

lower wages, to accept lower environmental standards, and to accept even more cuts to public and social services. [13]

Through this debate between labour and capital over NAFTA, we return again to the theme of choices between industrial policies. As we look toward the last years of this century, the industrial performance ledger shows clearly that many of the "fundamental adjustments" needed to address the "chronic" problems of Canadian manufacturing talked about in bureaucratic Ottawa since World War Two have still to be made. [14] Yet, in spite of the need, there seems to be nothing currently better on offer for Canada's industrial policy choices than capital's neo-liberal NAFTA project and labour's "hunker down" isolationist vision of full employment social democracy. While labour longs for a world of national economies superintended by interventionist states that simply does not exist for Canadians any more, the NAFTA genie in reality is capital's Frankenstein monster stumbling about without a social or political conscience. We have just seen that Canadian business has a wish list of specific future improvements to NAFTA. Political progressives would do well to adjust to current realities and map out their own alternative policy directions *within* the existing NAFTA framework. There is certainly a very large unsatisfied bloc in the electorate that might be attracted to a plan for imaginative improvements to the economic status quo. According to a 1993 Gallup Poll, three-fifths of Canadians were against the ratification of NAFTA, and, remarkably, considering the short memory of electorates on most issues, a plurality of Canadians still remained opposed to the FTA. [15]

With these factors in mind, let us list briefly those progressive features nascent in the evolving European Community model that might be grafted onto the existing base of NAFTA. In general, a "Community of the Americas" could provide for mechanisms to promote not just the economic growth of its members but also the social and political development of all the peoples of the Americas. At the heart of such a Community could be a social and environmental charter advancing for its residents a comprehensive package of minimum standards for wages and working conditions, labour organizational rights, human rights, and environmental protection. [16]

The framework for such a progressively oriented Community would need to be organized around an extensive program of political democratization. This would involve the forging of democratic supranational executive and legislative institutions with the power to develop and fully implement Community policies. Sustaining a Community executive council and elected parliament would be a permanent bureaucracy and an independent judiciary. The transfer of some degree of national sovereignty to Community institutions could act as at least a partial antidote to the techniques that both the FTA and NAFTA employ to weaken the ability of national states to control capital. Since capital has internationalized itself, so inevitably must the site of popular control of capital's activities become supranational if democracy is to be sustained.

Progressives could also work to add *persons* to the existing list of items – goods, services, and capital – that currently enjoy substantial freedom of movement under NAFTA. Only with the right to labour mobility can the tendency to create economic and political Bantustans be curbed. Mexican low-wage labour is *already* competing inside the FTA economy in the labour content of imported goods as well as in the human forms of millions of legal and illegal migrant workers. A 1992 study by the U.S. National Commission for Employment Policy indicated that between four and five million legal and illegal Mexican workers will enter the American economy during the 1990s.[17] The right to labour mobility for these workers would create upward pressure on wage rates in Mexico and would permit Mexican migrants access to the benefits of unionization and state protection of their social rights in their employment in the northern economies.

Finally, the pursuit of aggressive regional development strategies could also be high on the agenda of progressives for a Community of the Americas. With the objective of creating a better geographical spread of industrial activities and eliminating Third World poverty in the South, Community regional development funds could be used to restructure localities throughout the Americas. Special exemptions ancillary to the provisions of a Community-sanctioned regional development program might even allow disadvantaged regions in Mexico and Canada, for example, to recapture temporarily the ability to regulate United States capital that they have now surrendered under NAFTA.

Notes

~~~~~~

CHAPTER 1

1. Computed from Statistics Canada, *Historical Labour Force Statistics*, 1992 (Ottawa: Supply and Services, February, 1993), p. 158; and OECD, *Indicators of Industrial Activity*, 1985 (Paris, 1985-1).

2. J. Britton and J. Gilmour, *The Weakest Link: A Technological Perspective on Canadian Industrial Development* (Ottawa: Science Council of Canada, Background Study No. 43, 1978), p. 26; *Planning Now for an Information Society: Tomorrow is too Late* (Ottawa: Science Council of Canada, Report No. 33, 1982), p. 56.

3. OECD, *Indicators of Industrial Activity*, 1993, 2 (Paris, 1993).

4. Statistics Canada, *Historical Labour Force Statistics*, 1992, p. 158.

5. *Globe and Mail*, August 26, 1993, p. A5.

6. *Globe and Mail*, June 22, 1993, p. B1.

7. Michael E. Porter, *Canada at the Crossroads: The Reality of a New Competitive Environment* (Ottawa: Business Council on National Issues and Minister of Supply and Services Canada, 1991), p. 4.

8. Economic Council of Canada, *A Joint Venture: The Economics of Constitutional Options*, Twenty-Eighth Annual Review (Ottawa: Supply and Services, 1991), p. 7.

9. Science Council of Canada, *Reaching for Tomorrow: Science and Technology Policy in Canada 1991* (Ottawa: Supply and Services, June, 1992), p. 30.

10. *Montreal Gazette*, November 29, 1991, p. D2.

11. Canadian Manufacturers' Association, *The Aggressive Economy: Daring to Compete* (Ottawa, June, 1989), p. ES-3.

12. Canada, House of Commons, Standing Committee on Industry, Science and Technology, Regional and Northern Development, *Canada Must Compete*, Second Report (Ottawa, December, 1990), p. 2.

13. K. Levitt, *Silent Surrender* (Toronto: Macmillan, 1970).

14. G. Williams, "Canada – The Case of the Wealthiest Colony," *This Magazine*, 10, 1 (1976); L. Panitch, "Dependency and Class in Canadian Political Economy," *Studies in Political Economy: A Socialist Review*, 6 (Autumn, 1981).

15. M. Clark-Jones, *A Staple State: Canadian Industrial Resources in Cold War* (Toronto: University of Toronto Press, 1987), p. 11.

16. Statistics Canada surveys cited in a submission by the Canadian Export Association to the Minister of Industry, Trade and Commerce, January 9, 1973, entitled "View of the Export Community on an Industrial Strategy for Canada," and included in *A Compendium of Business Viewpoints on National Industrial Strategy* (Toronto and Montreal: Canadian Manufacturers' Association and Canadian Chamber of Commerce, March, 1973), p. 111.

17. Computed from Statistics Canada, *The Daily*, April 29, 1992, p. 6. In 1988, 32 per cent of provincial goods were imported while 22 per cent came from other provinces.

18. Computed from Statistics Canada, *Exports, Merchandise Trade*, 1992. Over one-half of Quebec's U.S. exports go to Massachusetts, Vermont, and the six easternmost Great Lakes states. Over one-half of the prairie provinces' U.S. exports go to Montana, North Dakota, and the Great Lakes states, and just under one-half of B.C.'s U.S. exports go to the four Pacific coast states.

19. J. Brodie and J. Jenson, *Crisis, Challenge and Change: Party and Class in Canada Revisited* (Ottawa: Carleton University Press, 1988); K. Sueuchi, "Tariff Out of Politics: Political Economy of Tariff Policy in Canada, 1875-1935" (Ph.D. dissertation, Carleton University, 1992).

20. The term "accumulation process" used in this text more commonly goes under the label of "economic growth." As a concept, however, it has the advantage of being a more precise way of capturing what goes on when economic growth occurs. In the capitalist marketplace, firms do not simply become larger and more profitable, thereby adding to aggregate economic activity, or conversely, smaller or bankrupt, thereby subtracting from the aggregate. Rather, when looked at collectively, all this frantic activity tends toward the transformation of the process itself. This occurs because the competitive units must "accumulate" in order to survive. That is, they are forced to reinvest a substantial portion of the economic surplus produced by their workers in order to keep up with the new efficiencies and technological breakthroughs being made by other firms in the world economy. Thus the accumulation process denotes qualitative as well as simply quantitative change. See S. Amin, *Accumulation on a World Scale*, 2 vols. (New York: Monthly Review Press, 1974.)

21. Stubborn public resistance by Canadians to hysterical pressure by their elites was most recently demonstrated in the extinction of the Meech Lake and Charlottetown Accords.

22. Slater found that if we use 1913 as an index base year, international trade volume in manufactures rose from 54 in 1896 to 446 in 1965 while trade volume

in primary produce only rose from 62 to 271 in the corresponding period. See D.W. Slater, *World Trade and Economic Growth: Trends and Prospects with Applications to Canada* (Toronto: Private Planning Association of Canada, 1968), p. 8. Throughout the 1970s and the 1980s, the growth rate in the export volume of manufactures continued to rise faster than the growth rate of non-manufactured commodities. See United Nations Conference on Trade and Development, Secretariat, *Structural Adjustment in the World Economy* (UNCTAD/ITP/25), 9 March 1990, Table 6.

23. *Ibid.*, p. 14.

24. OECD, *Industrial Policy in OECD Countries,* Annual Review, 1992, pp. 152-56.

25. A.K. Cairncross, *Factors in Economic Development* (London: George Allen and Unwin, 1962), p. 237. P. Lamartine Yates estimates that "some dozen countries" provided nine-tenths of the manufactured exports between 1913 and 1953. Slater's data suggest that these ratios remained constant up to the mid-1960s. P. Lamartine Yates, *Forty Years of Foreign Trade* (London: George Allen and Unwin, 1959), pp. 174-75; Slater, *World Trade and Economic Growth,* p. 30.

26. GATT, *International Trade 90-91,* Volume II (Geneva, 1992), Table IV.31, p. 52.

27. OECD, *The Newly Industrializing Countries: Challenge and Opportunity for OECD Industries* (Paris, 1988), p. 18.

28. R. Jones, "Developments in Trade between the OECD and the Dynamic Asian Economies," in *Economic Integration: OECD Economies, Dynamic Asian Economies and Central and Eastern European Countries* (Paris: OECD, 1993), Table 1, p. 21. For a useful short review of the historical development of the NICs and the limits of this pattern of development for the periphery of the world economy, see M. Castells and L. Tyson, "High Technology and the Changing International Division of Production: Implications for the U.S. Economy," in R. Purcell, ed., *The Newly Industrializing Countries in the World Economy: Challenges for U.S. Policy* (Boulder, Colorado: Lynne Rienner, 1989).

29. A. Maizels, *Industrial Growth and World Trade* (Cambridge: Cambridge University Press, 1963), pp. 158, 60-65. Maizels divided manufactured goods into finished manufactures and intermediate products that must undergo further processing. He argued that "a much more accurate picture of the incidence of industrialization can be obtained by excluding these intermediate products from the definition of exports of manufactures." A large proportion of Canada's exports have traditionally been of intermediate or semi-manufacture (e.g., metals, pulp and paper). For further clarification, see *ibid.*, Appendix D.

30. *Ibid.*, pp. 57-62.

31. Computed from Statistics Canada, *Canada's Balance of International Payments,* various years.

32. Computed from Statistics Canada, *Summary of Canadian International Trade*, various years.
33. OECD, *Labour Force Statistics, 1970-1990* (Paris, 1992). In 1990, 15.9 per cent of Canada's total civilian employment was in the manufacturing sector. In Germany, this percentage was 31.5; in Great Britain, 29.0; in Japan, 24.1; in France, 21.3; in Sweden, 21.1; and in the United States, 18.0.

CHAPTER 2

1. While it would be difficult to isolate the tariff as the only or even the principal cause of early Canadian industrial growth, it clearly played a central role. During the period following the proclamation of the National Policy tariffs of 1879, many small, inefficient enterprises either disappeared or were merged into more productive units. As a consequence, the total number of industrial establishments engaged in secondary production fell by approximately one-third between 1880 and 1929. Meanwhile, the total capital invested in secondary industry had increased, in relation to constant 1935-39 dollars, by three and a half times between 1890 and 1910 and had doubled again between 1910 and 1929. The decade 1900 to 1910 saw the highest rate of expansion of output in secondary industry before World War Two, featuring an average growth rate of 6.2 per cent per year. In summary, by the Great Depression, the basis for Canada's future as a modern industrialized nation had been secured. G.W. Bertram, "Historical Statistics on Growth and Structure of Manufacturing in Canada, 1870-1957," Canadian Political Science Association, Conference on Statistics 1962 and 1963, Tables 1 and 3; and Bertram, "Economic Growth in Canadian Industry, 1870-1915: The Staple Model," in W. Easterbrook and M. Watkins, eds., *Approaches to Canadian Economic History* (Toronto: McClelland and Stewart, 1967), Table 2. For a celebration of this growth, see D.G. Creighton, *Canada's First Century* (Toronto: Macmillan, 1970). For a critical perspective, see J.H. Dales, "Protection, Immigration and Canadian Nationalism," in P. Russell, ed., *Nationalism in Canada* (Toronto: McGraw-Hill, 1966).
2. R.T. Naylor, *The History of Canadian Business, 1867-1914* (Toronto: Lorimer, 1975), I, p. 38. For a critique of some of the more important contemporary approaches, see G. Williams, "The National Policy Tariffs: Industrial Underdevelopment Through Import Substitution," *Canadian Journal of Political Science*, XII, 2 (June, 1979), pp. 333-39.
3. A. Gerschenkron, *Economic Backwardness in Historical Perspective* (Cambridge, Mass.: Harvard University Press, 1966), p. 354. For an application of Gerschenkron to Canada, see G. Laxer, *Open for Business: The Roots of Foreign Ownership in Canada* (Toronto: Oxford University Press, 1989).
4. Canada, *House of Commons Debates*, March 7, 1878, p. 861.
5. *Ibid.*, March 14, 1879, pp. 413-14.

6. S.D. Clark, *Canadian Manufacturers' Association* (Toronto: University of Toronto Press, 1939), pp. 6-7.

7. *Debates*, April 22, 1879, p. 1440.

8. *Ibid.*, p. 1417.

9. *Ibid.*, p. 1442.

10. *Ibid.*, p. 1426.

11. *Ibid.*, May 12, 1887, p. 400.

12. *Journal of Commerce – Finance and Insurance Review*, February 4, 1881, p. 792. Bliss argues that such business publications "were almost certainly faithful representatives of their readers' opinions. They were self-consciously published in the interests of their constituency. Unlike the general press, all their news and editorial columns were designed to appeal to readers in a specific occupation; circulation and advertising depended on the success of that appeal." M. Bliss, *A Living Profit: Studies in the Social History of Canadian Business, 1883-1911* (Toronto: McClelland and Stewart, 1974), p. 145.

13. H.J. Morgan, *Canadian Men and Women of the Time, 1898* (Toronto: Briggs, 1898), p. 769, recorded that this journal, originally published by F. Nicholls, president of Canadian General Electric, was "the official organ and spokesman of the manufacturing interests."

14. *Canadian Manufacturer*, August 24, 1883, p. 605.

15. *Ibid.*, pp. 606-07.

16. *Ibid.*, January 2, 1885, p. 866.

17. *Journal of Commerce*, March 11, 1881, p. 111.

18. *Ibid.*, May 25, 1883, p. 1305.

19. *Ibid.*, July 26, 1889, pp. 151-52.

20. *Canadian Manufacturer*, August 15, 1890, p. 119.

21. *Ibid.*, June 3, 1892, pp. 324-25.

22. Opposition was by no means universal in this industry. Canada, House of Commons, *Journals*, 1874, Appendix 3, Report of the Select Committee on Manufacturing Interests, pp. 40, 57.

23. *Ibid.*, 1876, Appendix 3, Report of the Select Committee on the Causes of the Present Depression, p. 128.

24. *Ibid.*, p. 127.

25. *Ibid.*, p. 123.

26. *Canadian Manufacturer*, October 5, 1894, pp. 338-39.

27. *Ibid.*, July 19, 1895, pp. 55-56.

28. *Ibid.*, July 21, 1893, p. 49.

29. *Ibid.*, November 15, 1901, p. 13.

30. This is based on an estimate of the value of U.S. branch plants in Canada in 1913 of $135 million presented in F.W. Field, *Capital Investments in Canada*, third edition (Toronto: Monetary Times, 1914), p. 25, and the total value of capital invested in Canadian industries in 1910 of $1,248 million presented in *Census of Canada*, 1911, vol. 3. If other U.S. industrial investments reported

by Field of $90 million were included, total ownership share would increase to somewhere between 16 and 18 per cent.

31. E.J. Penrose, *The Economics of the International Patent System* (Baltimore: Johns Hopkins University Press, 1951), Chapters 1, 3.

32. *Debates,* June 4, 1869, pp. 619-23.

33. Computed from Naylor, *History of Canadian Business,* II, p. 46, Table X(1).

34. R.T. Naylor exhaustively documents many of the most significant licensing agreements of this period in *History of Canadian Business,* II, Chapter 10.

35. *Canadian Manufacturer,* December 7, 1894, p. 543.

36. *Ibid.,* January 15, 1892, p. 38.

37. M. Wilkins, *The Emergence of Multinational Enterprise: American Business Abroad from the Colonial Era to 1914* (Cambridge, Mass.: Harvard University Press, 1970), p. 95. Canadian General Electric was organized in 1892 with a majority of shares held by the parent U.S. company. Ownership passed to the Canadian shareholders in 1895 primarily because of a capital shortage in the U.S. firm. However, production in Canada was organized by means of patent and licence agreements with the U.S. firm until 1923, when American General Electric repurchased a majority interest. H. Marshall, F. Southard, and K. Taylor, *Canadian-American Industry: A Study in International Investment* (Toronto: McClelland and Stewart, 1976), pp. 72-73.

38. Computed from K. Buckley, *Capital Formation in Canada, 1896-1930* (Toronto: University of Toronto Press, 1955), pp. 130-31.

39. Computed from Canada, House of Commons, *Sessional Papers,* Trade of Canada, 1886-1915.

40. U.S., 58th Congress, Third Session, *Monthly Consular and Trade Reports,* Document 338, No. 302, November, 1905, pp. 24-25.

41. *Industrial Canada,* March, 1908, p. 619.

42. Naylor, *History of Canadian Business,* 11, p. 59.

43. *Industrial Canada,* June, 1905, pp. 717-18.

44. *Ibid.*

45. *Monetary Times,* November 5, 1926, p. 6.

46. E.J. Hobsbawm, *Industry and Empire* (Harmondsworth: Penguin Books, 1968), p. 174.

47. All the companies listed as "growth industry" U.S. branch plants may be found in Field, *Capital Investments,* pp. 39-52; and Marshall *et al., Canadian-American Industry,* Chapter 2.

48. Computed from A.K. Cairncross, *Home and Foreign Investment, 1870-1913* (Cambridge: Cambridge University Press, 1953), p. 185; and *Statesmen's Year Book,* 1913 (London: Macmillan, 1913), pp. 107, 123, 242.

49. Computed from Buckley, *Capital Formation in Canada,* pp. 22, 132, 135. Rail investment in the U.S. during this same period was only 7 or 8 per cent of total gross investment and had only been between 16 and 20 per cent during the peak construction era of the 1870s and 1880s. H.G. Vatter, *The Drive to*

Industrial Maturity, The U.S. Economy, 1860-1914 (Westport, Conn.: Green-wood Press, 1975), pp. 158-60.

50. India is perhaps the classic case. See P. Baran, *The Political Economy of Growth* (New York: Monthly Review, 1957), pp. 144-50.

51. *Sessional Papers,* 1916, No. 6, pp. 20-21.

52. F.H. Underhill, *The Image of Confederation* (Toronto: Canadian Broadcasting Corporation, 1964), p. 22.

53. Great Britain, *Parliamentary Debates,* March 20, 1879, p. 1312; *The Times,* March 19, 1879, p. 11.

54. S.B. Ryerson, *Unequal Union* (Toronto: Progress, 1968), p. 236.

55. Great Britain, House of Commons, *Papers,* "Correspondence Respecting the Canadian Tariff," August, 1887, No. C-5179, p. 4.

56. D. Farr, *The Colonial Office and Canada, 1867-1887* (Toronto: University of Toronto Press, 1955), p. 193.

57. Great Britain, House of Commons, *Papers,* "Correspondence between the Colonial Office and the Authorities in Canada, on the subject of the Removal or Reduction of the Duties charged on British Goods entering Canada," June 17, 1864, No. 400, p. 12.

58. *Ibid.*

59. *Ibid.,* "Dispatch from the Governor General of Canada respecting the New Customs Tariffs," April, 1879, No. C-2305, p. 19.

60. *Ibid.,* 1887, No. C-5179, pp. 39-40.

61. See C. Berger, *The Sense of Power* (Toronto: University of Toronto Press, 1970); D. Bell and L. Tepperman, *The Roots of Disunity* (Toronto: McClelland and Stewart, 1979), Chapters 2, 3.

62. Hobsbawm, *Industry and Empire,* p. 191; S.B. Saul, *Studies in British Overseas Trade, 1870-1914* (Liverpool: Liverpool University Press, 1960), p. 220.

63. G.A. Montgomery, *The Rise of Modern Industry in Sweden* (London: King and Son, 1939), p. 104.

64. J. Kuuse, "Foreign Trade and the Breakthrough of the Engineering Industry in Sweden, 1890-1920," *Scandinavian Economic History Review,* XXV, 1 (1977), p. 1.

65. In Canada, some have alleged that industrialization was inhibited by a form of species hostility toward manufacturers on the part of the merchants and financiers who organized Canadian resource capitalism. The Swedish experience directly contradicts this thesis, at least as it can be found in the work of R.T. Naylor in his "The rise and fall of the third commercial empire of the St. Lawrence," in G. Teeple, ed., *Capitalism and the National Question in Canada* (Toronto: University of Toronto Press, 1972).

66. L. Jorberg, "Structural Change and Economic Growth in Nineteenth Century Sweden," in S. Koblik, ed., *Sweden's Development from Poverty to Affluence, 1750-1950* (Minneapolis: University of Minnesota Press, 1975), p. 110. See also Kuuse, "Breakthrough of the Engineering Industry in Sweden," p. 7.

For the role of merchants and financiers in Japanese industrialization, see J. Hirschmeier, "Shibusawa Eiichi: Industrial Pioneer," and Yasuzo Horie, "Entrepreneurship in Meiji Japan," in W.W. Lockwood, ed., *The State and Economic Enterprise in Japan* (Princeton, N.J.: Princeton University Press, 1965).

67. Kuuse, "Breakthrough of the Engineering Industry in Sweden," pp. 5-6.
68. *Industrial Canada*, June, 1905, pp. 717-18.
69. United Nations, UNCTAD Secretariat, *Case Studies in the Transfer of Technology: Policies for transfer and development of technology in pre-war Japan (1868-1937)*, April 25, 1978, p. 16.
70. *Ibid.*, p. 34.
71. *Ibid.*, pp. 4-5.
72. W.W. Lockwood, *The Economic Development of Japan*, second edition (Princeton, N.J.: Princeton University Press, 1968), p. 381.
73. *Ibid.*, pp. 539-40.
74. *Ibid.*, pp. 345, 354, 365.

CHAPTER 3

1. For more on the institutional development of Trade and Commerce during this and later periods, see O.M. Hill, *Canada's Salesman to the World: The Department of Trade and Commerce, 1892-1939* (Montreal: McGill-Queen's University Press, 1977); G. Williams, "The Political Economy of Canadian Manufactured Exports: The Problem, its Origins, and the Department of Trade and Commerce, 1885-1930" (Ph.D. dissertation, York University, 1978), Chapters 3-5.
2. *Canadian Manufacturer*, January 2, 1885, p. 863; February 6, 1885, p. 937.
3. *Industrial Canada*, November, 1901, pp. 131-32. (Report of the Commercial Intelligence Committee to the Annual Convention of the Canadian Manufacturers' Association, November 5-6, 1901.)
4. *Ibid.*
5. National Archives of Canada (NAC), MG 28, I 230, vol. 36, nos. 154-163, July 16, 1907.
6. *Industrial Canada*, October, 1912, p. 373.
7. *Ibid.*, July, 1909, p. 1179.
8. *Ibid.*
9. *Ibid.*, July, 1903, p. 528.
10. *Ibid.*, July, 1907, p. 924.
11. *Monetary Times*, September 28, 1912, p. 492.
12. *Journal of Commerce*, December 15, 1893, p. 1144.
13. *Industrial Canada*, February, 1902, pp. 219-20.
14. *Ibid.*, November, 1903, pp. 209-11.

15. *Ibid.*, March, 1903, p. 363; April, 1904, p. 445; July, 1918, p. 146.
16. Canada, Trade and Commerce, *Weekly Report*, no. 293, September 7, 1909, p. 792.
17. *Ibid.*, no. 416, January 15, 1912, p. 41.
18. *Ibid.*, no. 181, July 15, 1907, pp. 371-72.
19. NAC, RG 20, vol. 1156, no. 5311, June 10, 1897.
20. *Weekly Report*, no. 19, June 6, 1904, pp. 3-4.
21. *Ibid.*, no. 377, April 18, 1911, p. 496.
22. *Ibid.*, no. 353, November 1, 1910.
23. *Ibid.*, no. 381, May 15, 1911.
24. *Ibid.*, no. 331, May 30, 1910, pp. 661-62.
25. *Ibid.*, no. 3, February 15, 1904, p. 12.
26. *Ibid.*, no. 266, March 1, 1909, p. 173.
27. *Ibid.*, no. 338, July 18, 1910, p. 857.
28. *Ibid.*, no. 17, May 23, 1904, p. 4.
29. *Journal of Commerce*, October 25, 1889, p. 718.
30. *Industrial Canada*, July, 1911, p. 1274.
31. *Weekly Report*, no. 252, November 23, 1908, p. 830.
32. *Ibid.*, no. 155, January 14, 1907, p. 31. For additional examples, see no. 122, May 28, 1906, p. 405; no. 128, July 9, 1906, p. 529; no. 541, June 8, 1914, p. 816.
33. *Ibid.*, no. 314, January 31, 1910, p. 136.
34. *Ibid.*, no. 432, May 6, 1912, pp. 417-18.
35. *Ibid.*, no. 336, July 4, 1910, p. 308.
36. *Ibid.*, no. 9, March 28, 1904, p. 11.
37. *Industrial Canada*, August, 1906, p. 33.
38. *Weekly Report*, no. 3, February 15, 1904, p. 23.
39. *Ibid.*, no. 139, September 24, 1906, p. 690.
40. *Ibid.*, no. 35, September 26, 1904, p. 13.
41. *Ibid.*, no. 242, September 14, 1908, p. 607.
42. *Ibid.*, no. 316, February 14, 1910, p. 192. See also no. 562, November 2, 1914, p. 1945. On this same subject, the *Monetary Times* pointed out that "the weekly reports of the Department of Trade and Commerce do not appear to receive the serious attention they deserve." (May 1, 1910, p. 1951.)
43. *Weekly Report*, no. 227, June 1, 1908, p. 331.
44. *Industrial Canada*, January, 1911, pp. 630-31.
45. NAC, RG 20, vol. 43, no. 18165, April 11, 1912.
46. *Canadian Manufacturer*, October 19, 1894, pp. 385-86.
47. *Monetary Times*, August 14, 1891, p. 193.
48. *Industrial Canada*, June, 1902, p. 381.
49. *Canadian Manufacturer*, November 2, 1894, p. 440.
50. The *Journal of Commerce* expressed this point elegantly. "Inter-colonial trade

or inter-imperial trade should develop equally with imperial sentiment, if it does not there is a screw loose somewhere in the machinery of the British Empire." (January 18, 1901, p. 148.)

51. *Industrial Canada,* September, 1902, p. 71.

52. *Ibid.,* October, 1907, p. 247. See also October, 1905, p. 151.

53. *Ibid.,* October, 1907, p. 283.

54. *Ibid.,* January, 1908, p. 498.

55. *Weekly Report,* no. 198, November 11, 1907, p. 639.

56. *Ibid.,* no. 113, March 26, 1906, p. 232.

57. *Ibid.,* no. 469, January 20, 1913, p. 37.

58. *Ibid.,* no. 542, June 15, 1914, p. 867.

CHAPTER 4

1. Williams, "The Political Economy of Canadian Manufactured Exports," Appendix I. Finished manufactures, the reader will recall from our discussion in Chapter 1, are products not normally subject to a further process of manufacture.

2. J.J. Deutsch, "War Finance and the Canadian Economy, 1914-20," *Canadian Journal of Economics and Political Science,* 6, 4 (November, 1940), p. 535.

3. *Debates,* January 22, 1917, p. 31; Deutsch, "War Finance."

4. Hill, *Canada's Salesman to the World,* p. 170; J.C. Hopkins, *Canada at War, 1914-1918* (Toronto: Canadian Annual Review, 1919), p. 66.

5. M. Bliss, in his biography of businessman J.W. Flavelle, chairman of the Imperial Munitions Board, recorded the Board's "impressive" achievement in pushing Canadian manufacturers "into reaching higher standards of precision and efficiency and a far higher volume of production than anyone had thought possible." *A Canadian Millionaire* (Toronto: Macmillan, 1978), p. 318.

6. R.G. Brown and R. Cook, *Canada 1896-1921: A Nation Transformed* (Toronto: McClelland and Stewart, 1974), pp. 198-200, 239-40.

7. NAC, MG 26 H, vol. 49, no. 22989, May 29, 1915.

8. *Ibid.,* no. 22986, May 27, 1915.

9. *Ibid.,* vol. 50, nos. 23150-23152, June 21, 1915.

10. *Ibid.,* nos. 23060-23062, June 11, 1915.

11. *Ibid.,* nos. 23075-23079, June 12, 1915.

12. *Ibid.,* no. 22998. See also no. 23096.

13. *Ibid.,* nos. 23142-23143, 23150-23152, June 21, 1915.

14. D. Carnegie, *History of the Munitions Supply in Canada* (London: Longmans, Green, 1925), p. 216. See also *ibid.,* pp. 14, 29, 33, 68, 72, 183, 215, 217; Bliss, *A Canadian Millionaire,* p. 239.

15. Bliss makes a similar point. "At best . . . Canada's manufacturing contribution to the war was primitive by British and American standards – Canadians

made ammunition; others made guns, tanks, and fighting aircraft. The long-term benefits of war industries to Canada in terms of new processes and methods were shared by other industrial countries, resulting in a treadmill situation and no comparative advantage." *A Canadian Millionaire*, p. 318.

16. Brown and Cook, *Canada 1896-1921*, p. 236.

17. NAC, MG 26 H, vol. 55, no. 27574, July 22, 1915.

18. *Ibid.*, nos. 27512-27518, June 11, 1915.

19. *Ibid.*, MG 27 II D 7, vol. 18, no. 1871, December 15, 1914.

20. *Ibid.*, MG 26 H, vol. 55, no. 27626, September 4, 1915.

21. J.W. Flavelle, before his appointment as chairman of the Imperial Munitions Board, wrote Borden: "I have frequently reminded my manufacturing friends that the orders which were secured for blankets, knitted goods, saddlery etc. during the early months of the war, originated solely with the Government, and that they, as manufacturers, showed little resource or capacity in finding business for themselves. . . . It occurs to me that where the manufacturing interests have failed, has been in organized effort in harmony with what was being done in Ottawa. . . ." NAC, MG 27 II D 7, vol. 18, no. 1984, June 25, 1915.

22. *Ibid.*, no. 27976, October 15, 1918.

23. *Ibid.*, vol. 19, no. 2550, April 12, 1916.

24. *Weekly Report*, no. 554, September 7, 1914, p. 1460.

25. *Industrial Canada*, July, 1915, pp. 331-32.

26. *Ibid.* For reasons well documented in Hill, *Canada's Salesman to the World*, pp. 211-20, this was to prove "an expensive and unproductive venture."

27. Canada, Trade and Commerce, *The German War and its Relation to Canadian Trade*, 1914. A sample of trade commissioner interest in replacing German goods in the Australian market can be found in *Weekly Report*, no. 564, November 16, 1914, p. 2087.

28. *Industrial Canada*, October, 1915, pp. 647-48; *Monetary Times*, February 23, 1917, p. 136; *Weekly Bulletin*, no. 641, May 8, 1916, p. 1020.

29. *Weekly Bulletin*, no. 638, April 17, 1916, p. 853.

30. *Ibid.*, no. 709, August 27, 1917, p. 443.

31. *Ibid.*, no. 669, November 16, 1916, p. 1177.

32. *Ibid.*, no. 832, January 12, 1920, pp. 93, 97.

33. *Ibid.*, no. 672, December 11, 1916.

34. *Ibid.*, no. 732, December 3, 1917, p. 1236.

35. *Industrial Canada*, July, 1918, p. 145.

36. *Weekly Bulletin*, no. 697, June 4, 1917, p. 1308; no. 641, May 8, 1916, pp. 1027-28.

37. *Industrial Canada*, August, 1916, p. 507.

38. *Ibid.*, April, 1918, p. 1754.

39. *Ibid.*, September, 1914, p. 164.

40. *Ibid.*, October, 1914, pp. 267-68.

41. *Ibid.*, March, 1916, p. 1171.
42. *Weekly Bulletin*, no. 633, March 13, 1916; no. 662, October 2, 1916, p. 769.
43. *Industrial Canada*, July, 1916, p. 384.
44. Canada, Senate, *Debates*, July 11, 1917, p. 226.
45. *Ibid.*, June 5, 1917, pp. 94, 97.
46. The Canadian Industrial Reconstruction Association included E.W. Beatty (Canadian Pacific Railway), T. Cantley (Nova Scotia Steel and Coal), H. Cockshutt (Cockshutt Plow), H.R. Drummond (Canada Sugar), R. Hobson (Steel Company of Canada), W. McMaster (Canadian Explosives), F. Nicholls (Canadian General Electric), and T.A. Russell (Willys Overland and Canada Cycle and Motor). For an examination of its domestic activities, see T. Traves, *The State and Enterprise: Canadian Manufacturers and the Federal Government, 1917-1931* (Toronto: University of Toronto Press, 1979).
47. "A National Policy," An Address delivered by Sir John Willison at Galt, Ontario, July 17, 1918, and published by the Canadian Industrial Reconstruction Association, pp. 6-9.
48. NAC, MG 26 H, vol. 93, nos. 48582-48585, November 7, 1918. Lloyd Harris, chairman of the London Mission, was, among other things: president of Russell Motor Car and of Canada Glue; vice-president of Canada Starch; and a director of the Steel Company of Canada. Sir Charles Gordon, chairman of the Ottawa Commission, was, among other things: president of Dominion Textiles, Penmans, and Dominion Glass; vice-president of the Bank of Montreal and Montreal Cotton; and a director of Royal Trust and Provincial Paper. B.M. Greene, ed., *Who's Who in Canada and Why* (Toronto: International Press, 1919-20), pp. 454, 351.
49. NAC, MG 26 H, vol. 93, no. 48606, November 15, 1918.
50. *Ibid.*, no. 48610, November 16, 1918.
51. *Ibid.*, RG 20, vol. 85, no. 22038, December 4, 1918.
52. *Ibid.*, MG 26 H, vol. 93, no. 48754, January 28, 1919.
53. *Ibid.*, no. 48622, November 26, 1918.
54. *Ibid.*, nos. 48951-48957, December 6, 1919.
55. *Industrial Canada*, July, 1919, p. 206.
56. NAC, MG 26 H, vol. 93, nos. 48951-48957, December 6, 1919.
57. *Ibid.*, no. 48885, April 14, 1919.
58. *Industrial Canada*, July, 1920, p. 157.
59. *Ibid.*, February, 1921, p. 126.
60. *Weekly Bulletin*, No. 838, February 23, 1920, p. 450.
61. *Ibid.*, no. 842, March 22, 1920, p. 651.
62. *Debates*, March 23, 1920, p. 621.
63. *Debates*, March 29, 1921, p. 1276.
64. *Industrial Canada*, November, 1922, p. 56.
65. Canada, Department of Marine and Fisheries, *Annual Report*, 1922-23, pp. 13-15.

CHAPTER 5

1. Examples of the following trade mispractices can be found in the *Commercial Intelligence Journal* of Trade and Commerce: failure to dispatch salesmen to foreign markets, no. 1263, April 14, 1928, p. 567; failure to send catalogues or samples, no. 1054, April 12, 1924, p. 467; refusal to quote foreign delivery prices, no. 997, March 10, 1923, p. 386; unwillingness to advertise, no. 1277, January 21, 1928, pp. 100-01; sloppy packing, no. 1045, February 9, 1924, p. 216. The department's 1924-25 *Annual Report* noted that "the most prolific source of complaint by Trade Commissioners on behalf of foreign business men is inattention by Canadian firms to correspondence" (p. 29).

2. *Industrial Canada*, July, 1916, p. 384.

3. NAC, MG 26 H, vol. 98, no. 52364, December 12, 1918.

4. *Industrial Canada*, March, 1922, pp. 53-54.

5. *Debates*, October 12, 1932, p. 119. For a descriptive account of the Imperial Conference, see Hill, *Canada's Salesman to the World*, Chapter 24.

6. *Monetary Times*, April 2, 1920, p. 15.

7. For example, *Industrial Canada*, July, 1918, p. 238; February, 1919, p. 79; September, 1920, p. 132; March, 1921, pp. 60-63; August, 1922, p. 81; June, 1923, p. 94; October, 1923, p. 78; March, 1927, p. 64.

8. Williams, "The Political Economy of Canadian Manufactured Exports," Appendix I.

9. *Debates*, April 13, 1923, pp. 1828-30. Robb's trade categories were so loosely defined that they had little meaning. "If we ship wheat that is a raw product. If we ship flour that is a manufactured product. If we ship milk that is a raw product. If we ship butter that is a manufactured product. If we ship pulpwood it is a raw product. If we ship paper it is a manufactured product. If we ship pulp it is partly manufactured." For further clarification, see Maizels, *Industrial Growth and World Trade*, Appendix D.

10. *Monetary Times*, April 6, 1928, p. 7.

11. *Debates*, February 11, 1929, p. 34.

12. *Debates*, June 1, 1931, p. 2164.

13. J. Laxer, "Lament for an Industry," *Last Post*, 2, 3 (December-January, 1971-1972), p. 34.

14. NAC, RG 20, vol. 95, no. 22693 F-1, October 21, 1922.

15. *Commercial Intelligence Journal*, no. 1354, January 11, 1930, p. 60. For automobiles, see no. 1291, October 27, 1928, p. 609.

16. NAC, RG 20, vol. 712, no. 4-U 2-32, February 8, 1947.

17. *Ibid.*, vol. 95, no. 22693 F-1, March 30, 1933.

18. *New York Times*, January 31, 1933.

19. M. Wilkins and F.E. Hill, *American Business Abroad: Ford on Six Continents* (Detroit: Wayne State University Press, 1964), pp. 18, 114-15, 130-31, 159.

20. *Debates*, May 21, 1926, p. 3672; February 21, 1927, p. 507.

21. *Ibid.*, May 21, 1926, p. 3644.
22. *Ibid.*, April 27, 1926, p. 2847.
23. *Ibid.*, May 21, 1926, p. 3655. G.H. Boivin, Minister of Customs, also stressed this point, pp. 3668-69.
24. C.H. Aikman, *National Problems of Canada: The Automobile Industry of Canada*, McGill University Economic Studies, No. 8. (Toronto: Macmillan, 1926), pp. 31, 40-41.
25. NAC, RG 20, vol. 124, no. 25007: C (1), March 26, 1934.
26. *Ibid.*, RG 2, 1, vol. 1778, no. 109, January 22, 1927; vol. 1818, T. 127996 B. April 19, 1929.
27. Canada, Advisory Board on Tariff and Taxation, Record of Public Sittings, Iron and Steel, vol. 3, Automobiles and their Parts, December 12, 1929; January 22, 23, 1930, p. 99.
28. Australia, House of Representatives, *Debates*, October 2, 1924, p. 5084.
29. Canadian automakers were disappointed that the content quotas were so high and that only certain parts had been included in the treaty, but they hoped for a future moderation in the regulations that would allow them preferential entry into the Australian market. T.A. Russell, president of Willys-Overland, wrote King: "I do not know that the Treaty at the present moment can be taken advantage of by any Canadian motor firm except the Ford Company, but we have all felt that it more or less prepared the way for the maintenance of preference within the Empire and were glad indeed to see a start made with Australia. Perhaps at some later date it may be possible to secure some further advantage, which would benefit the motor industry more directly." NAC, MG 26 J 1, vol. 123, no. 104625, July 17, 1925.
30. New Zealand, House of Representatives, *Debates*, September 30, 1924, p. 15.
31. NAC, MG 26 J 1, vol. 80, no. 67893, December 6, 1922.
32. *Ibid.*, no. 67895.
33. Australia, House of Representatives, *Debates*, October 2, 1924, p. 5073.
34. *Industrial Canada*, January, 1929, p. 222.
35. NAC, RG 20, vol. 162, no. 26725(3), July 23, 1932.
36. *Ibid.*, vol. 712, no. 4-U 2-40 A, January 27, 1950.
37. *Weekly Bulletin*, no. 858, July 12, 1920, pp. 70-71; no. 869, September 27, 1920, p. 890.
38. I.M. Drummond, *Imperial Economic Policy, 1917-1939* (London: George Allen and Unwin, 1974), pp. 33-36.
39. NAC, RG 20, vol. 162, no. 26725 (2) (3).
40. *Ibid.*, MG 26 J 1, vol. 104, no. 87927, January 15, 1924.
41. *Ibid.*, MG 26 E 1 (a), vol. 96, no. 7, February 1, 1894.
42. Australia, House of Representatives, *Debates*, August 27, 1925.
43. Union of South Africa, House of Assembly, *Debates*, July 1, 1925, pp. 5286-87.
44. Wilkins and Hill, *American Business Abroad*, p. 242. The trade commissioners recorded this decline. *Commercial Intelligence Journal*, no. 1152, February 17,

1926, p. 283 (South Africa); no. 1195, December 25, 1926, pp. 748-49 (New Zealand); no. 1225, July 23, 1927, p. 101 (Australia).

45. Sun Life Assurance Company of Canada, *The Canadian Automotive Industry,* prepared for the Royal Commission on Canada's Economic Prospects, September, 1956, p. 7.

46. J.V.T. Baker, *The New Zealand People at War: War Economy* (Christchurch: Whitcombe and Tombs, 1965), pp. 19-20; D.H. Houghton, *The South African Economy,* fourth edition (Cape Town: Oxford University Press, 1976), pp. 122-26; A.E. Safarian, *The Canadian Economy in the Great Depression* (Toronto: McClelland and Stewart, 1970), Table 50; A.G.L. Shaw, *The Economic Development of Australia,* seventh edition (Melbourne: Longman Cheshire, 1980), pp. 155-56.

47. *Debates,* February 21, 1927, p. 507.

48. NAC, RG 20, vol. 94, no. 22693: E, December 27, 1924, and January 5, 1925.

49. *Ibid.,* vol. 162, no. 26725 (2), October 13, 1930, October 21, 1930, and May 4, 1931.

50. *Debates,* March 13, 1928, p. 1262.

51. See Traves, *State and Enterprise,* Chapter 6. He observes: "the auto tariff revisions greatly appealed to King's imagination; at one stroke he increased jobs and reduced prices for the working man, he strengthened the Liberals' popular political base, and he furthered the Liberal-Progressive party alliance" (p. 108).

52. Advisory Board on Tariff and Taxation, Automobiles, pp. 68-69, 146.

53. *Debates,* April 26, 1932, pp. 2378-79.

54. *Monetary Times,* October 24, 1919, p. 11.

55. For example, *Weekly Bulletin,* no. 898, April 18, 1921, p. 627; no. 919, September 12, 1921, p. 433; *Commercial Intelligence Journal,* no. 968, August 19, 1922, p. 319; no. 1362, March 8, 1930, p. 368.

56. NAC, RG 20, vol. 178, no. 27725 (1), April 13, 1939, and November 7, 1947.

57. *Ibid.,* no. 27491, February 25, 1926.

58. *Ibid.,* March 30, 1926.

CHAPTER 6

1. Dominion Bureau of Statistics, *Indexes of Real Domestic Product by Industry* (1961 Base), July, 1968; Statistics Canada, *Fixed Capital Flows and Stocks, 1926-1978,* October, 1978; *National Income and Expenditure Accounts,* vol. 1, Annual Estimates, 1926-1974, March, 1976.

2. Ontario, *Debates,* June 13, 1968, p. 4427. For a thorough and insightful discussion of foreign investment after World War Two, see D. Wolfe, "Economic Growth and Foreign Investment: A Perspective on Canadian Economic Policy, 1945-1957," *Journal of Canadian Studies,* 13, 1 (Spring, 1978). For a defence of foreign investment during this era, see R. Bothwell, I. Drummond,

and J. English, *Canada since 1945: Power, Politics and Provincialism* (Toronto: University of Toronto Press, 1981), Chapters 5, 28.

3. Information Canada, *Foreign Direct Investment in Canada*, 1972, Tables 9 and 10, p. 25.

4. C.P. Kindleberger, *Foreign Trade and the National Economy* (New Haven: Yale University Press, 1962), p. 87.

5. *Industrial Canada*, July, 1939, pp. 100-02. The trade commissioners also remarked on the changing character of market demand as ISI became established in the countries where they were posted. For example, one wrote Ottawa that "in view of the apparent desire of both Chile and Bolivia to develop their own national industries of a secondary nature, we would be well advised, I believe, to centre our efforts toward the supply of those materials which entered into these said secondary industries, for I do not think that the tariff would permit much in the way of market development in the sale of finished consumers' goods." NAC, RG 20, vol. 270, no. 35226, May 27, 1943. See also *ibid.*, July 8, 1943.

6. *Industrial Canada*, May, 1939, pp. 39, 49.

7. Canada, Department of Reconstruction and Supply, *Canada's Industrial War Effort*, 1939-1945, 1947. See Chapter 4 for a review of Canadian technological dependence in World War One. Not only on the terrain of technology was the export performance of Canadian manufacturers during World War Two to be closely patterned on their Great War experience. Here again, their trade was export in destination only. The state, under the auspices of the Hyde Park arrangements, collected foreign orders and organized domestic production. Indeed, at the end of hostilities, C.D. Howe, Minister of Munitions and Supply, had to lecture manufacturers grown prosperous on guaranteed markets in the virtues of private enterprise. See R. Bothwell and W. Kilbourn, *C.D. Howe* (Toronto: McClelland and Stewart, 1979), Chapters 10-12; C.P. Stacey, *Arms, Men and Governments: The War Policies of Canada, 1939-1945* (Ottawa: Queen's Printer, 1970), Part VIII.

8. Stacey, *Arms, Men and Governments*, p. 489. He also reports that "largely because so many Canadian firms were subsidiaries of American or British corporations, comparatively little industrial research or development was then conducted in Canada, and of what was done a quite negligible amount had any military significance" (p. 507).

9. *Industrial Canada*, November, 1942, pp. 93-95.

10. Trade and Commerce, Economics Branch, *Canadian Machinery and Equipment Market*, September 1, 1949.

11. NAC, MG 27 III B 20, vol. 87, no. s. 48-10, August 15, 1947. For an informative discussion of Howe's role in economic policy formulation, see Bothwell and Kilbourn, *C.D. Howe.*

12. NAC, *ibid.*, September 2, 1947. W.A. Mackintosh, another important economic adviser to Howe, was to write about the process of getting economic

theories through to his boss that "Howe agrees but he does not know what he is agreeing with." Quoted in J.L. Granatstein, *The Ottawa Men: The Civil Service Mandarins, 1935-1957* (Toronto: Oxford University Press, 1982), p. 166.

13. For a more complete discussion of this legislation, see H.C. Eastman, "Recent Canadian Economic Policy: Some Alternatives," *Canadian Journal of Economics and Political Science*, XVIII, 2 (May, 1952); Wolfe, "Economic Growth and Foreign Investment."

14. *Debates*, March 1, 1949, p. 1002; *Industrial Canada*, February, 1948, pp. 49-52; NAC, MG 27 III B 20, vol. 86, no. s. 48, January 15, 1948.

15. *Industrial Canada*, February, 1948, pp. 49-52.

16. NAC, MG 27 III B 20, vol. 87, no. s. 48-10, October 23, 1947.

17. *Montreal Star*, June 27, 1979, p. D2.

18. C. Vaitsos, "Patents Revisited: Their Function in Developing Countries," in C. Cooper, ed., *Science, Technology, and Development* (London: Frank Cass, 1973).

19. *Foreign Direct Investment in Canada*, p. 118. For general reviews of Canadian technological dependence, see Science Council of Canada, Background Studies no. 23, P.L. Bourgault, *Innovation and the Structure of Canadian Industry*, October, 1972; and no. 43, I. Britton and J. Gilmour, *The Weakest Link: A Technological Perspective on Canadian Industrial Underdevelopment*, 1978.

20. Science Council of Canada, Background Study no. 35, A.J. Cordell and J. Gilmour, *The Role and Function of Government Laboratories and the Transfer of Technology to the Manufacturing Sector*, April, 1975, pp. 45-46.

21. Science Council of Canada, Background Study no. 22. A.J. Cordell, *The Multinational Firm, Foreign Direct Investment and Canadian Science Policy*, December, 1971, p. 56.

22. Industry, Trade and Commerce, Technological Innovation Studies Program, Research Report, D.A. Ondrack, *Foreign Ownership and Technological Innovations in Canada: A Study of the Industrial Machinery Sector of Industry*, October, 1975, pp. 29-30.

23. Canada, Department of Justice, Combines Investigation Commission, Report of the Commissioner, *Canada and International Cartels*, October 10, 1945, p. 49. It is unfortunate indeed that all the data collected by the Commission in preparing this report is missing and has either been destroyed or lost. Although the author was given permission to examine these documents, he was informed by an official of the Department of Consumer and Corporate Affairs that two extensive searches had produced no satisfactory results.

24. *Ibid.*, p. 43.

25. *Ibid.*, pp. 20-21.

26. NAC, RG 20, vol. 718, no. 7-983, June 5, 1945.

27. *Ibid.*, vol. 716, no. 7-C 1-1, March 2, 1949. For other examples, see vol. 650, no. 7-1586-F, October 24, 1961; vol. 722, no. 11872, September 15, 1947; vol. 723, no. 7-389, May 23, 1947; vol. 724, no. 19838, January 11, 19, 1950.

28. *Ibid.*, vol. 718, no. 7-983, June 3, 1946, Garner to McLeod.

29. *Ibid.*, vol. 665, no. 18-590-1 D (1), February 8, 1963: "Special Study on Export by Canadian Subsidiaries," pp. 11, 13.

30. *Ibid.*, vol. 650, no. 7-1586-E-1, May 2, 1961. Industry, Trade and Commerce kindly opened certain of their records from 1952 to the mid-1960s held by the National Archives for the examination of the author. This exception to the thirty-year secrecy rule was granted on condition that the identities of individuals and corporations not be disclosed.

31. *Ibid.*, vol. 665, no. 18-590-1 D (1), March 15, 1963: "Special Study on Export by Canadian Subsidiaries," p. 2.

32. *Ibid.*; also "Main Report Special Study on Export by Canadian Subsidiaries," Trade Commissioners' Conference, Ottawa, April 4-11, 1963, p. 2.

33. *Ibid.*, vol. 694, no. 18-171-3, April 15, 1958: "Universal Export Rights for U.S. Subsidiaries," Item 3.

34. *Ibid.*, vol. 650, no. 7-1586-E-1, May 11, 1961: "Summary of Discussions United States Group, 1960 Export Trade Promotion Conference."

35. "Special Study on Export by Canadian Subsidiaries," February 8, 1963, p. 4.

36. *Ibid.*, p. 3.

37. "Main Report Special Study on Export by Canadian Subsidiaries."

38. NAC, RG 20, vol. 921, no. T-7-1582, December 22, 1964.

39. Department of Industry, Trade and Commerce, Memorandum from an Assistant Deputy Minister to the Deputy Minister, *Export Performance of Canada-based Foreign Subsidiaries* with Annex I, "Examples of Export Market Limitations of Canadian Based Subsidiaries in Capital Equipment Manufacturing," April 13, 1977. (Access to this document was granted to the author by an unofficial source on the condition that the identities of individuals and corporations not be disclosed. Ian Waddell, a New Democratic MP, had his request to view this memorandum denied by J. Kelleher, Minister of State for International Trade, in a letter dated January 28, 1985, "because of the commercial confidentiality of the information on which the report was based.")

40. *Financial Post*, November 29, 1947, p. 1.

41. Bothwell and Kilbourn, *C.D. Howe*, pp. 219-20.

42. *Debates*, December 16, 1947, pp. 354-55, 398-99.

43. *Ibid.*, pp. 345-46.

44. *Ibid.*, June 10, 1954, p. 5768.

45. *Financial Post*, October 20, 1956, pp. 28-29; *Globe and Mail*, October 16, 1956, p. 22.

46. *Debates*, July 9, 1956, p. 5777; February 11, 1957, p. 1157.

47. *Ibid.*, July 15, 1959, p. 6096.

48. *Ibid.*, December 11, 1962, p. 2527.

49. *Ibid.*, June 13, 1963, p. 1001.

50. W. Gordon, *Walter L. Gordon: A Political Memoir* (Toronto: McClelland and Stewart, 1977), p. 256.

51. *Debates,* June 17, 1963, p. 1246; *Globe and Mail,* June 15, 1963, p. 4.

52. *Debates,* March 24, 1964, pp. 1398-99.

53. *Ibid.,* March 31, 1966, pp. 3713-14; November 18, 1966, p. 10052.

54. Department of Trade and Commerce, press release, Excerpts from an Address by the Hon. Robert H. Winters, Minister of Trade and Commerce, on Foreign Ownership and the Multinational Corporation delivered at the 42nd Canadian Purchasing Conference, Montreal, July 10, 1967, p. 10.

55. Department of Industry, Trade and Commerce, Memorandum from an Assistant Deputy Minister to the Deputy Minister, *Export Performance of Canada-based Foreign Subsidiaries,* April 13, 1977.

56. *Industrial Canada,* July, 1947, p. 121.

57. *Industrial Canada,* July, 1938, p. 107; July, 1939, pp. 104-05.

58. NAC, RG 20, vol. 718, no. 7-983, March 5, 1946.

59. *Industrial Canada,* January, 1939, p. 53.

60. *Ibid.,* July, 1944, p. 238.

61. *Ibid.,* January, 1948, p. 112.

62. *Ibid.,* July, 1958, pp. 44-50.

63. *Ibid.,* June, 1958, pp. 50, 54.

64. *Ibid.,* p. 61; September, 1958, p. 62.

65. *Globe and Mail,* September 21, 1963, p. 3; *Financial Post,* January 19, 1963.

CHAPTER 7

1. R. Whitaker, "Images of the state in Canada," in L. Panitch, ed., *The Canadian State: Political Economy and Political Power* (Toronto: University of Toronto Press, 1977), pp. 28-29.

2. For a detailed review of these debates spanning the half-century from the 1930s to the end of the 1970s, see Chapter 7 in both the first and the second updated editions of *Not For Export.*

3. NAC, RG 20, vol. 718, no. 7-983, June 3, 1946, Garner to McLeod.

4. *Debates,* November 9, 1976, p. 903.

5. *Debates,* March 9, 1983, p. 23593.

6. Department of External Affairs, *Statements and Speeches,* 47/21, November 17, 1947, p. 5.

7. Canada, Royal Commission on the Automotive Industry, *Report* (Ottawa: Queen's Printer, April, 1961), p. 18.

8. *Ibid.,* pp. 26-28.

9. *Ibid.,* pp. 48, 51, 53.

10. *Ibid.,* pp. 51-52.

11. *Debates,* May 5, 1966, pp. 4746-47.

12. Department of External Affairs, *Statements and Speeches,* 47/20, November 17, 1947, p. 3.

13. G.R. Winham, *International Trade and the Tokyo Round Negotiation*

(Princeton, N.J.: Princeton University Press, 1986), pp. 332-42. See also J.A. Finlayson with S. Bertasi, "Evolution of Canadian Postwar International Trade Policy," in A.C. Cutler and M.W. Zacheri, eds., *Canadian Foreign Policy and International Economic Regimes* (Vancouver: University of British Columbia Press, 1992).

14. *Debates*, November 24, 1978, p. 1470.

15. Canada, Senate, Standing Committee on Foreign Affairs, *Canada-United States Relations, Volume II, Canada's Trade Relations with the United States,* June, 1978, pp. 20, 111.

16. *Ibid.,* pp. 113-15.

17. *Ibid.,* p. 121.

18. Speech of H.W. Joly, President, Canadian Manufacturers' Association, to the 1967 Annual Meeting, *Industrial Canada,* July, 1967, p. 12.

19. R. Mahon, from the vantage point of the vulnerable and somewhat marginalized textile industry, approaches the question of tariff liberalization differently, emphasizing that it has been an arena of intra-class conflict in the sense that it "began to undermine the old basis for the accord between the staples fraction and capital based in manufacturing, raising the prospect of trade-induced deindustrialization." Mahon, *Politics of Industrial Restructuring: Canadian Textiles* (Toronto: University of Toronto Press, 1984), p. 17.

20. *Industrial Canada,* March, 1972, pp. 8, 9, 28.

21. Canada, Senate, Standing Committee on Foreign Affairs, *Proceedings,* December 9, 1980, p. 14:50.

22. Canada, *Report of the Royal Commission on the Economic Union and Development Prospects for Canada,* Volume 1 (Ottawa: Supply and Services, 1985), p. 336.

23. Special Joint Committee of the Senate and of the House of Commons on Canada's International Relations, *Minutes of Proceedings and Evidence,* August 1, 1985, p. 15:33.

24. *Ibid.*

25. *Debates,* May 8, 1972, pp. 2001-02.

26. *Debates,* June 23, 1975, pp. 7022-24.

27. *Debates,* October 14, 1975, p. 8192. See also the similar argument by Turner: "Unless we as a nation are able to conduct our affairs in a way that will maintain confidence at home and abroad in the soundness of our economy, we risk paying a heavy penalty in terms of lower capital investment, lower output, lower employment and lower real income." June 23, 1975, p. 7023.

28. Canada, House of Commons, Standing Committee on Finance, Trade and Economic Affairs, November 26, 1976, pp. 8:7-8:9.

29. Standing Committee on Foreign Affairs, *Canada-United States Relations, Volume II,* pp. 16, 21.

30. *Ibid.,* pp. 21, 109.

31. *Ibid.,* pp. 109, 121.

32. Canada, House of Commons, Standing Committee on Finance, Trade and Economic Affairs, February 21, 1978, p. 10:10. (Emphasis added.)

33. *Ibid.*, March 10, 1978, p. 12:22.

34. *Ibid.*, April 7, 1978, p. 19:22.

35. *Ibid.*, August 2, 1979, p. 39:7.

36. *Debates*, October 10, 1991, p. 3590.

37. Canada, House of Commons, Subcommittee on International Trade of the Standing Committee on External Affairs and International Trade, February 4, 1993, p. 30:27. Near the end of 1993, with the Canadian dollar trading in the 75 to 77 cent U.S. dollar range, the chief financial officer for Chrysler Corporation calculated that Canadian labour in his industry was between $12 to $14 an hour cheaper than U.S. labour. *Globe and Mail*, November 3, 1993, p. B1. For an illuminating discussion of the relation between Canadian wage levels and the location of North American automotive production, see J. Holmes and A. Rusonik, "The break-up of an international labour union: uneven development in the North American auto industry and the schism in the UAW," *Environment and Planning A*, Volume 23, 1991.

38. Canada, Privy Council Office, Report of the Task Force on the Structure of Canadian Industry, *Foreign Ownership and the Structure of Canadian Industry*, January, 1968, pp. 345-46.

39. Information Canada, *Foreign Direct Investment in Canada*, 1972, pp. 163-64, 168. For an excellent review of the Watkins and Gray reports, see Neil Bradford, "Creation and Constraint: Economic Ideas and Politics in Canada" (Ph.D. dissertation, Carleton University, 1994), Chapter 4.

40. For thorough examinations of FIRA, see Jack Layton, "Capital and the Canadian State: Foreign Investment Policy, 1957-1982" (Ph.D. dissertation, York University, 1983); Claire Sjolander, "Foreign Investment Policy-Making: The Canadian State in the Global Economy" (Ph.D. dissertation, Carleton University, 1989).

41. R. French, *How Ottawa Decides: Planning and Industrial Policy-Making, 1968-1980* (Toronto: Lorimer, 1980), pp. 103-18.

42. See, for example, the "Hatch Report": Department of Industry, Trade and Commerce, Export Promotion Review Committee, Final Report, *Strengthening Canada Abroad*, November 30, 1979.

43. F.J. Fletcher and R.J. Drummond, "Canadian Attitude Trends, 1960-1978," Institute for Research on Public Policy, Montreal, Working Paper no. 4, August, 1979, pp. 38-39.

44. *Ottawa Citizen*, June 21, 1980, p. 14.

45. Department of Industry, Trade and Commerce, *Framework for Implementing the Government's New Industry Development Policy During the Next Four Years and Proposals for Immediate Action*, July 3, 1980, pp. 7, 12, 13, 47.

46. *Globe and Mail*, September 17, 1980, p. 10. For insight into how the position of the continentalist faction within the Liberal cabinet was strengthened

during this period by U.S. government and business pressure on Ottawa to "shelve" these attempts to reform branch-plant performance through industrial strategy, see S. Clarkson, *Canada and the Reagan Challenge* (Toronto: Lorimer, 1982), Chapter 4. See, as well, J.L. Granatstein and R. Bothwell, *Pirouette: Pierre Trudeau and Canadian Foreign Policy* (Toronto: University of Toronto Press, 1990), Chapter 12.

47. Government of Canada, *Economic Development for Canada in the 1980s*, November, 1981.

48. *Globe and Mail*, February 13, 1982, p. 1. See also Trudeau in this period on the need for industrial restructuring in *Debates*, February 16, 1982, p. 15047.

49. *Debates*, December 7, 1983, pp. 2-3; June 18, 1984, p. 4721.

50. Canada, Senate, Standing Committee on Foreign Affairs, *Canada-United States Relations, Volume III, Canada's Trade Relations with the United States*, March, 1982, p. 33.

51. Keiko Sueuchi records the difficult move of the Canadian tariff from "the arena of explosive partisan politics into the routine operation of a state bureaucracy." See her "Tariff Out of Politics: Political Economy of Tariff Policy in Canada, 1875-1935" (Ph.D. dissertation, Carleton University, 1992), p. 410.

52. For a glimpse of the continentalist evangelists at work during this period, see G.B. Doern and B.W. Tomlin, *Faith and Fear: The Free Trade Story* (Toronto: Stoddart, 1991), pp. 46-57. For a useful review of the role of business during the FTA negotiations, see *ibid.*, Chapter 5.

53. Special Joint Committee on Canada's International Relations, *Minutes of Proceedings and Evidence*, July 15, 1985, pp. 2:62-63.

54. Prime Minister's Office, "Canada-U.S. New Bilateral Trade Initiative Communications Strategy," 1985. (Draft document, excerpted in the *Toronto Star*, September 20, 1985, pp. A1, A21.)

55. Special Joint Committee on Canada's International Relations, *Minutes of Proceedings and Evidence*, July 26, 1985, p. 11:6.

56. *Ibid.*, July 17, 1985, p. 4:10.

57. *Ibid.*, p. 4:36.

58. *Ibid.*, p. 4:46.

59. *Ibid.*, August 8, 1985, pp. 17:43-44.

60. *Ibid.*, July 26, 1985, p. 11:6.

61. *Ibid.*, July 15, 1985, p. 2:73.

62. *Ibid.*, August 8, 1985, p. 17:62.

63. *Ibid.*, July 17, 1985, p. 4:10.

64. *Ibid.*, July 18, 1985, p. 5:24.

65. *Ibid.*, July 17, 1985, p. 4:34.

66. For a fascinating inside description of how the FTA negotiations turned on the subsidies/countervail question, see Doern and Tomlin, *Faith and Fear*, Chapters 7, 8.

67. *Globe and Mail,* October 17, 1987, p. A4.

68. This argument is consistent with the view taken by Frank Stone in his comprehensive study of Canada and the GATT. He says that "the Canada-United States Free Trade Agreement (FTA) should be viewed neither as a replacement of GATT as the basic trade agreement between the two countries, nor as an alternative to GATT and its supplementary codes. . . . The Free Trade Agreement should . . . be viewed as extending and elaborating the longstanding commitments of the two countries to each other under GATT. It completes the process of crossborder trade liberalization which has been underway under GATT and on a bilateral basis since the mid-1930s." *Canada, the GATT and the International Trade System,* Second Edition (Montreal: Institute for Research on Public Policy, 1992), p. 236.

69. Statistics Canada, *Trade Patterns: Canada-United States, The Manufacturing Industries 1981-1991,* March, 1993, Table 7.3, p. 57.

70. Witness, for example, the complacency of most Canadian manufacturers in the face of the booming EC market. Canadian direct investment in the EC actually declined between 1987 and 1991 as the EC moved toward a single market. A 1990 Canadian Manufacturers' Association survey of their members found that while 35 per cent exported more than 20 per cent of their production to the United States, just over 3 per cent exported more than 20 per cent of their production to Europe. A 1991 survey of Canada's 1,000 largest businesses by a firm of chartered accountants found that only 36 per cent of Canadian firms were making plans to pursue European business, while 63 per cent of United States firms surveyed held such plans. See *Globe and Mail,* February 11, 1991, p. B5; February 15, 1991, p. B4.

71. See, for example, "Tape maker decides to stick with Canada," *Globe and Mail,* November 27, 1991, pp. B1, B5; "IBM building North American bloc," *Globe and Mail,* May 7, 1992, pp. B1, B4; "Inglis turnaround a 'heroic' effort," *Globe and Mail,* August 17, 1992, pp. B1, B2; "Head office flexes its might: 'What's left here is primarily a sales office'," *Globe and Mail,* January 18, 1994, pp. A1, A6.

72. See, for example, "An Apple in Quebec's eye to future: Montreal and U.S. firms team up to make circuit boards," *Globe and Mail,* September 23, 1992, p. B1.

73. Government of Canada, Prosperity Secretariat, *Prosperity Through Competitiveness* (Ottawa: Supply and Services, 1991), pp. 16, 32-33.

74. Michael E. Porter, *Canada at the Crossroads: The Reality of a New Competitive Environment* (Ottawa: Business Council on National Issues and Minister of Supply and Services Canada, 1991), pp. 15-16.

75. Government of Canada, Prosperity Secretariat, *Industrial Competitiveness: A Sectoral Perspective* (Ottawa: Supply and Services, 1991), p. 67.

76. Porter, *Canada at the Crossroads,* p. 16.

77. On the Conservative treatment of foreign investment during this period, see

Barbara Jenkins, *The Paradox of Continental Production: National Investment Policies in North America* (Ithaca, N.Y.: Cornell University Press, 1992), Chapter 4.

78. *Globe and Mail,* October 31, 1991, p. B7.

79. For a government denial of any secret deal, see *Debates,* June 23, 1988, p. 16765. For a lampoon of the rumours, see T. Corcoran, "Elvis lives – but the dollar deal is dead," *Globe and Mail,* February 19, 1992, p. B2.

80. Canada, House of Commons, Committee on Finance, Trade and Economic Affairs, November 2, 1979, pp. 6:14-16.

81. *Debates,* December 4, 1979, pp. 1979-80.

82. *Ibid.,* February 10, 1981, p. 7080.

83. *Ibid.,* June 21, 1982, p. 18662.

84. *Ibid.,* February 16, 1982, p. 15062.

85. *Ibid.,* February 16, 1982, p. 15063; June 21, 1982, p. 18662. For a similar analysis by John Crosbie, see May 13, 1981, pp. 9544-47.

86. *Globe and Mail,* June 25, 1984, p. 9.

87. *Debates,* June 27, 1984, p. 5168.

88. *Ibid.,* March 18, 1988, p. 13902. See also June 23, 1988, p. 16765.

89. *Ibid.,* December 4, 1989, p. 6445.

90. Canada, House of Commons, Committee on Finance, June 5, 1990, pp. 131:5, 131:8, 131:34, 132:6. See as well the analysis set out in the Mulroney government's "prosperity initiative." "Many observers suggest that a lower Canadian dollar would solve Canada's competitiveness problem. However, the record of the late 1970s and early 1980s shows that there are no quick fixes. When the fundamental inflation problem is not dealt with, gains from a lower dollar tend to be eroded by a vicious circle of rising costs, rising inflation and rising uncertainty. These factors work against improved competitiveness by discouraging investment and productivity, and creating pressures for further depreciation of the dollar." Government of Canada, Prosperity Secretariat, *Prosperity Through Competitiveness,* 1991, p. 4.

91. There had been no warning. On the contrary, John Crow, Governor of the Bank of Canada, in the period leading up to the 1988 FTA election had explicitly stated in reference to the exchange rate that "I do not think a great deal will happen; we are not talking about the difference between night and day." Canada, House of Commons, Committee on Finance, January 21, 1988, p. 132:18.

92. *Globe and Mail,* June 1, 1991, p. B3; September 14, 1991, p. B1.

93. Canada, House of Commons, Committee on Finance, May 28, 1990, p. 127:24.

94. *Ibid.,* May 29, 1990, pp. 128:25, 128:28.

95. *Ibid.,* May 24, 1990, p. 126:21.

96. J.D. Moore, Vice-President, Policy, Canadian Exporters' Association,

"Canada's Competitiveness and Export Performance," *The Parliamentary Weekly Quarterly Report,* 1, 3 (September, 1992), p. 27.

97. Canada, House of Commons, Committee on Finance, May 24, 1990, p. 126:18.

98. Canada, House of Commons, Committee on Industry, Science and Technology, Regional and Northern Development, February 13, 1990, p. 24:23.

99. Canada, House of Commons, Committee on Finance, May 24, 1990, p. 126:19.

CHAPTER 8

1. At the same time, Canadian business scolded the Tories for seriously impairing their adjustment to the NAFTA environment by maintaining an overvalued dollar. See, for example, the comments of J. Carter, Director of Policy Development of the Auto Parts Manufacturers' Association, before the Commons Committee on External Affairs and International Trade, September 27, 1990, p. 58:33.

2. *Ibid.,* September 28, 1990, p. 59:22.

3. For a useful summary of these events, see Jenkins, *Paradox of Continental Production,* Chapter 5.

4. Canada, House of Commons, Committee on External Affairs and International Trade, September 28, 1990, p. 59:26. See also p. 59:30.

5. M. Hart, *A North American Free Trade Agreement: The Strategic Implications for Canada* (Halifax: Institute for Research on Public Policy, 1990), p. 65.

6. Calculated from Statistics Canada, *Summary of Canadian International Trade,* December, 1991.

7. Canada, House of Commons, Subcommittee on International Trade of the Committee on External Affairs and International Trade, November 26, 1992, p. 19:5.

8. *Ibid.,* December 9, 1992, p. 27:9.

9. Canada, House of Commons, Committee on External Affairs and International Trade, September 28, 1990, pp. 59:25-26.

10. *Ibid.,* p. 59:25.

11. Canada, House of Commons, Committee on International Trade of the Standing Committee on External Affairs and International Trade, November 26, 1992, pp. 19:8, 19:11. Following this line, the Chrétien Liberal government quickly delivered on its 1993 electoral pledge to get the Americans to negotiate the subsidy and dumping code provided for in the FTA's article 1907. Mexico, the United States, and Canada have set December 31, 1995, as the target date for reaching a code on subsidies and anti-dumping measures. *Globe and Mail,* December 3, 1993, p. A2.

12. See, for example, Michael Wilson's defence of the FTA in *Debates,* December

1, 1992, pp. 14319, 14322-26. For an attack on the FTA, see B. Campbell, "Restructuring the Economy: Canada into the Free Trade Era," in R. Grinspun and M. Cameron, eds., *The Political Economy of North American Free Trade* (New York: St. Martin's Press, 1993).

13. House of Commons, Committee on International Trade, February 11, 1993, pp. 35:26-27. One cannot help but compare organized labour's position here in regard to Mexicans with the late nineteenth- and early twentieth-century attempts by labour to exclude Chinese workers from the Canadian labour market on the basis that "white people could not live on what the Chinese lived." See G. Williams, "Canada – The Case of the Wealthiest Colony," *This Magazine*, February-March, 1976. A useful discussion of the structural limits to northern U.S. (or Canadian) industry fleeing to Mexico to take advantage of Third World wages can be found in R. Ojeda and R. Morales, "International Restructuring and Labor Market Interdependence: The Automobile Industry in Mexico and the United States," in J.A. Bustamante *et al.*, eds., *U.S.-Mexico Relations: Labor Market Interdependence* (Stanford, Calif.: Stanford University Press, 1992).

14. NAC, MG 27 III B 20, vol. 87, no. s. 48-10, August 15, 1947. This memo from Alex Skelton to C.D. Howe is reviewed in Chapter 6.

15. Canadian Institute of Public Opinion, *The Gallup Report*, August 31, 1993.

16. I have argued elsewhere that the logic of the current North American production system is "ecohostile." See "Greening the New Canadian Political Economy," *Studies in Political Economy*, Spring, 1992.

17. As cited in G. Hufbauer and J. Schott, *NAFTA: An Assessment* (Washington, D.C.: Institute for International Economics, 1993), p. 25.

Index

~~~~~~